ROGERIAN PERSPECTIVES:

Collaborative Rhetoric for Oral and Written Communication

Writing Research

Multidisciplinary Inquiries into the Nature of Writing

edited by Marcia Farr, University of Illinois at Chicago

Arthur N. Applebee, *Contexts for Learning to Write: Studies of Secondary School Instruction*
Christine Barabas, *Technical Writing in a Corporate Culture: A Study of the Nature of Information*
Barbara Couture, *Functional Approaches to Writing*
Carole Edelsky, *Writing in a Bilingual Program: Habia Una Vez*
Lester Faigley, Roger Cherry, David Jolliffe, and Anna Skinner, *Assessing Writers' Knowledge and Processes of Composing*
Marcia Farr (ed.), *Advances in Writing Research, Volume One: Children's Early Writing Development*
Sarah W. Freedman (ed.), *The Acquisition of Written Language: Response and Revision*
George H. Jensen and John K. DiTiberio, *Personality and the Teaching of Composition*
David A. Jolliffe (ed.), *Advances in Writing Research, Volume Two: Writing in Academic Disciplines*
Judith Langer, *Children Reading and Writing: Structures and Strategies*
Bennett A. Rafoth and Donald L. Rubin (eds.), *The Social Construction of Written Communication*
Leo Ruth and Sandra Murphy, *Designing Writing Tasks for the Assessment of Writing*
Jana Staton, Roger Shuy, Joy Kreeft, and Leslie Reed, *Dialogue Journal Communication: Classroom, Linguistic, Social, and Cognitive Views*
William Teale and Elizabeth Sulzby (eds.), *Emergent Literacy: Writing and Reading*

IN PREPARATION

Anne Johnstone, *Uses for Journal Keeping: An Ethnography of Writing in a University Science Class* (revised and ed. by Barbara Johnstone and Valerie Balester)
Joy Kreeft Peyton and Jana Staton, *Dialogue Journals in the Multilingual Classroom*

ROGERIAN PERSPECTIVES:

Collaborative Rhetoric for Oral and Written Communication

Nathaniel Teich, Editor

Department of English
University of Oregon

ABLEX PUBLISHING CORPORATION
NORWOOD, NEW JERSEY

Printed in the United States of America

Library of Congress Cataloging-in-Publication Data

Rogerian perspectives: collaborative rhetoric for oral and written communication/Nathaniel Teich, editor.
p. cm.—(Writing research)
Includes bibliographical references and index.
ISBN 0-89391-667-6(cl).—ISBN 0-89391-668-4 (ppb)
1. Rogers, Carl R. (Carl Ransom), 1902-1987—Contributions in rhetoric.
2. Rogers, Carl R. (Carl Ransom), 1902-1987—Contributions in communication.
3. Rhetoric—Study and teaching. 4. Communication—Study and teaching.
5. Empathy. I. Teich, Nathaniel. II. Series: Writing research (Norwood, N.J.)
P92.5.R64R64 1991
153.6—dc20 91-32956
CIP

Ablex Publishing Corporation
355 Chestnut Street
Norwood, New Jersey 07648

DEDICATIONS

Carl R. Rogers (1902-1987)
who embodied his principles

Hyman M. Teich (1905-1987)
my father

Benjamin J. Teich
my son

CONTENTS

WRITING RESEARCH: Multidisciplinary Inquiries into the Nature of Writing

Marcia Farr, series editor
University of Illinois at Chicago

SERIES PREFACE

This series of volumes presents the results of scholarly inquiry into the nature of writing. The research presented comes from various disciplines, those which have emerged as significant within the last several decades in the burgeoning field of research on writing. These primarily include linguistics, anthropology, psychology, literary theory, philosophy, rhetoric, and education. In this series, research on writing is viewed as constituting a field, rather than a discipline. A field is seen as a multidisciplinary entity focused on a set of significant questions about a central concern (e.g., American Studies, or literacy), whereas a discipline is seen as sharing theoretical and methodological approaches which have a substantial tradition behind them. If research on writing evolves into a more unified discipline, rather than remaining a multifaceted field, much will be lost from the rich multiplicity of traditions which now contribute to it.

The history of this particular field is unique. Much early work, a great deal of which has been reported in this series, was conceptualized at and funded by the National Institute of Education, formerly of the U.S. Department of Education. Following a planning conference in June, 1977, a program of basic research on the learning and teaching of writing was developed and funded annually. During the 1980s, in spite of considerably reduced government support, this field flourished and expanded. New Ph.D. programs were created, primarily within English and education departments. At the same time, scholars from yet other disciplines (notably social historians) turned their attention to writing and literacy. The interest in literacy, in fact, reflected a growing awareness of the inner-relatedness of writing with other aspects of language, culture, and society. Simultaneously with the scholarly expansion, a serious concern for the apparent failure to achieve mass literacy in our educational institutions grew and deepened.

As we near the 21st century, unprecedented demographic changes in the United States (in which European-origin whites will become a minority) urge us to press on in this work. Scholarly grounding in a variety of disciplines continues to be of paramount importance, but no less so than grounding the scholarship in the concerns of mass literacy. What this literacy will consist of, and how it will be used in educational, work, and other institutional and personal domains remains, of course, to be determined. All scholarly work within the boundaries of these concerns continues to be invited for submission to this series.

PREFACE

If there is "one overriding theme in my professional life," Carl Rogers wrote in 1973, "it is my caring about communication."

> I have wanted to understand, as profoundly as possible, the communication of the other. . . . I have wanted to *be* understood. I have tried to facilitate clarity of communication between individuals of the most diverse points of view. I have worked for better communication between groups whose perceptions and experiences are poles apart: strangers, members of different cultures, representatives of different strata of society.[1]

The aim of this book is to discuss both theoretically and practically how Rogers' ideas inform communication in general, rhetoric and writing in particular, and the conditions of teaching in these fields. As the essays in this collection demonstrate, Rogerian principles, as theory, are inextricable from the dynamics of their practice—the performance of genuine communication in specific situations: from clinic to classroom, from interpersonal to communal relations.

This collection of essays is divided into three parts, and each part begins with a short introduction describing the essays that follow. As a starting point to reassess Rogers' contributions and influence, Part 1 reprints two representative examples of his work.

Part 1 includes two essays by Rogers: his 1951 paper on communication which originated the interest of rhetoricians in his principles, and a more recent report (1984) of his efforts to achieve mutual communication in world-wide contexts between politically opposed groups. Part 1 concludes with my 1985 interview with Rogers, in which he discussed the applications of his principles and practices to rhetoric and writing—contexts he had not previously addressed directly.

Part 2 presents new essays by the contributors. They reassess and extend Rogerian perspectives in a variety of situations: in the field of communication—broadly defined to include the theory and practice of rhetoric, written composition, interpersonal and communal discourse—and in the area of educational theory and pedagogical practices where Rogerian principles can be applied. Also included in Part 2 is the edited transcript of a 1987 forum discussion of Rogers' influences in these areas.

Part 3 focuses on the issue of empathy, which I find to be central in conceptions of genuine collaborative activities. I trace the origins and applications of empathy in literary history, psychoanalysis, and Rogerian communication in terms of the fundamental human intersubjectivity necessary for the understanding and interpretation of otherness. Part 3 concludes with the implications of Rogerian perspectives, grounded in empathic understanding, for carrying on our activities as speakers, writers, listeners, readers, and teachers.

In my general introduction, I summarize key issues in defining Rogerian principles as forming a collaborative rhetoric. In addition, I locate Rogerian approaches in relation to current controversies surrounding psychological-expressivist and social-epistemic approaches to discourse. My interest is in situating Rogerian perspectives in a mediating position, supporting a balanced pluralism of personal, social, and structural approaches within a contextual model of rhetoric. The unique contribution of Rogerian perspectives to rhetoric and pedagogy, as well as to discourse in general, lies in valuing the affective, pragmatic, humanistic dimensions of mutual communication, rather than privileging strictly cognitive, adversarial, and ideological perspectives.

I can trace back to 1985 the origins of this project to reassess Rogers' contributions to communication. After being encouraged by Linda Flower and Richard Young at Carnegie Mellon University (my undergraduate alma mater), I traveled to California to interview Rogers in La Jolla. We spoke about his ideas on communication and his attitude toward rhetoricians appropriating his principles for a Rogerian rhetoric of argumentation. At that point, I contemplated a volume that would include reprints of relevant articles by Rogers and others, the transcript of our interview, and new essays on the current value of Rogerian perspectives in communication.

As I initiated the project, I kept in touch with Rogers. He read and commented on the interview transcript. He wrote to me about his continuous professional activities, traveling the world to present workshops, including a first invitation to Russia in 1986. I had hoped that he could respond to the work in this collection at its completion. However, his death in February 1987, at age 85, precluded that response. Meanwhile, I had planned a forum to reassess Rogerian influences in rhetoric and writing at the March 1987 annual Conference on College Composition and Communication. There I chaired a panel of Paul Bator, Lisa Ede, Maxine Hairston, and Richard Young, who discussed the implications of Rogers' work. Our forum involved lengthy participation from the audience, as seen in the transcript (below, Chapter 4). At that point, I announced the call for contributions to this volume.

At this point of completion, I wish to thank the contributors for their informative work, commitment to the project, and patience during its growth to fruition. For her early encouragement, I thank Lisa Ede. For his identification of Rogerian principles as a collaborative rhetoric, I thank Bill Strong, who exemplifies collaboration at its best. Of those who read my introduction, I am particularly grateful to historian Stanley Pierson for his responses and suggestions. Suzanne Clark also carefully read versions of my introduction and Part 3. Her comments on contemporary theoretical matters informed and aided me. In the end, however, I retained the language of pluralism and humanism which I felt to be more congenial for my own and Rogers' thought.

Nathaniel Teich
Eugene, OR

NOTE

1. Rogers, "In Retrospect: Forty-Six Years," in his *A Way of Being* (Boston: Houghton Mifflin, 1980), pp. 64–65. Subsequent references to works cited are located at the end of each introduction and each chapter, except for cross-references to chapters in this volume, which are cited in text.

General Introduction

Nathaniel Teich

Carl Rogers' achievements continue to be influential. He has changed ways of thinking about and doing things in psychology, counseling, education, communication, and human relations in both the private and public worlds. He has contributed key words, as well as ideas and practices: *client-centered therapy, student-centered teaching, active listening, empathic understanding, unconditional acceptance*, reflecting (*saying back*) another's feelings and ideas (to show one's understanding of the other). These terms, and the ideas that they signify, have become so fully absorbed in various discourse and practical applications that often Rogers is not cited or even remembered as their originator or popularizer.

Although these and other Rogerian principles and practices originated in the oral, interpersonal context of psychological counseling, Rogers expanded their applications beyond therapeutic, helping relationships. Despite his own complaints about the distortions and misuse of his ideas, Rogers invited us to improve the quality of our communication by applying his principles in our personal, professional, and broader social and political interactions.

Yet, there have been, and continue to be, harsh criticisms of Rogers' humanistic (and often idealized) visions of self-reliant individuals interacting in authentic ways, engaging in honest dialogue to resolve personal and public problems cooperatively, rationally, and equitably. Rogers' critics often complained about his reliance on individualism, his faith that problems could be solved by simply improving communication, and his connections to the romantic idealism of the 1960s human potential movement.

While this volume is not intended as a defense of Rogers or a study of his reception, it is important at the outset to note the controversial aspects of his reputation. Why have Rogers' principles and their applications met with hostility and resistance from some specialists in psychology, rhetoric, and social criticism? One way to answer questions about this reception is to recognize that Rogerian perspectives challenge dogmatic and exclusivist approaches from psychotherapy and teaching to rhetoric and politics. Traditionalists and radicals alike have often sought to maintain their rationalistic standards and ideological purity, rather than acknowledge that the pragmatic pluralism of Rogerian theory and practice has valid applications in their fields.

1. ROGERIAN COMMUNICATION

Rogerian perspectives cut across the boundaries of established academic fields and their traditional approaches as a result of Rogers' identifying intersubjective modes of experiencing as fundamental to what he called "mutual communication."

> Mutual communication tends to be pointed toward solving a problem rather than toward attacking a person or group. It leads to a situation in which I see how the problem appears to you, as well as to me, and you see how it appears to me, as well as to you. (Rogers, 1961, p. 336)

Rogers extended his clinical model of empathy in the helping relationship to situations of functional or instrumental communication. In these situations, empathy and intersubjectivity could collaborate (as in therapy) to produce increased understanding and movement toward resolutions of problems. The pragmatic means and ends of Rogerian problem solving can be directed toward both individual and social/collaborative goals. In education, for example, Rogers believed that the teaching–learning relationship was best carried on by solving problems. In public conflicts over issues of social policy or ideology, Rogers sought to reduce tension and defensiveness to produce a climate favorable for problem solving.

While Rogerian principles may not be applicable in all discourse situations (especially forensic and adversarial contexts), they are not as limited and impractical as his critics assert. His principles of "active listening," "saying back," and empathic understanding are at the heart of both a Rogerian collaborative discourse relationship and the means of engaging in Rogerian communication.

> Real communication occurs . . . when we listen with understanding . . . to see the expressed idea and attitude from the other person's point of view, to sense how it feels to him, to achieve his frame of reference in regard to the thing he is talking about. (1961, pp. 331–332)

A curious irony arises, moreover, from contrasting the vehemence of the assaults on Rogerian theory and practice with Rogers' goal of reducing the climate of threat and defensiveness that results from antagonistic confrontations (e.g., Pounds, 1987). While Rogers' critics insist on banishing or severely restricting the use of his principles outside therapy, new and wider applications continue to emerge—as the essays in this volume attest.

This volume can serve as a concise casebook for students, teachers, and researchers who wish to examine the significance of Rogerian perspectives in oral and written communication. A broad representation of materials is offered, beginning with Rogers' 1951 paper on communication and introducing new work by current theorists and practitioners in the field of rhetoric and composition. The purpose of this volume is not simply historical, however; the new essays on the current value of Rogerian perspectives extend Rogers' "person-centered" principles into classroom interactions, peer response groups, and other collaborative activities. The reassessments of Rogers in this volume offer new ways of understanding and applying Rogerian principles to the central issues of rhetoric and literacy: speaking and writing about ideas, reading and writing about texts, listening to and understanding expressions of others' opinions and feelings.

2. ROGERIAN COLLABORATIVE RHETORIC

Claims for the centrality of Rogerian principles, in both theory and practice, to rhetoric and literacy may come as a surprise to traditionalists and radical social critics alike. The essays in this volume discuss Rogerian principles in relation to: classical and contemporary rhetoric, especially argumentation; pedagogical strategies and heuristics for the writing classroom and for foreign language learning; and the social construction of knowledge and understanding.

The applicability of Rogerian principles to rhetoric and communication is not limited to the level of the individual's separate activity, but rather encompasses more social and collaborative levels. Rogerian principles foster collaboration from their very origination in the interactions of persons seeking healthful growth. In terms of current rhetorical theory, Rogerian principles are fully operational within a contextual model of rhetoric—that is, one describing the interrelations of a discourser with other(s) (conversers or audience) using language in a particular social/historical context to produce (in varying degrees) new information and understanding.

The chapters in this volume demonstrate that Rogerian principles apply to the study of a broad range of discourse situations in their entirety. Although recent theorists, like LeFevre (1987) and Berlin (1987), place Rogers more restrictively within their theoretical models, their transactional and social/epistemic conceptions of rhetoric are incomplete to the extent that they minimize the collaborative characteristics of Rogerian principles.[1] Within the contextual model of rhetoric, Rogerian theory and practice can best be called *collaborative* because they apply to a broad range of intersubjective activities of communication.

Thus, what I am calling here Rogerian collaborative rhetoric applies to a broader range of oral and written communication than generally acknowledged. According to rhetoricians' early view of Rogers, his ideas were limited to argumentation. In this context, critics objected to the adaptations of such ideas as "active listening," "saying back," and empathy from oral dialogue to written texts. For example, assuming that the putative audiences for typical school assignments (e.g., persuasive essays) or actual public statements (letters to the editor) were distant and silent (unable to respond immediately, if at all), individual writers and their audiences could not engage in the interpersonal give-and-take necessary to work out resolutions acceptable to those with differing positions.

Now, however, as several of the new essays in this volume show, Rogerian argument constructed by a solitary, subjective, school-oriented writer is not the only, or most desirable, situation for Rogerian praxis. For many rhetorical situations, Rogerian principles offer initial guidance for one to engage in dialogue both internally (as self-generating interior conversation) and externally in actual discourse. In both instances, this dialogic process takes place as a social act by imaginatively internalizing and constructing others according to one's empathic understanding. This intersubjective activity, necessary for knowledge and interpretation of others (Agosta, 1984; Teich, Chapters 14, 17, this volume), places Rogerian principles in both individual and social/collaborative contexts. As a result, beyond the initial and ongoing internal empathic construction of the other, Rogerian principles provide the means for developing positive and productive external communication directed toward ends that are mutually acceptable to the parties involved.

With what has been called Rogerian argument, now it is clear that there is more than just conventional accommodation at issue. For situations of conflict or argumentation, Rogers' principles offer unique ways to reduce tension and personal threat, thereby increasing opportunities for understanding to the point that individuals may be willing to risk changing their positions. True, as critics claim, we can talk about objective statement, shared values, mutually acceptable resolutions, and reducing defensiveness without invoking Rogers; however, not only do Rogerian perspectives focus on these matters to a greater extent than forensic, adversarial approaches, but also Rogers' "person-centered" attitudes take these matters beyond conventional accommodation and make them central to a rhetoric of Rogerian principles and practices generally applicable to collaborative social communication. Consequently, Rogerian theory and practice provide radically different lenses through which we can view all discourse situations, not just conventional argumentation. As a result, new ways of looking at and generating oral and written discourse become available, as the chapters in this volume demonstrate.

3. ROGERIAN PRINCIPLES IN RHETORICAL PRACTICE

When Rogers discussed his basic principles, he variously described them as both attitudes and conditions: attitudes held by individuals, and the psychological conditions that these attitudes promoted (e.g., Rogers, 1980, 1961). Rogers identified three fundamental attitudes as promoting psychological growth—"congruence," "unconditional positive regard," and "empathic understanding" (see below, Part 3 for discussion). But these three attitudes are not limited to psychotherapy in bringing about an individual's "constructive change or significant learning" (1961, p. 282). The three attitudes (as expressed by such responses as active listening and restatement) are applicable to many communication situations beyond argumentation—to the discourses of teaching, parenting, supervising, negotiating—to circumstances, in short, where "person-centered" collaboration is important.

Rogerian principles, as applied beyond therapy to rhetoric, communication, and education, are both compatible with and contribute to the current inclusive approaches in these fields: from the writing process and problem solving to generative and epistemic rhetoric in social contexts. Rogerian principles in their practical applications support a theoretical model of balanced pluralism in these fields, in which separate approaches do not exclude or appropriate others, but can engage in respectful dialogue and collaborate within a contextual model of rhetoric. As chapters in this volume demonstrate, psychological approaches that represent personal and expressive modes of communication can be equally valued with linguistic/structural and social/historical approaches in a balanced pluralism.[2]

The pluralistic balance that Rogerian principles support is primarily evident in their focus on both the affective and the cognitive elements of all discourse situations. Because Rogerian principles address both the ideas and the feelings with which the ideas are held, when we take a Rogerian perspective, we seek to bring together the cognitive/rational and the affective/emotional qualities of ourselves and others as whole persons ("whole" in the sense of operating in and acknowledging both domains). Rogerian principles allow us to recognize and validate the affective as well as the cognitive dimensions of discourse situations.

For the affective and cognitive balancing necessary in teaching situations, for example, Rogers applied the principles of the "helping relationship" to facilitate growth for individual and social responsibilities. Teachers, like therapists, must start with each person's ideas and feelings evident in particular situations. The teacher then becomes a facilitator and collaborator through the three attitudes of congruence, positive regard, and empathic understanding. A facilitator (whether therapist, teacher, parent, supervisor) does not lead autocratically or coercively, but aids individuals and groups in becoming "self-directing" (Kirschenbaum, 1979, pp. 95, 367). The individual's goals are to become responsible for one's own learning, to learn about oneself (in both affective and cognitive domains), and to understand oneself in relation to others by "becoming more acceptant of others" (Rogers, 1961, pp. 280ff).

In the writing process, Rogerian principles can create conditions that foster supportive, nonthreatening dialogue both internally and in social contexts. Most phases in the process of generating written discourse are amenable to Rogerian collaborative rhetoric: invention, sharing and discussing ideas, changing one's opinions, responding to and revising drafts, interpreting finished texts. To the extent that particular subject matter and situations allow, Rogerian principles in the writing process can be engaged both alone and with others in the oral and written interactions that produce a final product.

Rogerian principles bridge the gap between the "internal dialogic perspective" and the "collaborative perspective," as defined by LeFevre (1987), given the connection between empathy and intersubjectivity in process of creating one's self and others (Agosta, 1984; Teich, Chapters 14, 17, this volume). The applications of collaborative Rogerian dialogue include both the internal imaginative constructions of external dialogues and the actual public dialogues themselves. In the solitary moments, when there is no other present to reflect and check one's perceptions, Rogerian principles offer internalized opportunities for cognitive and affective representations of the other, but within the constraints of actual-world conditions in order to be faithful to the ideas and feelings of the other.[3]

The transfer of Rogerian principles beyond the clinical situation calls our attention to the similarities and differences between their application in therapeutic situations and in other rhetorical situations. Therapeutic situations require empathy and the other facilitative attitudes that Rogers identified as necessary for mutual communication. If we consider the verbal discourse of psychotherapy, it is a specific form of communication (the collaborative construction of narrative discourse about the self). It represents and formulates both the affective and cognitive aspects of a person. But while such therapy is a kind of discourse, not all discourse situations would be appropriate for therapeutic Rogerian rhetoric. To the extent that rhetoric is assumed to be and practiced as forensic, adversarial, manipulative, and nonfacilitative, it is inimical to Rogerian principles and practices.

Yet as contributors to this volume stress, the adversarial mode, however dominant in the teaching of argumentation, may not be the best-suited or only workable mode for persuasion and problem solving in specific situations. Thus, in our teaching, the adversarial mode should not remain privileged by its exclusion of what Rogerian principles provide: attention to psychological affect and collaborative problem solving.

4. ROGERIAN PROBLEM SOLVING

In Rogers' pragmatic fashion, he regarded problem solving as applying not only to the therapeutic situation, but also to such fields as communication and education; moreover, he sought to transform structures and institutions in all the fields he encountered. "Significant learning" to Rogers (1961) "occurs most readily in relation to situations perceived as problems" (p. 286). This kind of learning is "learning which makes a difference—in the individual's behavior, in the course of action he chooses in the future, in his attitudes, and in his personality" (p. 280). It is from actual life, according to Rogers, that the important problems and challenges emerge; they are not simply assigned in class by teachers. In a rationalistic fashion, Rogers proposed that "the student as a self-respecting, self-motivated person" should be made aware of the immediate and long-range implications of the problems at hand and should be "free to choose whether he wished to put forth the effort" (p. 291) to solve the problem or strive for the goal.

Frequently from the 1950s, Rogers objected to the conformity which he found in American education and society. "Our whole culture—through custom, through the law, through the efforts of labor unions and management, through the attitudes of parents and teachers—is deeply committed to keeping young people away from . . . real problems of individual and group living" (1961, p. 293). Rogers recognized that the politics of person-centered education threatened the conventional roles of teacher, student, and administrator. To change educational policies, Rogers and his colleagues sought, not only to theorize about the transfer of power from authority figures to learners, but also to engage in experiments to transform educational institutions (Kirschenbaum & Henderson, 1989, pp. 299ff).

Yet Rogers focused on the individual as the basic agent of change.

> In our present educational culture, [the person-centered approach] cannot exist unless there is one precondition . . . : a leader or a person who is perceived as an authority figure in the situation is sufficiently secure within herself and in her relationship to others that she experiences an essential trust in the capacity of others to think for themselves, to learn for themselves. (Kirschenbaum & Henderson, 1989, pp. 326–327)

Rogers' rationalistic conception of problem solving in education and the helping professions connected individuals to ethical action in both personal and social/political spheres. Rogers' own connection to social action can be traced through John Dewey's ideas of progressive education. To Dewey, education should provide individuals with the means to live as responsible community members in a democratic society. Dewey's philosophy initially influenced Rogers through lectures he attended given by William Heard Kilpatrick, a prominent follower of Dewey, at Teachers College, Columbia University in the 1920s (Kirschenbaum, 1979, pp. 48–49; Evans, 1975, p. 111; Zappen, Chapter 10, this volume).

Two aspects of Dewey's ideas are notable in the formation of Rogers' principles. First, just as Dewey saw the teacher's role as engaging students' interests so that their learning would become self-motivated, so Rogers defined the facilitative role (whether assumed by self or others) as engaging the three person-centered attitudes (congruence, acceptance, empathy) that foster the self-directed growth of individuals. Rogers' concerns, like Dewey's, did not end with the individual (and did not glorify emotional indulgence or release), but carried through to social action with implications for improving society.

Second, Rogers' rationalistic assumptions for solving problems resembled Dewey's belief in reason as the means for negotiating social issues. While Rogers added emphasis on the affective characteristics of conflicts and sought to reduce psychological threat and defensiveness, his goal (like Dewey's) was to allow reason to operate for "objective resolutions to value conflicts."[4] For many of Rogers' critics, his approach to problem solving through improving communication assumed too much rationalism and reasonableness. To Rogers' colleague, Richard Farson, Rogers reduced complicated human dilemmas and conflicts by taking them out of such contexts as history, culture, class, and power (Evans, 1975). However, both in classroom and actual-life situations, those employing Rogerian collaborative principles can attempt to avoid these limitations, as essays in this volume describe.

For writing instruction the problem-solving approach has been criticized by some rhetoricians and composition specialists as too empirically positivistic, narrowly utilitarian, ideologically contaminated, and lacking the generative and epistemic qualities of current rhetorical theories. For example, in pedagogical terms, Fahnestock and Secor (1983) examined three major approaches for teaching argumentation and judged that their "rhetorical/generative" approach was superior to what they labeled "content/problem solving," given their aim of teaching transferable rhetorical skills. But their definition of problem solving narrowly linked it with specialized course content (interdisciplinary or case studies), thus undercutting their generalized charges against problem solving that it is preoccupied with content and that this focus "tends to crowd out the writing instruction" (p. 22).

Such a limited conception of problem solving can be corrected by a comprehensive "pluralistic theory of problems" that includes concepts of solving epistemic problems in writing (Carter, 1988). Recent discussions of problem solving have revealed its more extensive boundaries within the field of rhetoric and composition (Carter, 1988; MacDonald 1987; House & House, 1987). As I summarized above, and the essays in this volume show, Rogerian problem solving is not incompatible with the epistemic aspects of inquiry in a contextual model of rhetoric. Rogerian perspectives are not inherently vulnerable to the charges of being overly positivistic or detached from historical and cultural considerations.

5. IDEOLOGICAL CRITIQUES OF ROGERIAN, PSYCHOLOGICAL, AND EXPRESSIVIST APPROACHES

In addition to the specific challenges to Rogerian problem solving, broader critiques come from ideological criticism. At first, in the 1960s and 1970s, some cultural critics (from psychological perspectives) reacted harshly to what they perceived as self-indulgent and subversive about the human potential movement, in which Rogers was influential. According to Gross (1978):

> the human growth movement is blatantly romantic. It insists that each of us has within us the potential for emotional stability and happiness. By calling on humanistic techniques, we not only will grow emotionally but will find our authenticity. If the individual can be self-actualized, he will, in a new theological sense, be Saved. (p. 298)

Such theological analogies betrayed both theistic disdain and conservative alarm at a popular movement which produced powerful effects on individuals and society.

In the 1980s, criticism from Marxist perspectives replaced the earlier psychological and theological critiques of humanistic psychotherapy and Rogers. Tuman (1988) quoted Giroux, who condemned the privatized "concern for personal growth, inner happiness, and interpersonal relations which affirm the dignity and autonomy of the self" (p. 42). Pounds's (1987) rhetorical critique of Rogerian argument indicted the ideology of psychotherapy generally for seeking to "adjust" individuals to their established conditions.

Some 1980s proponents of postmodernist critical theory have presented epistemologically oriented ideological critiques, calling into question the idea of self and the status of individuals as subjects. According to Brodkey (1989), "in postmodern theories of subjectivity: (1) all subjects are the joint creations of language and discourse; (2) all subjects produced are ideological" (p. 126). Therefore, individuals who assume that they can construct a unified self that pervades and transcends all discourse situations are naive or deluding themselves; "we are at once constituted and unified as subjects in language and discourse" (p. 125), not outside or prior to them.

Such theorizing, however, does not predict the ideological outcomes of analysis; rather, it only enunciates general epistemological assumptions from which specific analysis begins. We might well agree with Brodkey that we should begin by questioning "the very notion of the unified self—the traditional Cartesian notion that the self is a transcendent and absolute entity rather than a creation of language and ideology" (p. 127). But what, in effect, such deconstructive analysis decenters is one historical conception of the individual—the bourgeois, autonomous, rational, self-regulating self as agent of all personal and social production (Venn, 1984; Sampson, 1989). This convenient figure of the bourgeois self turns into a straw man when it cannot contain and do justice to the multiple and complex notions of the individual subject and subjectivity in western culture during the last 200 years.

Rogerian and other self psychologies (like Heinz Kohut's, Chapter 16, this volume) resist being reduced to stereotypes. Rogers rejected the exclusive determinisms of biology and culture, including behaviorism and Freudian drive theory, for an eclectic, if less theoretical, synthesis of factors in which self-determinism was elevated. According to Farson, Rogers shifted psychotherapy from a medical model of curing illness to a focus on the healthful growth of ordinary people (Evans, 1975). Rogers emphasized the role of the self-aware individual as an agent of personal transformations which can lead to social transformations. A "whole person" would not be the only determinant of his or her life, unconstrained by other formative influences; but Rogers' emphasis was on helping individuals become more self-directed and personally responsible for their values and actions.

The "whole person" of humanist psychology signifies the recognition that such attributes as affective and cognitive, or rational and intuitive, comprise a self of multiple parts—or, we might now say, multiple selves in the various conditions and situations of one's existence. This multiplicity of selves, moreover, need not be integrated into an ideal organic unity; rather, the multiple self could function within the postmodernist environment of difference, indeterminacy, and contrastive individual and group qualities. The "whole person," then, is the sum of a variety of interrelated but not necessarily harmonious parts. A good way to describe this condition of the self would be Bakhtin's polyphonic dialogism. Treating the self as a polyphonic dialogue of multiple voices arises from a pluralistic and inclusionary approach to theory and practice (see Halasek, Chapter 8, this volume).

For rhetoric and composition instruction, unfortunately, deconstructive and social/epistemic approaches often take exclusionary turns in critiques of romantic, expressivist, humanistic, and psychological theories and practices. Such critiques deny the continuing usefulness and achievements of psychological and expressive approaches in the theory and teaching of writing. Berlin (1988), for example, linked humanistic psychologists, like Rogers, with expressivist rhetoricians, like Peter Elbow, as heirs to a romanticism which holds naive notions of the self. As a result, these cultural movements and their representatives are accused of presenting inadequate pedagogical, social, and political programs based on liberal humanist ideology. Expressivist rhetorical practices, as the charges read, lead to complicity with, if not support of, established conditions, rather than to the critique and correction of them.

But, despite the arguments by Berlin and others, it does not follow that romantic/expressivist approaches to writing, or psychological/epistemic rhetoric, need be limited by notions of a transcendent self or metaphysical conceptions of the individual as unconstrained agent of all personal and social production. Neither does it follow that applications of Rogerian and humanistic self psychology are incompatible with current epistemic approaches to rhetoric.

Taken in historical perspective, the arguments being presented against romanticism and the psychology of the self are imbalanced and incomplete. Romantic ideology, for example, is neither straightforward nor uncontested, as revealed by the history of its critical debates in the past 200 years (McGann, 1983). The critique of romanticism, moreover, can be understood as one extreme of the cycle of oscillating critical debates, which are themselves part of an ongoing historical dialectic, rather than final statements on the issues.[5] The self, to psychoanalyst Heinz Kohut (1984), for example, represented a construct, a shorthand for a variety of aspects of the individual personality evident in particular situations. Not only did Berlin fail to recognize the sophistication of theories held by self psychologists (e.g., Kohut, Chapter 16, this volume), but his charges also oversimplified the connections between ideology and praxis. Tuman (1988) has provided a more careful, class-based social analysis of college writing pedagogy, but, in recommending a limited, contextual goal ("emphasis on product over process or teacher as authority rather than facilitator," p. 50), his ideological critique remains unbalanced and unparticularized to individuals in specific classroom situations.

6. IDEOLOGY AND SELF PSYCHOLOGY

There seems to be a lack of distinction in postmodernist critiques between (a) the psychological theories of self, with their practical applications in clinical and pedagogical contexts, and (b) the ideologically contaminated notions of extreme individualism: the autonomous, aggrandizing, and rationally coherent self of capitalist, commodity society. In the current debates, I believe that operational distinctions need to be made between conceptions of the psychological self and ideological constructs of the bourgeois subject. The deconstruction of subjects conceived as bourgeois, humanist, or romantic needs to include the reconstitution of a psychological subject: a self allowing for the formation of identity and interactive personal agency within situational constraints (Shotter & Gergen, 1989).

To the extent that cultural critics reduce psychological approaches and explanations to social determinants, they would deny us opportunities to understand and aid the personal and social development of our students, as well as others with whom we wish to conduct empathic communication. The kind of development which I have in mind is not strictly cognitive and quantifiable. Rather it involves processes of interpersonal awareness and proceeds subjectively and affectively with identity formation and, ultimately, self-conscious awareness of authenticity and congruence in relation to one's self and others (see, e.g., Brooke, 1988, pp. 37–40). Rogerian empathy leads to modifying one's self or creating new subject selves in response to changing situations.

While it is useful to call into question outmoded assumptions which supported universal, unchanging, monolithic conceptions of the autonomous self, ideological critiques undermine the pluralistic balance within the contextual model of rhetoric. A balanced pluralism maintains multiple perspectives, so that one approach does not dominate and reduce or preclude others. No one approach in isolation, whether focused on self, on society, or on language and textuality, will be sufficient to explain and teach communication in theory and practice. In a balanced pluralism, each of us is assumed to participate in a reciprocal process of both determining and reflecting our discursive multiple selves. Just as we do not discover an objective reality, but create it (in conjunction with language systems and specific discourse situations), so too (within the same determinate contexts of language and discourse), each of us creates a self—or various discursively contextualized selves.

Psychologies of the self maintain a balance between subject and object at the moment when postmodernist epistemology goes beyond problematizing the status of the subject to the extreme of denying the agency of the psychological self—turning all selves into fictive selves and all reality into textuality. But the issues of human agency and subject–object relationships remain a function of their specific situations. From the advent of modern physics in the early 20th century, it became evident that a strictly objective rendering of events independent of the perceiving subject was not possible. This relativity, fundamental to all fields of inquiry, nevertheless, does not privilege one element over the others in any interpretive model, including the contextual model of rhetoric. The individual, the social communities, and the language of their transactions remain pluralistically interrelated. Just because we may be structured by the linguistic fictive selves which we or our culture invented, we have not negated the physical boundaries of the actual world or the contributing factors of human agency in constituting social reality (Brodkey, 1988, pp. 127–128).

To the extent that psychological matters, like concepts of the self, are reduced to social determinants, the psychological field is swallowed up by sociocultural ideology in a cannibalistic incorporation. Moreover, as psychoanalyst Theodor Reik (1948) recognized, such symbolic cannibalism involves exploitive power and control ("sublimated seizure and incorporation," pp. 232–234). Today, such ideological cannibalism (like ideological imperialism) can be further identified as having gender implications—the dominance (in a stereotypical masculine fashion) of the externalized, cognitive/rational study of history and material social forces over the internalized, affective/emotional aspects of psychotherapy and personal expression.

Just as Rogerian perspectives bridge the gap between the individual and collaborative approaches (balancing self and society), so they reconcile culturally inscribed gender attributes—interrelating feminine and masculine qualities without homogenizing their differences. Rogerian perspectives validate the qualities attributed to the feminine—by focusing on empathy, feelings, intersubjectivity, and interpersonal relationships. However, both feminine and masculine attributes collaborate in the person-centered conception of whole human beings, whose potentialities are not limited by culturally restricted stereotypes of masculinity and femininity.[6] Thus, Rogerian perspectives contribute to a fully engendered pluralism.[7]

7. SELF AND PRAXIS

Theoretically, there may remain a fundamental difference between psychological and social/epistemic theories regarding the concept of self as a construct; but this dispute will not be settled by rhetorical theorists alone. In fact, as with any foundational dispute, it need not be settled, if indeed it can be, in strictly theoretical terms. Theorists will continue to debate the nature of human nature and question if there are psychological entities (like a self) or affective states that exist outside—or prior to—language. Whether idealist or materialist answers are offered, they will not be benign or virulent in themselves, but rather in the practical applications that they spawn. For example, as both Rogers and Kohut recognized, empathy (whether a construct or capability) is value-neutral; it can be employed either positively or negatively, for mutual benefits or for manipulating others (Chapters 3, 16, this volume). In a pragmatic sense, therefore, the social value of theoretical constructs lies in their instrumental worth for producing ethical results.

There is something peculiarly American in Rogers' pragmatic efforts to transcend preoccupations with ideology by focusing on communication to reduce conflicts, solve problems, and improve relationships from the personal to the international political spheres. Although we are now rightly reminded that we cannot transcend ideology and theory, Rogerian principles also remind us that the ultimate social test is one of pragmatics; the best estimate of how theories translate into practice will be the performances that result—the kind and quality of personal and public actions that follow. In this test, we can unmask self-serving, autonomous individualism and exploitive social manipulations for what they are.

While there are significant differences between the therapeutic situation and the adversarial argumentative situation, the environment for teaching writing may well resemble that of counseling more than that of forensics. To maximize benefits for student writers, teachers must provide, directly or indirectly, safe and supportive conditions for facilitating personal expression, collaboration, and growth. The teacher who employs Rogerian principles displays such qualities as: respecting students, challenging and motivating them to assume responsibility for their learning, eliciting authentic discourse from them by being an authentic audience, and showing the teacher's own struggles and honest efforts at writing by participating with students in the writing process (Hairston, 1982).

In such conditions, I would assume that Ira Shor, Berlin's (1988) exemplary social constructivist classroom teacher, and Carl Rogers would be compatible in the classroom. Shor could not avoid relying on what, in effect, are Rogerian principles to bring about the classroom atmosphere for liberating students' social consciousness. And Rogers would support the personal awareness and social critique that would result. Although Rogers' *Freedom to Learn* (1969) and Paulo Freire's work, *Pedagogy of the Oppressed* (1970), did not influence each other, Rogers (1977) later praised Freire and pointed out similarities of their approaches, including empathy, collaboration, self-initiated learning, and real-world problem solving.

A balanced pluralism in rhetorical theory and composition instruction should recognize the ideological grounding of all perspectives, but not distort the influence of any one approach, be it personal/expressivist, linguistic/structural, or social/historical. To reject, diminish, or subjugate psychological and affective approaches under the domination of other major approaches is to ignore the powerful forces of intersubjective collaboration necessary to communication relationships.

Not only in the classroom, but also in other interpersonal situations, Rogerian principles provide a way of proceeding from the self to society, from the individual—with personal awareness, self-motivation, and increased learning—to larger social, economic, and political concerns. Rogerian perspectives allow individuals the opportunity to consider the affective and collaborative dimensions of communication, to negotiate among the possible discourses, to risk changing one's self-concepts and opinions, and, within situational constraints, to choose the language, texts, and stories that influence one's self and others.

NOTES

1. LeFevre is incomplete in her discussion of Rogers and incorrect in her statement that his "client-centered therapy . . . has as its aim the enhancement of the client rather than the solution of mutual problems or the achievement of social change" (1987, pp. 150–151, n. 21).
2. I use the term *pluralism* (which postmodernist critics eschew for its liberal humanist connotations) in the manner of Wayne Booth (1979). Pluralism appears to be accessible to a wider audience than, say, *multiplicity* or *heterogeneity*. Moreover, my use of *balanced pluralism* is intended to suggest to humanists and postmodernists alike that the ideologically contaminated aspects of liberalism and individualism can, with diligence, be factored out of a model fostering collaborative and contrastive approaches in order to avoid adversarial and exclusivist ones. Unfortunately, I do not have the space to discuss pluralism more fully; it may well be a key problematic of our time, as argued by Rooney (1989).
3. To the extent that one creates the "fiction" of one's audience, Rogerian principles insist on the fidelity of the construct to the actual psychological and social conditions, rather than distorted, incomplete, or wished-for fabrications of others. In the creation of fictive selves and audiences, Rogerian principles remind us that, to the extent that actual people are reduced to inaccurate fictional fabrications, there is a loss of the intersubjective recognition of the humanity of others.
4. In an interview, philosopher Sidney Hook (1987), one of Dewey's students and a major proponent of his ideas, commented on the strengths and limitations of Dewey's rationalism. "Some people

think he put too much faith in intelligence and reason, believing as he did that they could resolve value conflicts. Even I at one point thought he had ignored the necessity of violent struggle in some cases in which certain issues could not be negotiated. But I realized that, while Dewey would concede that certain issues could not be negotiated in particular situations, he did not believe that such conflicts involved a clash of ultimate values. He said that every actual conflict is actually over secondary, not final values and is, therefore, potentially resolvable by reason" (p. 46).

5. Over-reactions to Romanticism in the early twentieth century, for example, issued from such aesthetic and cultural critics as T. S. Eliot; his teacher, the neo-humanist Irving Babbitt; and T. E. Hulme, who called romanticism "spilt religion" and sought to resurrect what he considered to be the "hard," "dry classical spirit" in opposition to the "damp" and "drug"-like romantic poetry of his day (Gleckner & Enscoe, 1970). Such gender stereotypes need no further comment.
6. In their recent work, Carol Gilligan and colleagues proposed that the particular moral orientations of *care* and *justice* (which she identified earlier, *In a Different Voice* [1982], as essentially feminine or masculine, respectively) should not be taken as mutually exclusive categories of gender difference (Gilligan & Wiggins, 1987). Similarly, Rogerian perspectives avoid dichotomizing expressive qualities as stereotypically masculine or feminine, but integrate gender attributes to function collaboratively without compromising their differences.
7. Although Lassner (1990) reported that women in her "Women and Writing" course felt confined and forced to repress "a right to be angry" when instructed in Rogerian argument, the reassessments in this volume recognize that the applicability of Rogerian principles is situational. Just as some interpersonal and social situations might call for uncompromising advocacy, others might benefit from collaboration and mutual understanding for a satisfactory solution to a problem.

REFERENCES

Agosta, L. (1984). Empathy and intersubjectivity. In J. Lichtenberg, M. Bornstein, & D. Silver (Eds.), *Empathy I* (pp. 43–61). Hillsdale, NJ: Erlbaum.

Berlin, J. A. (1987). *Rhetoric and reality: Writing instruction in American colleges, 1900–1985.* Carbondale, IL: Southern Illinois University Press.

Berlin, J. A. (1988). Rhetoric and ideology in the writing class. *College English, 50*, 477–494.

Booth, W. C. (1979). *Critical understanding: The powers and the limits of pluralism*. Chicago, IL: University of Chicago Press.

Brodkey, L. (1989). On the subject of class and gender in "the literacy letters." *College English, 51*, 125–141.

Brooke, R. (1988). Modeling a writer's identity: Reading and imitation in the writing classroom. *College Composition and Communication, 39*, 23–41.

Carter, M. (1988). Problem solving reconsidered: A pluralistic theory of problems. *College English, 50*, 551–565.

Evans, R. I. (1975). *Carl Rogers: The man and his ideas*. New York: Dutton.

Fahnestock J., & Secor, M. (1983). Teaching argument: A theory of types. *College Composition and Communication, 34*, 20–30.

Freire, P. (1970). *Pedagogy of the oppressed*. New York: Seabury.

Gilligan, C. (1982). *In a different voice*. Cambridge, MA: Harvard University Press.

Gilligan, C., & Wiggins, G. (1987). The origins of morality in early childhood relationships. In J. Cagan & S. Lamb (Eds.), *The emergence of morality* (pps. 277–305). Chicago, IL: University of Chicago Press.

Gleckner, R. F., & Enscoe, G. E. (Eds.). (1970). *Romanticism: Points of view* (2nd ed.). Englewood Cliffs, NJ: Prentice-Hall.

Gross, M. L. (1978). *The psychological society*. New York: Simon and Schuster.

Hairston, M. (1982). Using Carl Rogers' communication theories in the composition classroom. *Rhetoric Review, 1*, 50–55.

Hook, S. (1987). Why "back to basics" isn't good enough. *American Educator, 11*, 22–28, 42–48.

House, E. B., & House, W. J. (1987). Problem-solving: The debates in composition and psychology. *Journal of Advanced Composition, 7*, 62–75.

Kirschenbaum, H. (1979). *On becoming Carl Rogers*. New York: Dell/Delta.

Kirschenbaum, H., & Henderson, V. L. (Eds.). (1989). *The Carl Rogers reader*. Boston, MA: Houghton Mifflin.

Kohut, H. (1984). *How does analysis cure?* Chicago, IL: University of Chicago Press.

Lassner, P. (1990). Feminist responses to Rogerian argument. *Rhetoric Review, 8*, 220–231.

LeFevre, K. B. (1987). *Invention as a social act*. Carbondale, IL: Southern Illinois University Press.

MacDonald, S. P. (1987). Problem definition in academic writing. *College English, 49*, 315–331.

McGann, J. (1983). *The romantic ideology*. Chicago, IL: University of Chicago Press.

Pounds, W. (1987). The context of no context: A Burkean critique of Rogerian argument. *Rhetoric Society Quarterly, 17*, 45–59.

Reik, T. (1948). *Listening with the third ear*. New York: Farrar, Strauss.

Rogers, C. R. (1951). Communication: Its blocking and its facilitation. In C. R. Rogers, *On becoming a person* (pp. 329–337). Boston, MA: Houghton Mifflin.

Rogers, C. R. (1961). *On becoming a person*. Boston, MA: Houghton Mifflin.

Rogers, C. R. (1969). *Freedom to learn*. Columbus, OH: Merrill.

Rogers, C. R. (1977). *Carl Rogers on personal power.* New York: Dell/Delta.

Rogers, C. R. (1980). *A way of being.* Boston, MA: Houghton Mifflin.

Rooney, E. (1989). *Seductive reasoning: Pluralism as the problematic of contemporary literary theory.* Ithaca, NY: Cornell University Press.

Sampson, E. E. (1989). The deconstruction of the self. In J. Shotter & K. J. Gergen (Eds.), *Texts of identity* (pp. 1–19). London: Sage.

Shotter, J., & Gergen, K. J. (Eds.). (1989). *Texts of identity.* London: Sage.

Tuman, M. C. (1988). Class, codes, and composition: Basil Bernstein and the critique of pedagogy. *College Composition and Communication, 39,* 42–51.

Venn, C. (1984). The subject of psychology. In J. Henriques, W. Hollway, C. Urwin, C. Venn, & V. Walkerdine (Eds.), *Changing the subject: Psychology, social regulation and subjectivity* (pp. 119–152). London: Methuen.

PART 1
Carl Rogers on Communication

INTRODUCTION

The chapters in this part present representative statements of Carl Rogers on communication, interpersonal relations, and sociopolitical interaction which he offered over a span of almost 35 years. Included are two previously published papers, plus an interview I conducted with Rogers in 1985. It is appropriate to begin (Chapter 1) with his 1951 paper, "Communication: Its Blocking and Its Facilitation." The jargon of the title notwithstanding, this paper became the reference point for rhetoricians (like Young, Becker, & Pike, 1970) and other social theorists (like Rapoport, 1960) to introduce Rogerian principles of communication into their fields. Here I will note only some key aspects of this paper, because it has been discussed frequently in the prior scholarship and in the new contributions below (Part 2).[1]

Among the broader implications of Rogers' entry into the field of communication is his extension of his "person-centered approach" from micro to macro contexts; that is, from (a) the therapist–client situation, situations of "small face-to-face groups . . . exhibiting industrial tensions, religious tensions, racial tensions, and therapy groups in which many personal tensions are present," to (b) situations involving larger groups, geographically separated groups, classes, nations, and negotiators representing such populations (Rogers, 1961, pp. 334–335).

While Rogers has been criticized as idealistic and politically naive—and while he appears to reduce conflict to matters simply of communication and understanding, apparently minimizing economic, social, and ideological components of conflict—he should not be dismissed merely as a Pollyanna. He does not propose that opponents will be converted, but rather that "real communication" will be established directed toward the goal of mutually satisfactory solutions to problems (Teich, 1987; Zappen, Chapter 10, this volume). As Rogers stated in his 1951 paper:

> Real communication occurs . . . when we listen with understanding . . . to see the expressed idea and attitude from the other person's point of view, to sense how it feels to him, to achieve his frame of reference. (1961, pp. 331–332)
>
> Mutual communication tends to be pointed toward solving a problem rather than toward attacking a person or group. (p. 336)

From interpersonal relations to international relations, Rogers proposed that his principles would produce "genuine understanding" if people would attempt "to increase the amount of listening *with*, and to decrease the amount of evaluation *about*" others (p. 335).

The key to applying Rogers' principles to communication is what I have called his *restatement rule*. It is an adaptation of his principle of "reflection of feeling" or "active listening," originating in his therapy and counseling practice (see *Interview*, this volume).

> Each person can speak up for himself only *after* he has first restated the ideas and feelings of the previous speaker accurately, and to that speaker's satisfaction. It . . . would be necessary for you to really achieve the other speaker's frame of reference—to understand his thoughts and feelings so well that you could summarize them for him. . . . However, once you have been able to see the other's point of view, your own comments will have to be drastically revised. You will also find the emotion going out of the discussion, the differences being reduced, and those differences which remain being of a rational and understandable sort. (pp. 332–333)

While we might question Rogers' optimistic and idealized expectations about the outcome of applying his rule, there is more here than his critics have given him credit for. Although his goal of rational and deliberative problem solving (reflecting the influence of Dewey)[2] valorizes democratic and socially harmonious processes and products, Rogers allows for the needs of resistance, hostile protest, and venting powerful feelings (see Chapter 2, this volume). Moreover, the previous commentaries on Rogerian rhetoric have not paid enough attention to the effects on the person who applies Rogerian restatement and gains genuine empathic understanding of the other's views (Teich, 1987). According to Rogers,

> If you really understand another person in this way, if you are willing to enter his private world and see the way life appears to him, without any attempt to make evaluative judgments, you run the risk of being changed yourself. You . . . might find yourself influenced in your attitudes or your personality. This risk of being changed is one of the most frightening prospects most of us can face. (1961, p. 333)

Accordingly, Rogerian principles are incompatible with rhetoric exclusively advocating adversarial confrontation, hostile refutation, and defeating opponents. The essential difference between Rogerian and forensic rhetoric lies precisely at the point of risking change—of being willing to transform fundamental aspects of oneself: one's identity, private or public beliefs, and positions. Moreover, Rogers proposes that such risking is as necessary for nations and their representatives as it is for individuals in their interpersonal relations.

In Chapter 2, I follow Rogers' suggestion at the end of our interview that I reprint one of his more recent papers showing his broader and deeper exploration of collaborative principles in communication. In "One Alternative to Nuclear Planetary Suicide" (1984), Rogers demonstrates his humanistic concern for a sane future for humanity on the planet, as he examines ways to engage the human collaboration necessary for mutually beneficial public policy and political negotiations of stubborn, highly charged issues. This essay includes reports of actual group work by Rogers and colleagues and an analysis of the 1978 Camp David negotiations with U.S. President Carter, Prime Minister Begin of Israel, and President Sadat of Egypt. Significantly, we should note the connections of writing with speaking and listening; written documents produced by the parties were embedded in and emerged from the oral and interpersonal contexts of the situation.

During our interview (Chapter 3), Rogers and I discussed the implications of his principles for communication, rhetoric, and writing. He conceded that problems of transferring his principles from oral to written communication had "never been a primary interest" of his. Nevertheless, he explored both the cognitive and affective aspects of empathic understanding and restatement, which should be helpful for those of us applying his principles to composition instruction. When questioned on the adaptation of Rogerian principles to conventional rhetorical argumentation, however, Rogers reacted harshly to the use of his principles for the adversarial purpose of winning an argument. He asserted:

> I regard that as quite the opposite of my thinking. And I also regard it as a perversion of my thinking. . . . I feel that's a trick . . . using my thinking in that fashion. (*Interview*, this volume, R.1-R.2)

Like other originative psychotherapists, (e.g., Jung),[3] Rogers strongly rejected the labeling and appropriation of his principles as strategies, techniques, or steps to follow. He resisted efforts to abstract his humanistic, interactive, and (we should now add) collaborative principles from the specific therapeutic situation and apply them formulaically. Thus, in my writing about Rogers, I deliberately use the term *principles* in a variety of contexts and refrain from calling the applications of these principles either *strategies* or *techniques*.

In addition to our lengthy discussion of the issue of empathy in oral and written contexts, I attempted to clarify with Rogers his concept of congruence (*Interview*, this volume T.16-T.21). I sought to explore connections between congruence and the Romantic/expressivist values of sincerity and authenticity in writing. My intent was to lead into an examination of Rogers' epistemological position on the issue of language as constituting meaning in individual and social contexts. I regret that I was not successful in formulating more pointed questions and focusing our discussion more cogently. Initially, I had in mind Ede's (1984) claim that

> Rogers' ontological and epistemological assumptions imply an arhetorical view of language, one in which language functions ideally as a transparent means of self-expression. (p. 40)

This interpretation of Rogers' assumptions about language in his 1951 paper is supported by his reference to Hayakawa (1941; Rogers, 1961, p. 333), who was a major influence in the "General Semantics" movement of the late 1940s and 1950s. Rogers' positivistic concept of language at this time would have been shaped by a technological model of communication theory; the semanticists sought to clean up the "noise" in the medium (language), which disrupted the message transmitted from sender to receiver. Whether Rogers still held a view of language as a transparent medium reflecting preestablished meanings was an issue I sought to explore with him.

In our interview, Rogers (like many other psychotherapists) spoke as if there were irreducible subjective qualities of affect; but whether he held a foundational position on the role of language as reflecting preestablished meanings was not as clear to me. While Rogers was puzzled by how "some words fit" better in articulating previously unarticulated feelings (*Interview*, this volume, R.19), he was less interested in the epistemological status of the medium (as providing socially constructed meanings) and more interested in the larger context of collaborative transactions of individuals and groups.

In the drift of our conversation, as I attempted to make clear the current epistemic ideas of language generating the constructs that determine meaning, I undoubtedly confused matters by introducing the "mirroring" analogies from Shakespeare and from Abrams' contrast between the mirror and the lamp (*Interview*, this volume, T.20-R.21). Nevertheless, I would conclude from our discussion in and beyond the transcript that Rogers' views of language are less epistemologically naive in the context of his practice than his critics contend. While he may not have accommodated his views to current assumptions of the discourse basis of psychoanalytic communication, he did not appear to hold extreme, monistic views. Given his interest in clinical practice rather than abstract theorizing, it is understandable that Rogers did not propound either of the extremes: that language exclusively creates reality, or that language directly reflects reality.

Such issues as the epistemological implications of Rogerian principles, the relations between oral and written communication in applying Rogerian principles to rhetoric and composition, the interconnections of cognitive and affective aspects of communication from the Rogerian perspective, and the appropriateness and practicality of Rogerian principles beyond the clinical situation—these and other issues which emerge from Rogers' own statements will be treated directly and indirectly by the contributions in the remainder of this volume.

Regarding Rogers' own language, we note that he used masculine universal terms in his early publications; however, his sensitivity to nonsexist language is evident in his writings from the late 1970s (Rogers, 1977, p. ix) and in our interview.

NOTES

1. See, e.g., Teich (1987). Rogers' paper was reprinted in full by Young, Becker, & Pike (1970) as the core of their chapter introducing "Rogerian argument" to the field of rhetoric and composition. In the various contributions to the present volume, citations to Rogers' 1951 paper have not been conformed to the pages of this volume or to a single source; citations are either to Young, Becker, & Pike (1970) or to Rogers' (1961) volume, *On Becoming A Person*.
2. See Introduction, this volume, section 4; Zappen, Chapter 10, this volume.
3. See, for example, the interview with Jung included in the documentary film about him, *Matter of Heart* (1983), in which he rejects the reduction of praxis to strategies and formulae.

4. Hayakawa's popular textbook, *Language in Thought and Action*, was first published in 1941. In the 1949 edition, it cited both Rogers and Rapoport (who was writing on "General Semantics"). Rogers shared a humanistic ethical stance with the semanticists of the 1940s and 1950s, who focused on language pragmatics for the purposes of cooperation, reducing conflict and discomfort, and keeping communication channels open to produce mutual understanding and social harmony.

REFERENCES

Ede, L. (1984). Is Rogerian rhetoric really Rogerian? *Rhetoric Review 3*, 40–48.

Hayakawa, S. I. (1941). *Language in thought and action*. New York: Harcourt Brace.

Matter of Heart. (1983). C. G. Jung Institute of Los Angeles. New York: Kino International.

Rapoport, A. (1960). *Fights, games, and debates*. Ann Arbor, MI: University of Michigan Press.

Rogers, C. R. (1961). *On becoming a person*. Boston, MA: Houghton Mifflin.

Rogers, C. R. (1977). *Carl Rogers on personal power*. New York: Dell/Delta.

Teich, N. (1987). Rogerian problem-solving and the rhetoric of argumentation. *Journal of Advanced Composition 7*, 52–61.

Young, R. E., Becker, A. L., & Pike, K. L. (1970). *Rhetoric: Discovery and change*. New York: Harcourt Brace.

CHAPTER 1
Communication: Its Blocking and Its Facilitation (1951)*

Carl R. Rogers

[Rogers' note: *It was written in 1951 for presentation at the Centennial Conference on Communications at Northwestern University, where it was given the title, "Communication: Its Blocking and Its Facilitation." It has since been reprinted a half-dozen times, by different groups and in different journals, including the* Harvard Business Review *and* ETC, *the journal of the Society for General Semantics.*

Although some of its illustrations now appear a bit dated, I am including it because it makes what I feel is an important point regarding group tensions, national and international. The suggestion regarding Russian–U.S. tensions appeared hopelessly idealistic at that time. Now I believe it would be accepted by many as good sense.]

It may seem curious that a person whose whole professional effort is devoted to psychotherapy should be interested in problems of communication. What relationship is there between providing therapeutic help to individuals with emotional maladjustments and the concern of this conference with obstacles to communication? Actually the relationship is very close indeed. The whole task of psychotherapy is the task of dealing with a failure in communication. The emotionally maladjusted person, the "neurotic," is in difficulty first, because communication within himself has broken down, and second because, as a

---

* This chapter originally appeared in *On Becoming a Person*, by Carl Rogers. Copyright © 1961 by Houghton Mifflin Company. Reprinted with permission.

result of this, his communication with others has been damaged. If this sounds somewhat strange to you, then let me put it in other terms. In the "neurotic" individual, parts of himself which have been termed unconscious, or repressed, or denied to awareness, become blocked off so that they no longer communicate themselves to the conscious or managing part of himself. As long as this is true, there are distortions in the way he communicates himself to others, and so he suffers both within himself, and in his interpersonal relations. The task of psychotherapy is to help the person achieve, through a special relationship with a therapist, good communication within himself. Once this is achieved he can communicate more freely and more effectively with others. We may say then that psychotherapy is good communication, within and between men. We may also turn that statement around and it will still be true. Good communication, free communication, within or between men, is always therapeutic.

It is, then, from a background of experience with communication in counseling and psychotherapy, that I want to present to you tonight two ideas. I wish to state what I believe is one of the major factors in blocking or impeding communication, and then I wish to present what in our experience has proven to be a very important way of improving or facilitating communication.

I would like to propose, as an hypothesis for consideration, that the major barrier to mutual interpersonal communication is our very natural tendency to judge, to evaluate, to approve or disapprove, the statement of the other person, or the other group. Let me illustrate my meaning with some very simple examples. As you leave the meeting tonight, one of the statements you are likely to hear is, "I didn't like that man's talk." Now what do you respond? Almost invariably your reply will be either approval or disapproval of the attitude expressed. Either you respond, "I didn't either. I thought it was terrible," or else you tend to reply, "Oh, I thought it was really good." In other words, your primary reaction is to evaluate what has just been said to you, to evaluate it from *your* point of view, your own frame of reference.

Or take another example. Suppose I say with some feeling, "I think the Republicans are behaving in ways that show a lot of good sound sense these days," what is the response that arises in your mind as you listen? The overwhelming likelihood is that it will be evaluative. You will find yourself agreeing, or disagreeing, or making some judgment about me such as "He must be a conservative," or "He seems solid in his thinking." Or let us take an illustration from the international scene. Russia says vehemently, "The treaty with Japan is a war plot on the part of the United States." We rise as one person to say "That's a lie!"

This last illustration brings in another element connected with my hypothesis. Although the tendency to make evaluations is common in almost all interchange of language, it is very much heightened in those situations where feelings and emotions are deeply involved. So the stronger our feelings the more likely it is that there will be no mutual element in the communication. There will be just two ideas, two feelings, two judgments, missing each other in psychological space. I'm sure you recognize this from your own experience. When you have not been emotionally involved yourself, and have listened to a heated discussion, you often go away thinking, "Well, they actually weren't talking about the same thing." And they were not. Each was making a judgment, an evaluation, from his own frame of reference. There was really nothing which could be called communication in any genuine sense. This tendency to react to any emotionally meaningful statement by forming an evaluation of it from your own point of view, is, I repeat, the major barrier to interpersonal communication.

But is there any way of solving this problem, of avoiding this barrier? I feel that we are making exciting progress toward this goal and I would like to present it as simply as I can. Real communication occurs, and this evaluative tendency is avoided, when we listen with understanding. What does this mean? It means to see the expressed idea and attitude from the other person's point of view, to sense how it feels to him, to achieve his frame of reference in regard to the thing he is talking about.

Stated so briefly, this may sound absurdly simple, but it is not. It is an approach which we have found extremely potent in the field of psychotherapy. It is the most effective agent we know for altering the basic personality structure of an individual, and improving his relationships and his communications with others. If I can listen to what he can tell me, if I can understand how it seems to him, if I can see its personal meaning for him, if I can sense the emotional flavor which it has for him, then I will be releasing potent forces of change in him. If I can really understand how he hates his father, or hates the university, or hates communists—if I can catch the flavor of his fear of insanity, or his fear of atom bombs, or of Russia—it will be the greatest help to him in altering those very hatreds and fears, and in establishing realistic and harmonious relationships with the very people and situations toward which he has felt hatred and fear. We know from our research that such empathic understanding—understanding *with* a person, not *about* him—is such an effective approach that it can bring about major changes in personality.

Some of you may be feeling that you listen well to people, and that you have never seen such results. The chances are very great indeed that your listening has not been of the type I have described. Fortunately I can suggest a little laboratory experiment which you can try to test the quality of your understanding. The next time you get into an argument with your wife, or your friend, or with a small group of friends, just stop the discussion for a moment and for an experiment, institute this rule. "Each person can speak up for himself only *after* he has first restated the ideas and feelings of the previous speaker accurately, and to that speaker's satisfaction." You see what this would mean. It would simply mean that before presenting your own point of view, it would be necessary for you to really achieve the other speaker's frame of reference—to understand his thoughts and feelings so well that you could summarize them for him. Sounds simple, doesn't it? But if you try it you will discover it is one of the most difficult things you have ever tried to do. However, once you have been able to see the other's point of view, your own comments will have to be drastically revised. You will also find the emotion going out of the discussion, the differences being reduced, and those differences which remain being of a rational and understandable sort.

Can you imagine what this kind of an approach would mean if it were projected into larger areas? What would happen to a labor–management dispute if it was conducted in such a way that labor, without necessarily agreeing, could accurately state management's point of view in a way that management could accept; and management, without approving labor's stand, could state labor's case in a way that labor agreed was accurate? It would mean that real communication was established, and one could practically guarantee that some reasonable solution would be reached.

If then this way of approach is an effective avenue to good communication and good relationships, as I am quite sure you will agree if you try the experiment I have mentioned, why is it not more widely tried and used? I will try to list the difficulties which keep it from being utilized.

In the first place it takes courage, a quality which is not too widespread. I am indebted to Dr. S. I. Hayakawa, the semanticist, for pointing out that to carry on psychotherapy in this fashion is to take a very real risk, and that courage is required. If you really understand another person in this way, if you are willing to enter his private world and see the way life appears to him, without any attempt to make evaluative judgments, you run the risk of being changed yourself. You might see it his way, you might find yourself influenced in your attitudes or your personality. This risk of being changed is one of the most frightening prospects most of us can face. If I enter, as fully as I am able, into the private world of a neurotic or psychotic individual, isn't there a risk that I might become lost in that world? Most of us are afraid to take that risk. Or if we had a Russian communist speaker here tonight, or Senator Joseph McCarthy, how many of us would dare to try to see the world from each of these points of view? The great majority of us could not *listen*; we would find ourselves compelled to *evaluate*, because listening would seem too dangerous. So the first requirement is courage, and we do not always have it.

But there is a second obstacle. It is just when emotions are strongest that it is most difficult to achieve the frame of reference of the other person or group. Yet this is the time the attitude is most needed, if communication is to be established. We have not found this to be an insuperable obstacle in our experience in psychotherapy. A third party, who is able to lay aside his own feelings and evaluations, can assist greatly by listening with understanding to each person or group and clarifying the views and attitudes each holds. We have found this very effective in small groups in which contradictory or antagonistic attitudes exist. When the parties to a dispute realize that they are being understood, that someone sees how the situation seems to them, the statements grow less exaggerated and less defensive, and it is no longer necessary to maintain the attitude, "I am 100% right and you are 100% wrong." The influence of such an understanding catalyst in the group permits the members to come closer and closer to the objective truth involved in the relationship. In this way mutual communication is established and some type of agreement becomes much more possible. So we may say that though heightened emotions make it much more difficult to understand *with* an opponent, our experience makes it clear that a neutral, understanding, catalyst type of leader or therapist can overcome this obstacle in a small group.

This last phrase, however, suggests another obstacle to utilizing the approach I have described. Thus far all our experience has been with small face-to-face groups—groups exhibiting industrial tensions, religious tensions, racial tensions, and therapy groups in which many personal tensions are present. In these small groups our experience, confirmed by a limited amount of research, shows that a listening, empathic approach leads to improved communication, to greater acceptance of others and by others, and to attitudes which are more positive and more problem-solving in nature. There is a decrease in defensiveness, in exaggerated statements, in evaluative and critical behavior. But these findings are from small groups. What about trying to achieve understanding between larger groups that are geographically remote? Or between face-to-face groups who are not speaking for themselves, but simply as representatives of others, like the delegates at the United Nations? Frankly we do not know the answers to these questions. I believe the situation might be put this way. As social scientists we have a tentative test-tube solution of the problem of breakdown in communication. But to confirm the validity of this test-tube solution, and to adapt it to the enormous problems of communication breakdown between classes, groups, and nations, would involve additional funds, much more research, and creative thinking of a high order.

Even with our present limited knowledge we can see some steps which might be taken, even in large groups, to increase the amount of listening *with*, and to decrease the amount of evaluation *about*. To be imaginative for a moment, let us suppose that a therapeutically oriented international group went to the Russian leaders and said, "We want to achieve a genuine understanding of your views and even more important, of your attitudes and feelings, toward the United States. We will summarize and resummarize these views and feelings if necessary, until you agree that our description represents the situation as it seems to you." Then suppose they did the same thing with the leaders in our own country. If they then gave the widest possible distribution to these two views, with the feelings clearly described but not expressed in name-calling, might not the effect be very great? It would not guarantee the type of understanding I have been describing, but it would make it much more possible. We can understand the feelings of a person who hates us much more readily when his attitudes are accurately described to us by a neutral third party, than we can when he is shaking his fist at us.

But even to describe such a first step is to suggest another obstacle to this approach of understanding. Our civilization does not yet have enough faith in the social sciences to utilize their findings. The opposite is true of the physical sciences. During the war when a test-tube solution was found to the problem of synthetic rubber, millions of dollars and an army of talent was turned loose on the problem of using that finding. If synthetic rubber could be made in milligrams, it could and would be made in the thousands of tons. And it was. But in the social science realm, if a way is found of facilitating communication and mutual understanding in small groups, there is no guarantee that the finding will be utilized. It may be a generation or more before the money and the brains will be turned loose to exploit that finding.

In closing, I would like to summarize this small-scale solution to the problem of barriers in communication, and to point out certain of its characteristics.

I have said that our research and experience to date would make it appear that breakdowns in communication, and the evaluative tendency which is the major barrier to communication, can be avoided. The solution is provided by creating a situation in which each of the different parties comes to understand the other from the *other's* point of view. This has been achieved, in practice, even when feelings run high, by the influence of a person who is willing to understand each point of view empathically, and who thus acts as a catalyst to precipitate further understanding.

This procedure has important characteristics. It can be initiated by one party, without waiting for the other to be ready. It can even be initiated by a neutral third person, providing he can gain a minimum of cooperation from one of the parties.

This procedure can deal with the insincerities, the defensive exaggerations, the lies, the "false fronts" which characterize almost every failure in communication. These defensive distortions drop away with astonishing speed as people find that the only intent is to understand, not judge.

This approach leads steadily and rapidly toward the discovery of the truth, toward a realistic appraisal of the objective barriers to communication. The dropping of some defensiveness by one party leads to further dropping of defensiveness by the other party, and truth is thus approached.

This procedure gradually achieves mutual communication. Mutual communication tends to be pointed toward solving a problem rather than toward attacking a person or group. It leads to a situation in which I see how the problem appears to you, as well as to me, and you see how it appears to me, as well as to you. Thus accurately and realistically defined, the problem is almost certain to yield to intelligent attack, or if it is in part insoluble, it will be comfortably accepted as such.

This then appears to be a test-tube solution to the breakdown of communication as it occurs in small groups. Can we take this small scale answer, investigate it further, refine it, develop it, and apply it to the tragic and well-nigh fatal failures of communication which threaten the very existence of our modern world? It seems to me that this is a possibility and a challenge which we should explore.

CHAPTER 2
One Alternative to Nuclear Planetary Suicide (1984)*

Carl R. Rogers and David Ryback

It is certainly not news that our planet and all the people on it are threatened by the incredible build-up of nuclear arms. This threat has led to vigorous efforts in a great many countries to halt the arms race: the production, testing, and deployment of the increasingly deadly missiles. It seems strange and tragic that we may destroy our global culture and most of life on the planet at the very moment when, technologically and psychologically, we have the capability of moving into a new era in which we could all live richer lives.

It needs to be recognized that, in the last analysis, it is not nuclear arms which pose the threat. A missile resting in its silo is not a threat. It is the intercultural and international feuds, the hatreds between groups, the religious animosities, the interracial bitterness, the hostile feelings of the "have-nots" toward the "haves." It is these social tensions which endanger us, since any one of them might trigger a nuclear war.

In my own country, and in others as well, it seems that the primary method of dealing with these tensions at the international level is through force or the threat of force. Intimidation appears to be the

---

* The first part of this paper is the work of the senior author. The second portion, beginning with the Camp David material is a joint effort.

This chapter is a slightly shortened version of what originally appeared in *The Counseling Psychologist*, Vol. 12, No. 2, pp. 3–12.

mode most commonly used in our diplomacy. It is the escalation of such threats that has led to the increasing possibility of all-out nuclear war.

Is there, then, any hope, or are we on a collision course leading to our own destruction? It is the purpose of this presentation to say that there is a body of knowledge, and there are ways of being and acting, which can reduce or even resolve these fundamental situations of social tension. This body of knowledge, these skills, these attitudes, need to be developed, promoted, enlarged, researched, and improved. It is vital to our very survival that we learn how to deal constructively with hatreds and competition between groups.

In this paper I present several personal experiences with such feuding or antagonistic factions. I would like to try to draw from my experience some principles which seem to emerge that might guide us in handling other conflictual situations. Then I use the Camp David experience, where the leaders of Egypt, Israel, and the United States met for 13 days, to show that the principles which we have learned in smaller groups are evident in the Camp David meetings and hence seem definitely applicable at the international level. I would like to point to the fact that there are alternatives to our present form of diplomacy by armed threat: A person-centered approach to intergroup hostility is one such alternative.

THE PATTERN

It is important to recognize that, in any serious dispute between groups, the underlying pattern is exceedingly simple. Group A is convinced of the fact that "We are right and you are wrong. We are good and you are bad." Unfortunately, Group B has the identical point of view. They firmly believe that "*We* are right and *you* are wrong. *We* are good and *you* are bad." This simple pattern at the level of the neighborhood squabble also holds true at the highest international level. A recent striking example is the statement by President Reagan that the government of the Soviet Union is "the incarnation of evil." The Soviet leaders, for their part, see the U.S. government as a diabolical enemy, intent on nuclear war, and concentrating on first-strike missiles.

If we are to achieve reduction in tension or any resolution of differences, the existence of this pattern must be recognized, at least dimly, by both sides. Group A must recognize that the certainty with which they believe in their own rightness and goodness is equalled by the certainty with which Group B believes in its own rightness and goodness. By what process can this recognition be achieved? Here I will turn to some personal examples, describing them at sufficient length to indicate something of the process which takes place.

HEALTH "PROVIDERS" VERSUS HEALTH "CONSUMERS"

The National Health Council is an organization made up of representatives of the American Medical Association, the American Dental Association, nurses' organizations, health insurance companies, health-oriented agencies, and many other similar groups. A few years ago these "health providers," as they termed themselves, decided to include in their annual conference a group of "health consumers" from the urban ghettos and the rural underprivileged. They should receive full credit for this humane and courageous decision, which clearly involved risk to themselves. The "health consumers" were elected or selected by local groups in their own areas. They were all poor persons: many black, some Mexican-American. As the time of the conference approached, the planners became uneasy and invited the staff of the Center for Studies of the Person to act as facilitators of groups at the conference. The invitation was accepted.

When the conference opened, the hostility of the "consumers" was so thick it was palpable. After the usual bland opening events, the conference threatened to split wide open. The "consumers" were going to withdraw. The conference was seen as just another attempt by the establishment group to give a meaningless token representation to the poor. They would have none of it. Only the statements of the facilitators that they had come all the way across the country, for no fee, simply to make certain that *everyone* in the conference would be *heard* and that everyone would have a truly representative voice, held the conference together temporarily.

Twenty groups of 20 to 25 each were formed, with "providers" and "consumers" in each group. I remember the group I facilitated. The bitterness of the poor erupted in full force. Their anger at white professionals, at the lack of health services, and at the lack of any voice in their own health care was so strong that some of the professionals were frightened, while others were self-righteously angry in response. The value of a facilitator who could truly understand and clarify the feelings expressed was most clearly demonstrated. Without the facilitators there is no doubt the conference would have blown apart. Voicing his hatred of oppression, one black man said that the Marines had trained him to kill, and if need be he would use that training against the people and institutions that were holding him down. A black woman with little formal education was undoubtedly the most influential person in the group. Highly skeptical of everyone's motives, including mine, she spoke out of a long and terrible personal struggle against poverty, prejudice, and oppression. Whenever she spoke, everyone listened and learned.

As the group sessions continued, there was a small but significant growth in understanding. The white professionals really began to see their functioning as it appeared to the recipients. A ghetto member who hated health insurance companies realized that the insurance company executive in our group was not all bad, and that they could communicate. A white social worker finally gained the courage to tell how she had constructed a "cover story" for herself as an unemployed worker needing health care, and how, playing this role, she had approached various health-oriented "helping" agencies. The appalling treatment she had received had disillusioned her about her own profession, but now she could begin to see some hope. Some blacks began to differ with others of their color, to their great embarrassment, because they felt they should keep a united front against whites. A Mexican-American woman finally told tearfully of how she felt scorned and uncared for by *both* blacks and whites.

To put the process in more general terms, the existing conflicts, such as those between haves and have-nots, between blacks and whites, between professionals and recipients, and between establishment and radicals, burst into the open. But these violent outpourings occurred in a climate in which each person was respected and permitted to state his or her feelings without interruption: a climate in which the facilitators showed that their caring concern was for the dignity of each person, and their primary purpose was to foster open communication. In this atmosphere the issues became greatly clarified, and, what is perhaps equally important, persons emerged as separate, unique individuals, each with his or her own perception of those issues. Little by little real interpersonal communication began. This is the essence of the process which a person-centered approach puts in motion.

At this point, some radicals will say, "See, what you are accomplishing is better, less angry communication! You are destroying the possibility of revolutionary change! You are defusing the hatred and bitterness which alone can spark any real change for the oppressed!" I would only ask such readers to hear the rest of the story.

Although the "health consumers" had never known one another before, they quickly coalesced and began to formulate resolutions which were circulated to the various groups where they were discussed, revised, and amended. Then we were all told that it was "the established policy" of the National Health Council to be a forum only, and that it did not take stands on health issues, so no resolutions could be adopted. Undaunted, the "consumers" waited until the final meeting of the whole conference, which was scheduled to be a series of talks "summarizing" the conference, though some of the speakers had not even attended. A "consumer" spokesman immediately moved that the whole program be dropped and that the time be spent considering and voting on the resolutions that had been circulating. Excitement was high, and the pros and cons emotional. The motion carried by a large majority, and the scheduled speakers were thanked and dismissed. The conference ended with highly affirmative feelings, not only on the part of the "consumers" but on the part of most of the establishment members as well.

During the following year, a surprising thing happened. A very large number of these resolutions was carried out. The power of the "consumers" continued to have its effect (Rogers, 1977, pp. 110–112). What are some of the principles that emerged from this experience or some of the learnings from which we might profit? Here are a few.

It is important that a person with facilitative attitudes and a facilitative way of being be present in such a dispute, and that this person be sensitively empathic to the whole range of feelings and opinions expressed by members of each group. It is equally important that this empathic understanding is nonjudgmental and acceptant. When group members experience themselves as being truly heard, and accepted, in their bitterness, their yearnings, or whatever, they are able to view themselves and their feelings more objectively, and with less irrationality.

When the facilitator hears and understands the feelings of Group A, members of Group B can gradually take somewhat the same understanding stance, and when he or she is empathically sensitive to members of Group B, Group A can begin to hear them, too. They begin to recognize that there are two sides to the dispute, two ways of seeing the situation.

In an atmosphere which contains more mutual understanding, steps can be taken toward dealing with the issues on a more realistic basis, with consideration of all of the interests involved.

A particularly important learning is that the facilitator is able to give equality to the groups, even though normally one is a low-status group and the other a high-status group. The equality provided by the facilitator grows out of the fact that he or she treats each individual as a person of dignity and worth and shows as much respect for the feelings and attitudes of low-status members as of high-status members. Thus, often for the first time, people who normally cannot talk to each other can communicate as equals, temporarily equal in power.

What the facilitator does *not* do is perhaps as important as what he or she does do. A facilitator committed to a person-centered way of being does not guide, push, or prod. He or she is content to go with the process of the group, whether rapid or slow. He or she does not persuade or take sides. The facilitator does not offer solutions. His or her basic trust is in the wisdom which, from experience, he knows resides in the group, if he can only create the psychological climate in which it can emerge.

DEALING WITH LONGSTANDING ENMITIES

I experienced a deep feud when I worked with a group from Belfast, Northern Ireland. It was possible to observe what happens in a group where the bitterness involves generations of economic, religious, and cultural hatred. There were five Protestants—including one Englishman—and four Catholics in the group. The nine were carefully chosen to include on both sides extremists and moderates, men and women, older and younger. The Englishman was a retired army colonel. We wanted to facilitate straightforward communication and to film this interaction.

In the early sessions the bitterness, horror, and despair of everyday life in Belfast was abundantly clear. Tom's sister was blown to bits by a bomb which might have been thrown by terrorists of either side. Dennis and his family have hidden behind mattresses as bullets struck their home during a wild burst of shooting on their street. Dennis has on several occasions had to help carry away the torn bodies, living and dead, from bomb explosions. Becky spoke repeatedly of the brutality of the British army patrols to her teenaged sons. After one episode where the boy was made to believe he would be shot, "That child came in and I never saw fear like it on anybody's face in my whole life."

Gilda, young and attractive, spoke of hopelessness, "I just get so full of despair. I just give up, you know." Becky said, "I really feel hopeless. . . . If something is not done, the bitterness is just going to keep eating away at those kids and eventually they could become IRA men."

The bitterness was on both sides. Pretty Protestant Gilda said, "If I seen an IRA man lying on the ground—this is the wrong thing I suppose in your eyes—I would *step* on him, because to me he has just went out and taken the lives of innocent people."

All the violent feelings leave their mark. Sean, a sensitive young Catholic teacher, told how he had been forced to pull down a "steel shutter" between his functioning self and the seething feelings within. Otherwise he would go berserk. In a very quiet, soft voice he spoke of this inner wild beast: "Yeah, I know myself. I'm quite aware of this kind of thing, and it scares me to know that it is there. 'Cause it is violent and emotional and daft. . . . I take long walks and let this thing inside of me talk. It isn't quite the same as human feelings—it isn't quite the same as having a beast inside you—some sort of animal feelings, you know."

The whole mixed stream of hatred and violence, of fear and despair, seems so powerful that to think one weekend could possibly make *any* difference seems incredibly quixotic. Yet changes did occur. . . . There were only 16 hours of group interaction, yet during that incredibly short period these centuries-old hatreds were not only softened but in some instances deeply changed. It is evidence that facilitative attitudes can create an atmosphere in which open expression can occur. Open expression, in this kind of a climate, leads to communication. Better communication very often leads to understanding, and understanding washes away many of the ancient barriers. So rapid was the progress, so significant the changes, that some of the statements I have quoted here had to be deleted from the film. To show such understanding of the opposition would have endangered the lives of the speakers when it was shown in Belfast.

When the group returned to Belfast, almost all of them continued to meet at the home of the British colonel, whose neighborhood was the safest. After the film was completed they formed teams—one Protestant, one Catholic—and showed the film to many church groups of both sects, and led discussions. None of this had been planned. There were no funds to help out. It was done on their own spontaneous initiative.

For one group to make progress toward reconciliation has not ended the killings in Belfast. True, but suppose there had been one thousand or two thousand groups. The expense would be a fraction of what private Catholic armies, the British occupation army, and private Protestant armies have cost. As for facilitators, there are hundreds already sufficiently trained, and with three months' notice they could be on the job. . . .

When will all this come about? It will happen when the concerned public makes up its mind that the problem is so serious that something *must* be done. It is not experience or personnel or solid evidence that is lacking. It is the public will. The public is not yet sufficiently informed or convinced that there are any possible solutions, and even if there were, it is not yet willing to take the risk. When it is, a humanistic, person-centered approach has something to offer, even in situations of deadly antagonism (Rogers, 1977, pp. 129–133).

When can we learn from this experience? It seems evident that, even in the space of 16 hours, centuries-old feuds can be modified and reduced. This comes about in a situation in which both factions are entirely removed from their own locale, meeting in a residential retreat setting. The informality encouraged by the facilitators is another factor in the process. One striking outcome is that, even in this short space of time, people can move so far from their own constituency, from the beliefs of their own group, that their lives may be endangered. This is a problem which needs to be recognized.

OTHER EXPERIENCES

I have described these two experiences at some length, but I could add a number of others. At various international conferences, conflicting groups have made progress in understanding each other. At Escorial in Spain, 177 people from 22 different countries gathered for a workshop and during the 10-day period began to form a genuine community; this, in spite of the fact that the group contained Marxists and conservative businessmen, Catholic priests and atheists, members of national and cultural groups that hated each other.

I could also cite a brief experience with a black/white encounter group in South Africa, where, though the time was very short, some progress was made in mutual understanding in a most complex, difficult, and tragic situation. In short, we have a very considerable body of experience on which to build.

DEALING WITH AN INTERNATIONAL SITUATION—THE CAMP DAVID EXPERIENCE

You may feel that what has been presented is all very well with small groups such as conferences, workshops, encounter groups, but such a process could not possibly help with international issues where we are dealing with large political entities. In this connection it is of great value to consider the Camp David experience. I wish to discuss the dynamics of the process which occurred at the Camp David meetings in September, 1978. I will not go into the political aspect, or the complexity of the specific issues involved. I will not consider the enormous amount of groundwork which preceded the conference. I will focus primarily on what I see as the similarities and the differences between the Camp David experience and the groups I have described. I will endeavor to indicate the way in which this examination of the process points toward future steps.

Some Significant Similarities

In a number of important ways, the experience at Camp David was definitely parallel to what we have experienced in intensive group meetings in which there were tensions and hostilities between antagonistic groups. I will endeavor to list these similarities, later pointing up some of the significant differences.

1. The sessions were held in a residential retreat setting. This is a highly important fact. None of the factions is on their own conventional turf. They are free from the distractions of their ordinary offices or meeting places. It helps to be faced with a new environment in which fresh perceptions crowd in upon one. It is important that the meeting was residential, because this means that they are in daily casual contact with members of the other groups. They see them at meals. They see them as they take walks, play tennis, or whatever. There is not necessarily communication in these casual contacts, but there is at least the chance to observe the others in a variety of situations. Camp David showed, as we have found, that a residential retreat setting is most conducive to a positive group process.

2. The meetings were highly informal. The accommodations were comfortable but not pretentious. The three leaders lived in neighboring cabins, and their staff members in other cabins not too far away. Informality of dress was encouraged. A zippered jacket was given to each person upon arrival. Whether they were worn or not is inconsequential. It signified that causal dress was quite satisfactory. It was informal in manner of speech. Though titles were sometimes used, they were not regarded as necessary. One aspect of the informality was certainly sharply different from the usual diplomatic gatherings. Individuals sat wherever they wished at meals. There was no protocol, no special tables.

Beyond the informality of the setting, President Carter bravely encouraged an informality of interpersonal interactions which allowed for more genuine and sincere expression on the part of the dialoguing factions.

The three major participants responded somewhat differently to this informality. "Prime Minister Begin was the soul of propriety. He preferred to wear a tie and coat and strictly observed protocol, always reminding President Sadat and me that he was not a head of state and therefore did not rank as an equal with us" (Carter, 1982, p. 331).

A most unusual feature of the conference was that the wives were invited. Sadat did not bring his wife, but Carter says of Rosalynn and Mrs. Begin, "the two wives were, in effect, an integral part of their own national delegations" (Carter, 1982, p. 346).

One example, reported by Dayan, shows that informality was not only encouraged, but existed. Aharon Barak, of the Israeli delegation, had been asked by Carter one night, after a joint session, to reformulate a particular memorandum and to bring it to him, no matter how late. Barak completed his task at 1:00 a.m. There was no phone in his cabin, so he went looking for one. He saw a barefooted woman, presumably a secretary, sitting on the steps of the Camp David cinema. He approached her and asked if she could help him get in touch with the President by phone. "Certainly," she answered, "follow me. There's an office with a telephone in a nearby hut." Only when the lights were switched on did he find that his guide was Rosalynn Carter. She cut off his apologies, saying "I'd better connect you with the President myself. The operator would hesitate to ring him at this hour" (Dayan, 1981, p. 156). Can one imagine such an incident at a conventional diplomatic conference? The incident helps to point up the tremendous contrast between the Camp David attitudes and those of the usual formal diplomacy.

In many of these informal respects the meetings resembled intensive groups that we have known, where people tend to be on a first-name basis and the whole atmosphere has a cordial informality.

3. Partly because of this informality the three leaders were able to be present as persons and to meet as persons. They could, of course, withdraw into their roles and into their status positions, but the opportunity was there for them to meet simply as three individuals. Carter and Sadat, according to the best information, frequently did meet as persons without any facade. Begin was more rigid in his role, with one very crucial and important exception, which will be mentioned later.

Another important aspect of their meetings as persons was that they could speak with authority. It was not necessary for them to consult with their superiors or to follow a party line. They could speak for themselves and in general could speak for their constituents, even though their final decisions needed to be ratified by parliaments back home.

In the intensive groups of which I have spoken, it was simply natural for the people to meet as persons and to speak for themselves. However, this aspect of Camp David is most unusual in diplomatic conferences, where ordinarily a delegate must consult the home office or the party central committee before expressing any position or any point of view.

4. The conference was self-contained and private. There was no press or TV coverage. Members of the media were not admitted. The

one important exception to this shows how devastating it would have been to the conference had reporters been present.

At the very outset, President Sadat insisted on reading an 11-page paper to the other two leaders. It purportedly set forth the Egyptian position. It was a shocking document, to which the Israelis especially listened with some horror. It showed none of the conciliatory attitudes which had brought Sadat to Camp David. It presented a position which the Israelis could not possibly accept. Carter, too, was astonished at the belligerent and rigid stand that it took.

The silence was long and heavy. Carter "tried to break the tension by telling Begin that if he would sign the document as written, it would save all of us a lot of time. . . . I was surprised when everyone broke into gales of genuine laughter" (Carter, 1982, p. 345). It later developed that Sadat had given this document to the Arab newspapers in order to prove to the Arab countries that he was adopting a very hard line in dealing with the Israelis. Had each portion of the conference been reported in the press, it would, of course, have been necessary for the leaders to take very conservative and rigid stands.

As it was, however, it was possible for the leaders to make tentative, and even uncertain, statements. It was possible to change one's mind. It was at least possible to move away from the pattern of "I am right and good, and you are wrong and bad."

We, too, have found that the most progress is made when an intensive group is similarly self-contained and private. When such a group is not in a residential setting, and members talk with others between sessions, often they find it necessary to retreat to more rigid or conservative positions, influenced by the attitudes of those to whom they have spoken.

5. There was no set agenda for the meetings. This is unheard of in a diplomatic conference. There was, of course, a profound and well-understood general purpose: that of arriving at some sort of formulation which would advance the peace. But the steps toward that goal were not rigidly outlined in advance. Problems were taken up and dealt with and discussed as they arose, not in some preset order. There were no regular working hours: another contrast with the usual diplomatic conference, with meeting times carefully set and agreed upon.

Similarly, there were no preconditions to the meeting, no rules which had been set up in advance. Sadat, prior to the conference, had formulated certain preconditions, but after discussing the matter with Cyrus Vance, he dropped his insistence on such conditions.

In our experience in situations of social tension, the agendaless meetings are far more fruitful than those that attempt to follow an agenda. In this respect, our experience coincides with that of Camp David.

6. The meetings were basically very emotional. Statements were often made which were very intemperate and full of feeling. The differences between Israel and Egypt ran very deep and had lasted for many years. From the beginning Sadat and Begin had difficulty communicating. "There was no compatibility between the two men, and almost every discussion of any subject deteriorated into an unproductive argument, reopening the old wounds of past political or military battles" (Carter, 1982, p. 355). (That these "shouting matches" might have been better handled will be discussed later.) . . .

In any sessions with antagonistic or hostile groups, there is bound to be a high degree of feeling, and emotional, even irrational, statements are not uncommon. If handled well, these often serve a positive purpose in releasing tension.

7. President Carter made many facilitative efforts. Though he was at times a persuader rather than a facilitator, he nonetheless was able to take a more neutral stance than either of the other two and to bend his efforts toward increasing understanding. In one of the early meetings of the three leaders, Begin and Sadat were arguing bitterly over a whole range of issues. Carter said practically nothing, but continued to take notes, which he frequently did in the meetings. At the end of the session he simply read from his notes the issues which had divided them and the stand of each party in regard to the issues. This certainty served a most facilitative function, since, in stating the issues calmly and clearly, those present could understand them better and could see the issues in a more rational light.

President Carter consciously endeavored to be a mediator and facilitator. When mistrust deepened between the other two, "I acted as a referee and put them back on track, and on occasion explained what was meant when there was an obvious misinterpretation. Strangely enough, every so often laughter broke out. Once, for instance, one of them referred to kissing Barbara Walters, the television journalist, and wondered if the cameras were on and what his wife might think" (Carter, 1982, p. 353).

As the tension heightened and Begin and Sadat frequently refused to meet with each other, Carter served a facilitative function by talking first with one and then with the other, presenting to each leader in a calm and cool way the views and positions taken by the other.

Sometimes he could not quiet the turmoil and had to simply wait for it to die down. In one situation, "All restraint was now gone. Their faces were flushed, and the niceties of diplomatic language and protocol were stripped away. They had almost forgotten that I was there, and there was nothing to distract me from recording this fascinating debate. . . .

"Begin had touched a raw nerve, and I thought Sadat would explode. He pounded the table" (Carter, 1982, p. 351). Eventually, the discussion cooled down of its own accord.

In our experience, it is rare that people have refused for any length of time to meet with others. But certainly Carter's role as a more neutral party, able to understand and voice the views of the contending leaders, was a major facilitative help.

8. The "pressure cooker" aspect of the conference: In every intensive group lasting over a period of a number of days, feelings become intensified and the group process becomes more dynamic, because persons are in contact or potential contact all day, every day, with just one focus in mind. It has been our experience that the highs and lows of feelings become much more marked. This was very evident at Camp David. In describing this aspect, Dayan says that they were "cooped up in the high pressure chamber of the Camp David Conference" (Dayan, 1981, p. 169).

To be continually in face-to-face contact for 13 days with a person with whom you violently disagree, together with a person who seems to understand each of you, is a powerful dynamic which leads toward better understanding. There is no doubt that Carter helped to keep this high-pressure aspect from exploding and turned it into a positive force.

9. The meeting is experienced as a failure. It is of interest that there were separate times when each of the three leaders experienced the conference as a complete failure. Sadat and his entourage packed up their bags and were ready to leave the morning of the eleventh day. It was only a very intense plea on the part of President Carter that led Sadat to say that he would stay to the end. Begin, even on the last day of the conference, decided that he would not sign anything, that no agreement was possible, and that the conference was a failure. Carter's experience came on day 11, when he learned that Sadat was leaving. In this "terrible moment" he recognized that the conference was a failure and "prayed fervently for a few minutes that somehow we could find peace" (Carter, 1982, p. 392).

This is an aspect with which I (Rogers) am very familiar. It has sometimes seemed to me that, in intensive group sessions with hostile groups, it is only when I recognize that no progress can be made, that the cause is hopeless, that somehow a turning point is reached. I have no explanation of the reasons for this. I simply know it has happened on several occasions that only when I have felt the session had come to a dead end has there come a turn toward the positive.

10. The incident which seems to have turned the Camp David Con-

ference from a complete failure into a significant success was a highly personal one, involving none of the issues relevant to the conference. President Carter describes this incident, and it is a very moving one. On the last day of the conference, when it seemed that all efforts were failing and when Begin was adamant about not signing anything, Carter took a very personal step. Photographs had been taken of the three leaders together, and Sadat had autographed all of these photographs. Begin has requested that three be autographed for his grandchildren. Susan Clough, Carter's secretary, suggested that he obtain the names of the grandchildren, so that President Carter could personalize the inscriptions. This was done. He went to Begin's cabin. He found Begin

> sitting on the front porch, very distraught and nervous because the talks had finally broken down at the last minute.
>
> I handed him the photographs. He took them and thanked me. Then he happened to look down and saw that his granddaughter's name was on the top one. He spoke it aloud and then looked at each photograph individually, repeating the name of the grandchild I had written on it. His lips trembled and tears welled up in his eyes. He told me a little about each child and especially about the one who seemed to be his favorite. We were both emotional as we talked quietly for a few minutes about grandchildren and about war. (Carter, 1982, p. 399)

It is worth pausing for a moment to consider the message which was contained in Carter's behavior. He was saying, mostly nonverbally, "I know the conference has failed, as far as you are concerned. Yet I want you to know that I care for you as a person, and I value those whom you love. I think of their future in the world we are creating. I think of the possibility of war and its effect on them." Certainly he touched not the Prime Minister, but the man. They connected as persons with common concerns.

Although there was further conversation—Begin objecting to the statement about Jerusalem—his attitude was changing. Within the hour he phoned to say that the just-drafted new letter about Jerusalem was acceptable to him. Then he took an unprecedented step. He went to Sadat's cabin. Carter, being told of this, went over, determined to interrupt if they were arguing. He arrived as Begin was leaving Sadat's cabin. "He was quite happy as he told me they had had a love feast and that Sadat had agreed to Begin's language on the Knesset vote" (Carter, 1982, p. 400).

To some it may seem very strange that the turning point of an international conference of great significance was based on tearful discussion of grandchildren, rather than the issues of the conference.

Yet to us who have experienced intensive groups, this seems quite natural. It is when the deepest personal feelings are touched that change takes place in the individual's attitude. This definitely seems to have been the case here.

11. All three of the leaders experienced an intense emotional "high" when the agreements were finally reached, after the conference had been so perilously close to failure. "All three of us were flushed with pride and good will toward one another because of our unexpected success" (Carter, 1982, p. 403). It is convincing evidence of this heightened feeling that Sadat and Begin, who had for so long been violent enemies and who even at Camp David had difficulty in communicating with each other without anger, embraced each other warmly on public television at the signing ceremony. There can be no doubt of the sincerity of this feeling at the moment, even though it undoubtedly had existed very recently and probably would fade in the days to come.

Such intensive emotional highs are common indeed, in the closing moments of an intensive group. They are even more marked when tensions have been reduced and there is a feeling of great relief as well as great pleasure. They certainly do not last with this intensity. They are in part possible because of the limited nature of the experience. Whether or not they continue to exist as close bonds depends on the situation and the people involved.

Some Differences—With Comments

There are a number of ways in which the experience of Camp David differed, sometimes rather sharply, from the intensive groups described earlier. Some of these differences will be pointed out and comments made as to ways in which the situation might have been handled differently. These suggestions are certainly not given in any presumptious way. The achievements at Camp David were outstanding and speak for themselves. The suggestions are simply to induce thoughtful consideration if other similar diplomatic conferences are held.

1. Although President Carter's facilitative efforts were unusual and often effective, there was no attempt to understand the leaders at a more profound emotional level. Some might feel that this would be inappropriate, but this was not the opinion of Dayan, who was one of the major participants. He says, after speaking favorably of the attitudes of both Carter and Vance, "But there were times—and that evening was one of them—when I felt that neither the President nor the Secretary of State had sufficiently penetrated the core of the problems of the Middle East. They did not put themselves in the

shoes—or rather the hearts—of either side. They knew what the Israeli and the Arab representatives were saying, but they did not always distinguish between what was being uttered for bargaining purposes and external consumption and what was the profound expression of the spirit and the yearning of a nation" (Dayan, 1981, p. 183).

The task of the experienced facilitator is to do exactly what Dayan describes: to step into the shoes, and into the hearts, of the antagonists, to be thus sensitively empathic and to voice this deep understanding. Equally important, he would be nonjudgmental. He would understand, in a profound and acceptant way, the spirit and yearnings of each of the contending parties. He would not be concerned with solving the complex issues, but solely with clarifying and bringing into the open the feelings, attitudes, concepts, and opinions of the participants. It is our experience that this delicate "indwelling" in the inner world of each person leads most rapidly to improved communication, and gradually, to improved relationships and movement toward reduction of tension. . . .

2. There was no attempt to hold continuing meetings which included the three delegations. It seems reasonable that the primary meetings were among the big three, since their status was sharply different from that of the other members of the delegations. However, it is interesting to speculate what might have happened if the remaining 24 members of the delegations had met together with experienced facilitators. Since 24 is a rather large group, it would have been well to divide them into two groups of 12 each, with four members of each delegation participating in each group. Their meetings would have had much the same intensity and the sharp differences that we observed among the big three. They would have resembled the intensive groups described earlier in this paper. It would have been understood that their meetings did not have official weight, but I believe they could have served as very good breeding grounds for innovative and stimulating ideas which could have been communicated to their leaders. Such meetings would have served several important purposes. It would mean that the members of the delegations would have gone through much the same kind of experiences as Sadat, Begin, and Carter. Consequently they would be aware, within themselves, of the kind of mutual understandings that had been achieved. Thus they would have constituted an important support group when the leaders returned to their respective countries. The leaders paid a large price for not having such sensitively understanding support groups. Even before the conference ended, two of Sadat's major delegates resigned because they did not approve of what they saw as concessions that he made. Likewise, Begin met a storm of criticism when he returned . . . [home], as did Sadat. . . .

3. Partly because the conference was touch-and-go right up to the

last moment, there was little opportunity for consideration of "back-home" problems. It has been frequently found that, in the intense emotional interaction of such a group, the participants tend to forget the distance they have come from their constituents. It is very fruitful for them to become aware of the attitudes of those they will meet on their return, and to be more ready to cope with the differences, the criticisms, and the lack of understanding which they will meet when they are again with their constituents. It is unfortunate that there was no such opportunity for these considerations.

4. It would seem that all parties could have profited from more consultation with people in various fields such as group dynamics, labor negotiations, and the like, to learn more of what was already known about the handling of frictional situations. It is known that Carter, through Cyrus Vance, did consult the Harvard Negotiation Center and, whether because of their advice or spontaneously, followed a "one text procedure," which was part of their counsel (Fisher & Ury, 1981, pp. 118–122). Very simply put, it meant that, when Sadat had started his position in extreme terms and the Israelis had responded with a position paper of their own, the only avenue to peace seemed to be through making concessions, which neither side would be willing to make. Carter then introduced an American proposal, the single document strategy, which came as close as possible to meeting the demands of both sides and in which there was no investment. It was a document made to be improved upon, and it meant that both sides were working to improve a single document rather than standing by their own separate documents. This is simply one example of the help that might have been obtained through consultation with those persons outside the diplomatic world, with long experience in handling disputatious groups.

WHAT OF THE FUTURE?

We have presented a way of working with antagonistic factions which has proven effective in our experience. Looking through the prism of this viewpoint, we have examined the negotiations at Camp David. The similarities in the process are striking. But where does this lead us?

Research and Development

There are many people with wide experience working in the field of conflict resolution. We have spoken of our experience, working in a person-centered way, but that is only one view. What is needed is to recognize this as an important field of study and fund deeper and broader investigations into all of the ways in which intergroup tensions may be resolved. In the United States, the proposed Peace Academy (to be on equal terms with the military academies) would be an excellent base for such studies. Internationally, the New University for Peace, established by the United Nations (and aided by its first million-dollar gift from Japan) would be an ideal place for the intellectual and experiential pursuit of pathways to peace. Similar institutions would hopefully be established in other countries.

At present we spend billions on research and development leading to new and more destructive weapons of war. We spend almost nothing on research and development of new and more effective means of moving two feuding parties toward peace. Such funding is essential.

At present only a small amount of research and experimentation is going on, usually with inadequate funding. Such an experiment is the "Fermeda experience" (Doob, 1970), in which unofficial representatives of two African nations were brought together to see if they could find solutions (unofficial, of course) to an important border dispute. In many ways, they implemented the factors which have been pointed out as being effective in our experience and in the Camp David experience. In the philosophy and manner of leadership, the experiment differed considerably from a person-centered approach. The process appeared positive up to a point, but due to special frustrating circumstances, the final outcome was disappointing. The investigators are to be congratulated on conducting this experiment, and in reporting their findings and their learnings so fully. There should, however, be dozens of such studies and experiments going forward with generous funding from national and international sources. There is much we could learn about new and more effective ways of reducing intergroup hostilities and resolving intergroup problems.

A PROPOSAL

As an immediate step, which could be taken without such massive support, a seminar or workshop might be held for diplomats, executives of multinational corporations, international labor leaders, and others with influence in international affairs. The purposes of this workshop would be for such individuals: (1) to *experience*, during a period of 10 days or more, the reduction in their own intercultural and interpersonal prejudices and animosities and the building of a sense of community; (2) to contribute from their own backgrounds new ways of working with tensions; (3) to plan a suitable long-term training program for persons such as themselves, to sharpen and improve understanding of and skills in dealing with feuding groups. Such a workshop could be carried out with international sponsorship.

CONCLUDING COMMENTS

We have endeavored to make clear that a person-centered approach is one way, a unique way, of increasing communication and reducing tension in situations "bristling with malice." A process is initiated in a pervasive psychological environment springing from the special way of being of the facilitator or facilitators. This process leads to improved understanding, more mutual trust, and steps toward resolution of differences.

We have pointed to the Camp David experience as having many similarities to this approach. Camp David indicates that this kind of way may be effective, not only with small groups, but at an international level.

We have called for national and international sponsorship of well-funded centers for research and development of this and every other promising approach to peaceful settlement of the tensions which now plague our planet and may lead to its destruction. We have pointed out that it is high time we invest in the means of bringing peace, and not only invest in the means of making war. We need to enlarge the knowledge and develop the appropriate attitudes and skills so necessary in resolving hostilities.

We have suggested one step which could be taken now: an extended seminar or workshop for those working with international issues, where they might experience a person-centered approach and determine whether it would improve their own abilities to work toward peaceful solutions.

Finally, we know of no more strategic area for study and practice than the expansion of ways of resolving bitterness and animosity. Our modern world will perish in a holocaust unless we learn new and more effective means of reducing and resolving the competitions, hatreds, and enmities which are leading us toward our doom. But the purpose of this paper is to say—there is hope.

REFERENCES

Carter, J. (1982). *Keeping faith*. New York: Bantam.

Dayan, M. (1981). *Breakthrough: A personal account of the Egypt-Israel peace negotiations*. New York: Knopf.

Doob, L. W. (Ed.). (1970). *Resolving conflict in Africa: The Fermeda workshop.* New Haven, CT: Yale University Press.

Fisher, R., & Ury, W. (1981). *Getting to yes: Negotiating agreement without giving in.* Boston, MA: Houghton Mifflin.

Rogers, C. R., (1977). *Carl Rogers on personal power.* New York: Delacorte.

CHAPTER 3
Conversation with Carl Rogers (1985)

Nathaniel Teich

[Carl Rogers spoke with me on April 19, 1985 at his home in La Jolla, CA. He had just returned from a late afternoon walk on the beach. I edited the following selections from my tape recording of our conversation and submitted them to Rogers, who made a few minor revisions for clarity. In a preliminary letter to Rogers, I informed him of the continuing interest on the part of some rhetoricians and composition specialists in applying Rogerian principles to the teaching of writing, and especially argumentation.]

T.1. What is your opinion of the use of Rogerian principles for the purpose of conventional argumentation? Some rhetoricians suggest that a writer try to demonstrate empathic understanding of another's point of view, but for the purpose of winning an argument or changing the other person's mind.

R.1. I regard that as quite the opposite of my thinking. And I also regard it as a perversion of my thinking. My belief is that, by extending sensitive empathy to another person, it enables him or her to come forth and gain a better understanding of himself and what direction he's going.

T.2. You seem to be using empathy in a more therapeutic context. Your focus is on the other person, the one who receives the empathy, in somewhat of an I–Thou relationship.[1]

R.2. Yes, I have nothing but criticism for using my thinking in that fashion [initially described]. I feel that's a trick. . . .

T.3. Perhaps it's a kind of tricking, although those rhetoricians who first adopted your principles had laudable motives of attempting to increase understanding and humanize the process of teaching argumentation to college students. But it seems as if they do not fully understand your conception of empathy.

R.3. Well, the way I have considered empathy, in my experience of it, it's constructive and growth producing in interpersonal relationships. A person feels relieved when someone else really understands what his or her inner world is like. But I have also recognized that the understanding gained from the empathic attitude can be used in ways hurtful to the other person.

Heinz Kohut, a leading radical thinker in psychoanalysis who died recently, was the first analyst who really recognized the great importance of empathy. He pointed out that it is a dangerous thing. He empathized with a patient to gain an understanding of what's going on within the other person. And then he formulated an interpretation of the dynamics of the situation to feed back to the patient. But he recognized that by going too far too fast, it can be really hurtful to the patient.

Similarly, way back in my early years of training young counselors, some of the most sensitive of them were so empathic that they understood material the client was not yet aware of, was quite frightened of. And when it was verbalized, the client vanished. We began to call them "blitz therapists." They had the makings of very good counselors, but they had to learn that you don't verbalize an understanding that is deeper than the client needs, or wants, or can deal with consciously.

This reminds me of the fact that a number of years ago I was much interested in brainwashing, because I felt that brainwashing was sort of psychotherapy turned upside down. The expert at brainwashing is also empathic; he's warm and understanding. He gets the prisoner to open up, to reveal a lot of himself and his personal attitudes, and then turns around and uses that material to put terrible pressure on the prisoner. So, empathy is both one of the most constructive elements of a relationship, but it also can be used in ways that are damaging—from mild hurt or fright to something really personally destructive.

T.4. In your chapter on empathy (Rogers, 1980), you wrote that in the act of empathic understanding "you lay aside your own views and values in order to enter another's world without prejudice. In some sense it means that you lay aside your self. . ." (p. 143). Isn't this very different from the attitude of rhetoricians who wish to employ empathic understanding for the purpose of wining an argument? According to your view, people must be prepared to change in order to come to some mutually satisfactory solution to a conflict or difference of opinion.

R.4. To discuss it at another level, I've been interested in recent years in the use of empathy in groups which contain hostile factions. In Belfast, for example, we worked with a group of Protestants and Catholics and filmed our efforts to facilitate better communication.[2] It is essential to have a genuinely facilitative person who is capable of being empathic to persons on both sides of the fence. He or she makes it possible, step by step, for each side to achieve a somewhat better understanding of the other.

By being empathic to members of group A, and really understanding their point of view and accepting it in a nonjudgmental fashion, the facilitator helps to reduce their tension and increase their openness. Then, by being equally empathic to members of group B, he or she encourages the same efforts, and meanwhile members of group A can see: "Oh, there is another way of looking at this. Members of group B do have something to be said for their views." This process leads toward reconciliation and helps the resolution of concrete issues, because a lot of the irrational feeling has been dissolved.

This was particularly evident in the Belfast group. We had only a short time with them, but by the process I was just describing, they came much closer. We filmed the interaction but had no money for any kind of follow-up. After our filming was over, we were quite surprised to find that these people, who had been very hostile toward each other initially, began meeting on their own initiative. They planned to show the film to church groups of both sides and lead discussions about reconciling their differences. The final proof that this was pretty effective was that a number of copies of the film were stolen and destroyed by members of paramilitary groups, both Protestant and Catholic. They did not want that film to be seen, because it showed that reconciliation was possible. So empathy can be significant on a group level, as well as on the individual level.

T.5. As a result of your own experience, then, you do not believe it is overly optimistic to assume that the process of empathic understanding will lead to a resolution of differences. But in the give and take of an argument or a problem-solving situation, how do we get people to realize that they need to modify their own positions to produce a mutually satisfactory solution? As you said in your original [1951] paper (Rogers, 1961), this is very frightening to people. They would rather win than compromise.

R.5. I feel that we've shown that it is effective in a number of instances. I don't regard it as a cure-all, although some people may say that I do. One critic I read the other day said that my position is that international hostilities and disagreements are simply the results of misunderstanding and would be resolved if there were better communication. And this critic said that's just not possible; some differences are irreconcilable.

Well, that may be true. But I know that many tensions exist because of failures in communication, and each group has arrived at the pattern of feeling: "I'm right and you're wrong. I'm good and you're bad." And the trouble is that the other group feels exactly the same way: "I'm right and you're wrong, and I'm good and you're bad." An example of that is President Reagan saying that Russia is the Empire of Evil. This destroys communication; it is also a good example of an absolute lack of empathy.

T.6. Yes, I'm afraid that's true. Let me take a little tangent here. The complication, which those of us concerned with written communication find, is that the facilitation you talk about occurs either in the face-to-face therapist/client relationship or some other interpersonal oral situation. What can you say about the use of empathy from the perspective of written communication? How do we get the feedback?

R.6. That has never been a primary interest of mine. But I can think of a number of instances in my correspondence where I have certainly used an empathic approach as a means of reestablishing or improving a relationship. In fact, there is a tense situation right now with some people we're trying to work with. The letter I just wrote contains quite a bit of empathy and also a request for empathy on their part. I understand that they felt misunderstood, too. What is hard [whether orally or in writing], and particularly hard in close personal relationships, is to extend an acceptant, nonjudgmental empathy. It's so tempting to use the empathy in a destructive fashion: "I understand how hurt you are, but you have no reason to feel hurt."

T.7. When you describe empathy as accepting and nonjudgmental, you are connecting two of the basic conditions which you have defined, repeatedly in your writing, as necessary for effective therapy or relationships.[3]

R.7. That's right. Let me give another example. If I get a quite emotional letter, I go through it to try to figure out what this person is feeling. What are the strongest feelings? Then I write a letter in which I recognize and accept these feelings. I do not try to argue the feelings down, though sometimes I express my own quite different feelings. It has less to do with empathy than it does with relationships. I think that, by showing a nonjudgmental acceptance of their feelings, it makes them more able to read about my feelings, which may be quite different. Because when we don't feel understood, we're defensive.

If you have feeling about something and you're sure someone else is not understanding it, then internally and sometimes in words you'll be trying to defend your feeling—that you're justified in what you are doing. "He doesn't understand, but I'm justified." It's only when you realize: "Oh, he understands what I mean!" Then you experience a particular physical letting down or relaxation, because you realize, "Oh, ok, he understands what I'm feeling."

Significant empathy, I think, has more to do with feelings, not so much with intellectual contents. A lot of intellectual ideas are held with passion, and that passion needs to be understood. But understanding the idea is something in my mind a little different from empathy as I use the term.

T.8. It's more than just cognitive.

R.8. That's right. It is primarily attitudinal, carrying with it an understanding of feelings, emotions, and perceptions.

T.9. And for both the oral and written attempts to show empathy and to gain understanding, there is, what I have been calling your restatement principle—the idea of "saying back," which appeared in your original [1951] paper (Rogers, 1961, p. 332).

R.9. The so-called reflection of feeling or, as you call it, restatement has no value in itself except as a means of checking my understanding. If I'm really trying to understand you, then I need to check my understanding, and this is where it has been misunderstood. Every reflection of feeling, everything that looks like a restatement in print, is really a question saying: "I'm trying to understand you; is this what you're feeling?" "Is it that you're angry with your father? Is that what you're telling me?" "Is it that you despise your job? Is that what you're telling me?"

In other words, it's a sensitive attempt to capture the most subtle—the major but also the most subtle—elements of feelings the other person is expressing and to check that. And I would also add, if I say: "It sounds as though what you're talking about is that you really hate your father." And if he says, "No, that's not it." I would accept that immediately. In other words, the person with the feelings knows whether I'm right or wrong. I'm just trying to check it. If my understanding is wrong, then I try to correct it.

T.10. But beyond feelings, can we use the restatement principle to check our understanding of intellectual positions? Can we show empathic understanding of the ideas someone holds by restating them?

R.10. Yes. If I can capture your concern about the strategy of restatement, the question you've had about it and the objections you've had about some uses of it, that would be understanding the idea and also the feelings associated with it. Because you wouldn't be working on this problem if you didn't have some feelings about it. The objections you raise are not purely intellectual. You feel something wrong is going on here.

T.11. Exactly; others are not accurately or satisfactorily applying your principles. So we come back to the point that a construct is not totally cognitive or ideational, but there is an affective or emotional dimension, although some people may not choose to admit it.

R.11. My guess is that Einstein couldn't have explained his theory of relativity or his equation $E = mc^2$ without putting feeling into what he was saying. To understand it, you need to understand the equation, but to really understand Einstein, you would need to understand the passion he must have felt about that, too.

T.12. Now to go back to the origin of the restatement rule itself: you said, in your original paper, try a little experiment, which was to restate.[4]

R.12. The phrase "restatement rule" is brand new to me this afternoon [chuckles].

T.13. Well, yes, I've just made this name up; but the idea of it: was it original with you? This principle of restatement has been used by others as more than just a check for understanding feelings. Gendlin calls it "say back" as part of "absolute listening." Gordon calls it "active listening."[5]

R.13. Richard Farson and I wrote the paper "Active Listening." It was first published as a little pamphlet [1957]. Tom Gordon was a student of mine and developed a program on parent/child and teacher/student relationships, in which he tried to popularize some of these ideas.

T.14. The concepts of "active listening" and "say back" are very powerful. In your original [1951] paper, I see you did call it a "rule" for discussion.

R.14. I'm glad to be reminded of the form in which I cast it in that paper. I'd really sort of forgotten—that you can't state your point until you can restate your opponent's point to his satisfaction. Yes.

T.15. But you see why the transfer of this form from an oral to a written context poses problems. For many of us teaching writing, we are now using more student groups, peer groups either before writing or with drafts. But for writing at home on your own, wouldn't it take an act of imagination on the writer's part to try to create an imaginary empathic dialogue without the face-to-face oral feedback?

R.15. Yes, it does. It's not too different from making an assignment: Read this chapter about somebody's theory and restate it in your own words in a couple of paragraphs. That does demand an empathic understanding in a sense. You are convincing me that it does apply to the intellectual-cognitive realm as well as the emotional. I realize that's partly where I started from.

T.16. One last theoretical question. It has to do with the concept of congruence, which is one of the three basic conditions you mention frequently in your writing. As it applies to teaching writing, I've tried to interpret congruence in two ways: one has to do with the self; honesty to oneself (as you have said many times) without false persona, so that there's a kind of transparency of the self. This is an important idea beginning in 19th-century literature, very romantic. I don't mean it in a pejorative sense, but as opposed to the neo-classic idea of playing a role. . .

R.16. That's right.

T.17. . . . the romantics rejected it as insincere and artificial. Wordsworth and other writers rejected role playing. They wanted immediacy and sincerity and authenticity.

But the issue of congruence with substance, or with the content of communication, seems to be more problematical. There are disagreements in some of the sources I've read commenting on your work. So, I'm not clear on whether congruence is valid in this context or not. One view of language and making meaning is that there's something inside us that preexists, and we want to reveal it, to find the forms that will articulate it. But another view stresses the more spontaneous. You don't know what you really think about something until you say it or write it. You don't know in advance what's going to come out or where it's going to lead. And it turns out in a way that's new, unexpected. Do you see a distinction here?

R.17. Partly. I think congruence means that one is aware of what one is experiencing inside, and consequently one is able to express it if it seems appropriate in the situation. The most important part is that one is aware of what one is experiencing. And experiencing, as we have said, has both content and feeling in it.

T.18. Yet the dynamic process of language is such that it's not as if new thoughts preexist already formed inside, and I'm simply reproducing them in getting them out. The dynamic process makes them new in the act of speaking and writing. In your letter to me, it seemed to me that you view both your writing and your response in oral dialogue as spontaneous, not preplanned or premeditated.

R.18. That's right. How to put what I am experiencing into words is a really creative and spontaneous process.

T.19. So you feel that there's a distinction between what's inside and putting it into words?

*R.19.*Yes, because often that's a lot of what therapy is about. When a client is experiencing something, and we know it's bad or frightening, we don't quite know at first what it is. To put words to what's he's experiencing is freeing, and a very significant aspect to therapy.

Now here's what has interested me about this. (Let's just say this off to one side, but it's always puzzled me.) Some words fit what is being experienced and others do not. I've noticed that, in trying to check my understanding, I might say: "Is it that you are so angry at your father?" "No, that's not quite it." "Is it that you hate him?" "No." "Is it that you feel contempt?" "Yes! Contempt. That's what I feel." That's the kind of response, as though at some level there is a verbal form which really fits what's being experienced. It's quite striking sometimes. I don't pretend to understand it, but it's something that has intrigued me. How is it that, if he hadn't been able to describe his feelings, one word fits exactly and another word quite similar to it doesn't fit at all? Puzzling. . . .

T.20. But then it seems to me that the therapeutic context is more of a mirroring context. I'm borrowing a metaphor from a literary critic who used it to show the difference between classical and romantic theories. The romantic idea of creativity was more spontaneous, organic, and subjective; and the classical more controlled, objectified: as Shakespeare said, holding a "mirror up to nature"[6] and reflecting what's already there.

R.20. Even the mirroring process is not something passive; it's creative, too.

T.21. That's right. That's right. You have made some useful clarifications of your views on language and how your principles can be applied to writing. Congruence and empathic understanding have some relevance for personal expression and creativity, in addition to establishing a humane, considerate atmosphere for communication.

R.21. Yes. And I realize we've had our own difficulties in communication, with my trying to understand your more literary interest in my ideas, and also, I realize, my trying unconsciously to persuade you to see that they are therapeutic concepts.

T.22. Well, I think that I'm getting a better grasp of the difference between those rhetoricians who too narrowly deny the applicability of your ideas to written argumentation, and others who have adopted them but not given appropriate weight to their therapeutic basis.

R.22. They haven't seen the roots of it deeply enough. Yes, that's what I feel. I hope that if you reprint the [1951] paper, because it was an attempt to popularize something that had deeper roots, you will reprint some more recent work, to show more of the depth this has for me. [Here he handed me a copy of "One Alternative to Nuclear Planetary Suicide" (1984), reprinted as Chapter 2 of this volume.]

NOTES

1. On the influence of Martin Buber, see Evans (1975, pp. 25, 70–71).
2. See Rogers (1984), reprinted as Chapter 2, this volume.

3. For a recent, concise statement, see Rogers (1980, pp. 114–116); also Chapter 15, this volume.
4. Rogers (1961, p. 332) and (1980, p. 154), connecting empathic understanding to nonjudgmental acceptance of another's world.
5. Gendlin (1978, p. 116); cf. Rogers (1980, p. 145); Gordon (1970a, b).
6. I was thinking of Abrams' (1953) contrast of the mirror and the lamp; *Hamlet*, III, ii.

REFERENCES

Abrams, M. H. (1953). *The mirror and the lamp: Romantic theory and the critical tradition*. New York: Oxford University Press.

Evans, R. I. (1975). *Carl Rogers: The man and his ideas*. New York: Dutton.

Gendlin, E. (1978). *Focusing*. New York: Everest House.

Gordon, T. (1970a). *PET: Parent effectiveness training*. New York: Wyden.

Gordon, T. (1970b). *TET: Teacher effectiveness training*. New York: Wyden.

Rogers, C. R. (1951). Communication: Its blocking and its facilitation. In C. R. Rogers, *On becoming a person* (pp. 329–337). Boston, MA: Houghton Mifflin.

Rogers, C. R. (1961). *On becoming a person*. Boston, MA: Houghton Mifflin.

Rogers, C. R. (1980). *A way of being*. Boston, MA: Houghton Mifflin.

Rogers, C. R. (1984). One alternative to nuclear planetary suicide. *The Counseling Psychologist, 12*, 3–12 (Reprinted as Chapter 2 of this volume.)

PART 2
New Views on Rogerian Theory and Practice

INTRODUCTION

The contributions in this part offer reassessments and wide-ranging applications of Rogerian principles to the fields of rhetoric, composition, and communication. After more than 20 years of scrutiny and use in these fields, Rogers' theory and practice remain relevant, provocative, and uniquely suited to certain discourse situations. The contributors have considered, but not limited themselves to such key issues as: (a) whether Rogerian principles constitute a *rhetoric* as distinguished from traditional Aristotelian rhetoric and argumentation; (b) how Rogers' clinically developed approaches can be transferred from oral to written discourse; and (c) how Rogers' humanistic attitudes and values of mutual communication and empathic understanding can be taught and practiced as more than a strategy or technique.

Rogerian principles were brought to the attention of writing teachers and rhetoricians in 1970 by Young, Becker, and Pike in *Rhetoric: Discovery and Change*. They came to Rogers through Anatol Rapoport's work in the area of conflict resolution. According to Rapoport (1960), Rogerian principles provided a means "to convey to the opponent the assurance that he has been understood, so as to reduce his anxiety on that account and to induce him to listen" (p. 289). From this, Young et al. developed a "Rogerian strategy" of argument to apply especially "in those dyadic situations that involve strong values and beliefs," in which traditional argument "tends to be ineffective." This "Rogerian strategy seeks to reduce the reader's sense of threat," thus making possible a more reasoned consideration of the writer's views (1970, p. 274).

Maxine Hairston (1976) subsequently emphasized that Rogers provided a unique approach for reducing threatening and defensive behaviors in certain communication situations. She proposed the "Rogerian approach" as a new and alternative attitude or stance which the rhetor could take. While she acknowledged the gap between the origins of Rogers' principles in the oral dialogue of therapy situations and their transfer to written discourse, nevertheless she asserted that "we can use . . . [Rogers'] approach to rhetoric in composition because the *attitude* is transferable, and . . . that is the unique and crucial element" (p. 376).

Since then, Rogerian theory and practice have been used by rhetoricians and writing teachers in various ways. The most prevalent application has been to argumentation, where Rogers' approach has been considered, at the least, a supplement, complement, or contrary to traditional argument and, at the most, an alternative rhetoric. A second prevalent application has been to pedagogy in general, employing Rogers' body of writing on education which fosters his student-centered approach. Another approach, suggested more recently by a few composition specialists, has been to engage Rogerian principles at the early stages of the invention process, when writers are exploring and developing their opinions. Stephens (Chapter 5) illustrates the heuristic value of Rogerian principles for invention (see also Forum, Chapter 4).

From Young et al. (1970) and Hairston (1976) to the new contributions in this volume, Rogers' principles have been treated most persuasively when applied to argumentation in dyadic rather than triadic situations.[1] The situational contexts appropriate for Rogerian argument and pedagogy are key factors in many of the discussions that follow. Several contributors directly address the assumption that the ethos and intent of the rhetor determine the success of assuming a Rogerian stance (Coe, Chapter 5; Young, Chapter 6; Baumlin & Baumlin, Chapter 7). In contrast, for example, Lunsford's (1979) formalistic efforts to absorb Rogerian principles into Aristotelian rhetoric proved unconvincing, because she ignored ethos and dispensed with the distinctions "based on audience" between dyadic and triadic situations.[2]

Ede (1984), although aware of the issues of ethos and context, has been most critical of importing Rogerian principles into rhetoric and composition, stating that "what has been called Rogerian rhetoric . . . is not Rogerian," and that it "represents a distortion of Carl Rogers' own principles" (p. 40). She maintained her objections to the appropriateness, usefulness, and validity of Rogerian rhetoric in the 1987

Forum (see Chapter 4); however, as Richard Young stated at the outset of the forum, Rogers had

> a good deal to say about the conflict situation, and it's a mistake to confuse it with the therapeutic situation. It was Rogers' proposal that he knew something that could be useful in the conflict situation that attracted us [Young, Becker, and Pike].

Young closed the forum by elaborating the particular kind of situations in which he envisioned Rogerian argument would be applicable.

The transcript of the forum, "Reassessing Carl Rogers' Principles in Composition Instruction,"[3] is drawn from the discussion among audience and panelists. It is organized under three headings to include most of the questions and comments. First, the section headed "Institutional Demands" contains discussion on the issues of how Rogerian principles facilitate the process approach (including honest writing and honest relationships within the composition class), educational reform, and evaluation procedures. As a transition to the second section, "Ethos in Rogerian Argument," Toby Fulwiler's comment—that Rogers' attitude toward language is "profoundly respectful"—qualifies a prevalent opinion of rhetoricians that Rogers was epistemologically naive and arhetorical in his understanding of language. In the third section, "Applications of Rogers to Composing and Persuading," specific approaches and strategies are described and debated by both panelists and audience.

Richard M. Coe, in "Classical and Rogerian Persuasion: An Archaeological/Ecological Explication," extends his prior work on Rogers and provides a basis for considering Rogerian persuasion by examining Classical argumentation and stressing the importance of "the context of situation," since the use of the rhetorical strategies and structures of persuasion inevitably involves matters of ethics. Coe distinguishes the social and political contexts of Classical rhetoric from situations in which Rogerian rhetoric would be appropriate. But rather than continuing the debate between Classical and Rogerian strategies, Coe undertakes to "specify the distinctive features of Rogerian persuasion and define the sorts of situations" where it would be necessary and effective. He provides many examples of how Rogerian persuasion could be developed (including an appendix presenting one student's Classical and Rogerian texts on the same issue). Moreover, he extends Rogerian rhetoric to encompass "all rhetorical strategies and structures that facilitate empathy, consensus, non-antagonistic communication, mediation of disputes, problem solving" (including discussion of constructive criticism and consensus building).

Richard E. Young, in "Rogerian Argument and the Context of Situation: Taking a Closer Look," reconsiders Rogerian argument in the light of the 20 years of reactions since he, Becker, and Pike introduced it as an alternative strategy to "traditional argument." Like Coe, Young locates classical persuasion primarily in "the conduct of public affairs"; but now Young specifies that Rogerian argument is most appropriate in "highly conflicted," "value-laden dyadic situations." He urges that we pay more attention to the "considerable variation" in dyadic situations, which Young et al. (1970) did not recognize. In particular, Young pushes beyond such constraints (of assuming shared interests in a mutually satisfactory solution and a willingness to compromise) as proposed in Teich's (1987) pedagogical applications for initially teaching Rogerian principles in writing classes. Young explores "the intractable situation" of "unyielding" opponents, which "constitutes some sort of boundary condition" for rhetoric. Finally, the opportunity offered in reassessing Rogerian principles for rhetoric, according to Young, is that renewed attention to ethos and pathos directs us toward "the dialogic character of rhetorical argument" and away from excessive emphasis on logos, dialectic, and exclusively logical appeals.

In "Rogerian and Platonic Dialogue in—and beyond—the Writing Classroom," James S. Baumlin and Tita F. Baumlin offer a new perspective for Rogerian dialogic by tracing parallels with Platonic dialogue. They shift our focus from considering Classical persuasion only in terms of Aristotelian adversarial and public appeals to explore a rhetoric of dialogue. They reveal similarities between the dialogue that the Platonic "philosopher/therapist" seeks to establish through "companionable and interrogative" discourse intended to reveal the truth, heal the soul, and restore harmony to the interlocutor; and the dialogue that the Rogerian therapist seeks through the facilitative attitudes of congruence, acceptance, and empathy. With these attitudes, the therapist enters the client's mental life ("an approximate if demystified equivalent of the Platonic soul") and helps the client change and grow. In the last part of their essay, the Baumlins describe in detail a practical assignment that necessitates genuine written dialogue—a personal letter and a response. The goal is to create the "healing language" of Rogerian therapy. The Baumlins describe a climate of genuine communication generated within the classroom, emerging from it, and returning to it from caring respondents on the outside.

Kay Halasek's chapter on "The Fully Functioning Person, the Fully Functioning Writer: Carl Rogers and Expressive Pedagogy" continues the focus on both the person of the writer and the extension of Rogerian principles beyond argumentation, here to include expressivist rhetoric. Halasek explores important connections between Rogers and expressivists such as Macrorie, Murray, Stewart, and Elbow, especially their shared values, methods, and goals. She reveals the social, collaborative, and dialogic dimensions of both expressivist rhetoric and Rogerian principles as applied to rhetoric and composition instruction. Halasek discusses in detail the social nature of "the helping relationship," in which Rogerian therapeutic principles and practices inform expressivist pedagogy. Finally, Halasek examines the development of Elbow's believing and doubting strategies as methods of inquiry and their similarities to Bakhtin's dialogic. As a result, Halasek describes new ways of conceiving the relationship between Rogerian and Aristotelian approaches to argument. As believing (the nonconfrontational Rogerian approach) and doubting (the more adversarial Aristotelian approach) are regarded "as equally necessary contraries . . ., they become knowledge-generating, epistemic activities"; for, "as Bakhtin argues, . . . meaning is constructed out of dialogue and difference."

Rebecca Stephens, in "Rogerian Principles and the Invention Process," offers a new direction for Rogerian principles to be applied in the composing process. After briefly surveying the primary applications of Rogerian theory and practice in argumentation and pedagogy, Stephens provides a detailed description of a Rogerian heuristic for the invention process. She describes an example of its use in exploring one issue with her writing class. Rather than focusing exclusively on strategies of arrangement for Rogerian argument (as found in several texts and articles), Stephens proposes that Rogerian principles are profitably used in the early stages of invention as questioning strategies. In this manner, starting with one's initial investigation of an issue, Rogerian questioning strategies facilitate engagement, empathy, and consideration of multiple perspectives. While many of the questions in Stephens' example could well be used in the six-part Classical structure (cf. Coe, Chapter 5), it is not traditional rhetoric, but rather Rogerian theory and practice that originate and validate the collaborative ethos, intent, means, and ends of such questions.

James P. Zappen (1980), in an important prior essay, advanced the discussion of Rogerian rhetoric by analyzing its political and social implications and by offering a composite strategy of arrangement for proceeding with Rogerian argumentation. This strategy, according to Zappen, resembled "Dewey's procedure for problem solving" (1980, pp. 103–104, 107–108). In his new essay, "Dewey, Kilpatrick, and Rogers on Expert Communication," Zappen extends his earlier comments on Rogers' "indebtedness to Dewey" by discussing the influences of John Dewey and William Heard Kilpatrick as they informed Rogers' radical views on "expertise" and "expert communication." In Dewey's view, experience and, thus, learning are cooperative as well as individual; to Kilpatrick, group sharing and discussion are a method of inquiry and communication. Zappen illustrates how Rogerian principles and practices could apply to a variety of situations in science and engineering in which a broader view of technical communication should include alternative personal, cultural, and political considerations.

Wayne Pounds, in "Community Language Learning: Charles Curran's Application of Rogerian Counseling," comments on broader theoretical issues of collaborative learning as he discusses examples of Rogerian pedagogy in teaching English to Japanese students. Within the specialized field of foreign language teaching, Pounds describes the pedagogical practices of Charles Curran (a student of Rogers) and Paul La Forge (a student of Curran). Curran's approach, called Community Language Learning, is based on the strategies of nonthreatening "group experience" and "reflection" on the transactions occurring during that experience. Pounds distinguishes between the "more socially oriented" collaborative theories of Bruffee and Curran's more personally oriented approach. Although raising the issue of personalism and conservatism in Rogerian psychotherapy (the principles and practices of which may not lead to "inquiry into the social determinants" of power, control, and one's alienation), Pounds does not find the ideological implications of Rogerianism to invalidate its praxis. From a basis in Rogerian principles, according to Pounds, "Curran's work . . . provides solutions to practical problems with which collaborative learning is still grappling, particularly the problem of developing the group's self-critical consciousness."

In "Attitudes and Expectations in a Shared Responsibility Classroom," Chris Madigan discusses Rogerian pedagogy in specific personal and operational terms. What Madigan calls the shared responsibility classroom is one in which, "within the limits imposed by the institution and the teacher, students help decide and implement class content, activities, schedule, course and student evaluations." His guidelines for setting up and trouble-shooting such classes demonstrate his commitment to Rogerian principles, sensitivity to students, and psychological acumen in adapting the principles and perspectives of a therapist to those of a teacher. Madigan candidly reports his successes and difficulties, pleasures and painful experiences, in his efforts. He tells us what to expect: from students' initial resistance to collaboration, from pain to trust and growth. As he describes his teaching experiences, Madigan emphasizes the importance of the Rogerian principles of genuineness, acceptance, and empathic listening. He relates not just the changes taking place in his students over short- and longer-run periods, but also his own changes and growth, particularly in trusting the pedagogy to work. Finally, Madigan realistically faces the institutional, specifically political, implications of such potentially controversial, radical pedagogy. Yet, he concludes, "if we expect that students given freedom will work hard . . . they'll tend to fulfill those expectations."

Paul Bator's "Carl Rogers and the Teaching of Rhetoric and Composition" concludes by presenting students' reactions to Rogerian rhetoric in writing classes that he taught. In an important prior essay, Bator (1980) distinguished between Aristotelian and Rogerian rhetorics. In this chapter, Bator states that "many teachers I've worked and talked with have found it theoretically sound and pedagogically effective to teach Rogers' ideas as part of a larger rhetorical framework that encompasses a rhetoric of inquiry and good reasons." Since students often have difficulty accepting and applying Rogerian approaches, Bator describes their feelings and thoughts: from their initial reactions of acceptance or resistance, and their problems at various stages in their writing, to their new insights into the use of dialogue, their relations with the audience, and the ethics of Rogerian rhetoric. This focus on students demonstrates that those teaching Rogerian principles are concerned not just with theory, but with the individuals for whom theory becomes practice.

NOTES

1. The dyadic (two-sided) situation involves the direct interaction of the parties. The triadic (three-sided) situation may involve direct interaction of opponents (e.g., lawyers in court), but their goal is to convince some third party or group (who may or may not take an active part in the dialogue, e.g., judge and jury, legislators, members of a discourse community) to adopt or change an opinion, or render a decision; see Young et al. (1970, pp. 273–274); Coe, Chapter 5, this volume.
2. Lunsford contended that the "distinctions between dyadic and triadic arguments" were "minimal." But by regarding these two different situations as "arguments" rather than contexts, she confused form with the substance of rhetorical situations. Similarly, Lunsford proposed an unconvincing formalistic reduction of "the techniques used in Rogerian argument" to a prerequisite: "necessary before successful argumentation begins" (assuming Aristotelian arguments begin on the basis of shared assumptions, opinions, and values as expressed in an enthymeme). The broader applicability of Rogerian principles is a common theme of the contributions in this volume.
3. This forum was held at the Conference on College Composition and Communication National Convention, March 1987, Atlanta, GA. The panelists

were Paul Bator, Lisa Ede, Maxine Hairston, and Richard Young; Nathaniel Teich served as moderator. In Rogerian fashion, discussion among audience and panelists occupied most of the session, after brief opening remarks from the five speakers.

REFERENCES

Bator, P. (1980). Aristotelian and Rogerian rhetoric. *College Composition and Communication, 31*, 427–432.

Ede, L. (1984). Is Rogerian rhetoric really Rogerian? *Rhetoric Review, 3*, 40–48.

Hairston, M. (1976). Carl Rogers' alternative to traditional rhetoric. *College Composition and Communication, 27*, 373–377.

Lunsford, A. A. (1979). Aristotelian vs. Rogerian argument: A reassessment. *College Composition and Communication, 30*, 146–151.

Rapoport, A. (1960). *Fights, games, and debates*. Ann Arbor, MI: University of Michigan Press.

Teich, N. (1987). Rogerian problem-solving and the rhetoric of argumentation. *Journal of Advanced Composition, 7*, 52–61.

Young, R. E., Becker, A. L., & Pike, K. L. (1970). *Rhetoric: Discovery and change*. New York: Harcourt Brace.

Zappen, J. P. (1980). Carl R. Rogers and political rhetoric. *PRE/TEXT 1*, 95–113.

CHAPTER 4
Forum: Reassessing Carl Rogers' Principles in Composition Instruction

Transcribed and edited by Nathaniel Teich

[This forum was held at the Conference on College Composition and Communication National Convention, March 1987, in Atlanta, GA. The panelists were Paul Bator, Lisa Ede, Maxine Hairston, and Richard Young; Nathaniel Teich served as moderator. Each panelist presented brief introductory remarks, summarizing and extending his or her previous views on Rogers' work. In true Rogerian fashion, discussion among audience and panelists occupied most of the session. Unfortunately, not all the names of the audience speakers can be identified in the following transcript. I have organized the discussion under three heads: (1) institutional demands, (2) ethos in Rogerian argument, and (3) applications of Rogers to composing and persuading.]

1. INSTITUTIONAL DEMANDS

AUDIENCE (man). I am interested in the panel's responses to the relationship between the Rogerian approach to teaching and the institutions in which many of us teach. In the institutional setting, colleagues who do not think of themselves primarily as teachers of writing expect us to teach certain kinds of competencies and at the end of the semester to give letter grades. It seems to me the tension between letter grades and the Rogerian approach is more intense than between the Rogerian approach and other kinds of argument. I raise this question not as a skeptic [of the Rogerian approach], but as one who is laboring with the problem.

LISA EDE. I would like to comment because I think that it does reveal a weakness in Rogers' theories, in that Rogers is basically ideologically neutral. There is no way by means of Rogers' theories to ask questions like you just asked. Rogers assumes that you are beginning in a privatized client relationship, that the client has chosen this relationship, that you are working under mutually controllable conditions. I don't think that Rogers can say very much to us about these kinds of questions because of the way he separates the individual from society.

RICHARD YOUNG. I think we need to separate what Rogers has to say about the therapeutic situation from what he has to say about the conflict situation. He does have a good deal to say about the conflict situation, and it's a mistake to confuse it with the therapeutic situation. It was Rogers' proposal that he knew something that could be useful in the conflict situation that attracted us [Young, Becker, and Pike] in our book [*Rhetoric: Discovery and Change* (1970)]. I don't think Rogers is irrelevant to situations in which individuals disagree and judgments must be made.

MAXINE HAIRSTON. I don't think it is ever possible to take all of any theory and make it apply to other situations. I don't think that prevents us from taking what is valuable and using it, and I don't feel that it violates the original principles. We also need to remember that Carl Rogers wrote a great deal about teaching. He was very interested in teaching, and I have looked as much at his teaching ideas as I have his ideas on therapy and conflict. He stresses having a positive regard for one's students, trusting one's students. I have found this to be a very important principle.

I think, in the grading situation we are talking about, that we can use what he says. It is important to have positive regard for one's students, even in the face of institutional constraints. I give grades and am known as a really tough grader. What I do, however, is have students work on drafts and work in situations where they can get feedback that is nonthreatening and nonjudgmental before they submit the paper for a grade. I don't think this exempts them from being judged in the end. Therapists may not judge, but we judge. We are paid to judge; we are qualified to judge; and that's what we are expected to do. I see no conflict with teaching students competencies and using a nonthreatening, process-centered, student-centered approach. I tell them when they turn in their final papers to me that this is a public appearance. And they are going to be judged on everything that they have published in this public appearance.

PAUL BATOR. It seems to me that we ought not to feel compelled to take Rogers' every word in our adaptations and applications of his practices to our writing classrooms. Yet, at the same time, we can use some of his theory directly in our teaching. For grading, what one might take from Rogers is a shifting of the point of view from the therapist to the client, in Rogers' terms. From this, manifold possibilities arise regarding questions about how to make judgments about writing and how to assign grades.

AUDIENCE (TOBY FULWILER). I really appreciate what Maxine Hairston has to say about the process approach and working with drafts as a helpful response to the question about grading. Rather than accepting that Rogers has little to offer us as composition teachers, I would argue that Rogers has a lot to offer. He would have been glad to accept the challenge that he can contribute to composition teachers and, in fact, to issues of education at all levels. There is something profoundly wrong with education, as the conflict about grades reveals. We have taken our responsibilities for certifying students all out of proportion to educating them, with wildly destructive results.

Rogers had much to say about educational reform in *Freedom to Learn* [1969]. His assumptions seemed right to me then, and they still seem right to me now. You . . . panel, seem to be speaking from these assumptions. As someone concerned and disturbed about what's wrong with education, I invite you to comment on any of these assumptions.

LISA EDE. I want to make clear that my criticisms are directed to what has been called Rogerian rhetoric and not necessarily Rogers' own work. I agree with Maxine, in that I found Rogers a rich and compelling figure from whom I learned a great deal. As a composition teacher, however, I find his views less helpful to me, in trying to understand what is going on in my classroom, than, say, Burke's [1969] concepts of identification and division, and his understanding of the way we form ourselves through language. But I wouldn't disagree that Rogers has a great deal to offer us and that he stands as a monumental figure arguing for a particularly humane view of education and relationships.

AUDIENCE (man). To follow up on what Paul Bator said, I would like to comment on rearranging the authority in the classroom in the Rogerian sense. I think students should be involved in assessing their own work.

MAXINE HAIRSTON. I think students learn from evaluating each other's work. They learn about their own work from it. And it's very pragmatic; it may save the teacher's life by transferring some of the paper load we have. Also it has helped me to respect my students, because I find that they can do it quite well. If you put trust in them, they recognize that, and they do better. So, I think that this is a very positive stragegy. It does not mean abdicating our authority at all. We are still the final judge. We still have the responsibility to give grades, however unpleasant we find it.

AUDIENCE (same man). So you would not share that responsibility? You would not accept negotiating with the students about their own assessments of their work?

MAXINE HAIRSTON. Oh, I think it's fine to have students come in and talk about what grades they think they should get in the class. Often they are realistic about it. That doesn't mean you abdicate the responsibility for putting your grade on the grade sheet.

PAUL BATOR. Let me add that these comments illustrate some of the manifold options that I suggested would follow from applying Rogers' principle of shifting the point of view from the therapist to the client. For the student to become a grader of his papers implicates him in your situation, just as it demands from you a radical reorientation of yourself, a divestment of selfhood. But to what extent we as teachers, particularly in the grading situation, are willing to shift our point of view, as Rogers does as a therapist, I'm not sure.

AUDIENCE (woman). I want to bring up the issue of honesty in the writing class. According to Rogers' views, sincerity of the teacher would probably promote sincerity in students' writing. And this would eliminate something we all hate, and that is writing for the teacher. This would avoid a lot of anxiety. I was worried about an anti-Rogerian incident in my home as I was packing to come here. I decided to check on my college-freshman son, who was writing a paper. "How's it going?" I asked. "Great," he replied. I asked what position he was taking, and he said, "I'm writing that the massacre was correct." I was appalled. "This is not your style. You are nonviolent, a pacifist, anti-war." He said, "I'm going for an *A*. [Laughter] The teacher made signals in class that she believed the massacre to be right." I was really upset on the plane coming here. I believe that there is dishonesty in my son's class, which I will discuss with him postconference.

MAXINE HAIRSTON. You can get angry about this incident, but it's hard to be angry with him. You can understand why in this atmosphere he can choose to do that. It's survival, what Abraham Maslow called "deficit motivation." I think this is a very serious issue: how do you move students from deficit motivation—performances to avoid penalty, to avoid being hurt—to growth motivation. You don't do it without a profound change in the teacher.

PAUL BATOR. I certainly agree with what Maxine said about the seriousness of this matter. If I can relate it to a method of rhetoric or dialogics, if you will, as I would with my students: we would attempt to turn it all back in on itself and focus on the truth of the situation (whether it was good to lop off all these people's heads in the massacre or not). That is, we would turn it back on the person and his own ideas. In that sense, it is what Rogers always moves us toward, and we as teachers can move students toward in discussing papers, or perhaps even sons.

AUDIENCE (TOBY FULWILER). I was struck, Nathaniel, by the report of your interview with Rogers that you judge his views of language to be arhetorical. In a sense, I would not disagree with the statement that Rogers is arhetorical. He is, in a way, distrustful of language. But there is a certain kind of distrust that is absolutely bonded to respect. I would much prefer to say that he is profoundly respectful of language. That's what the empathic response means—be more rhetorical.

NATHANIEL TEICH. Yes, that's good to phrase it positively. In his writings and in our interview, Rogers expressed his concern for clear and genuine communication. I get the impression that he does not think about language as we do now—as making meaning. His concerns with language seem more functional, as a referential medium to reflect feelings in terms of his principles of congruence, unconditional positive regard, and empathy.

2. ETHOS IN ROGERIAN ARGUMENT

AUDIENCE (JOHN BEAN). We have been talking a lot about attitudes toward students. What's the difference between Carl Rogers and Dale Carnegie? The issue is, what's the difference between authentic positive regard and a positive regard which you just assume? Looking at what authentic positive regard is in Rogers, I find problems in that I don't think he has a developed sense of paradox, or of evil or grace. You wouldn't say of Cordelia and Kent that they have a positive regard for Lear. There is something not profound enough in Rogers. I wonder if the panel could comment on that.

NATHANIEL TEICH. Very briefly, I think this issue has to do with *congruence*; in Rogers' terms, there should be congruence between what you feel inside and what you say outside about how you feel inside. The artificiality you're talking about seems more to do with using a kind of device as a Dale Carnegie technique. But with Rogers, there is a sense of authenticity and sincerity that is not a technique or assumed. It is a genuinely romantic perspective. It seems to me that Rogers fits on the romantic side of the romantic vs. neoclassic controversy. If you see that there's no irony, no paradox, that's probably right. But the romantic is sincere and talks about genuine feelings, in contrast to Dale Carnegie techniques, which are superficial and manipulative.

RICHARD YOUNG. I think that the dichotomy you set up between what the romantic might call "the authentic voice" and the classicist might call "assumed personae" is a very interesting one. It also comes out in a distinction that Jim Corder draws between his work and Paul's. If I recall it right, Paul doesn't see Rogerian argument as essentially an appeal to ethos. To Corder, that's what it is fundamentally. So we can translate the dichotomy between Carl Rogers and Dale Carnegie into another dichotomy: whether there is an appeal to ethos or to something else. My inclination is to come down on Corder's side, particularly if you look at his really elegant discussion of ethos in *Freshman English News* a few years back [Corder, 1978].

MAXINE HAIRSTON. John, I think what you brought up is the crucial underlying question about rhetoric and the criticism that has always been made against it: that you're using it to manipulate people, it's fake, you're using it to appeal to emotions. . .

RICHARD YOUNG. Maxine, I don't think assuming different roles is necessarily being fake. We all do it. My question is, can you escape it?

MAXINE HAIRSTON. I agree. We can't escape it. What I'm saying is that criticism has always been lodged against rhetoric that, well, you're simply using language, you're shifting with the wind. But going back to classical rhetoric, it's the character of the speaker, the character of the writer; ethos is the heart of it; ethos is the anchor. This is what keeps rhetoric anchored in an ethical base, in honesty. One has to assume that the Dale Carnegie's don't necessarily get away with it. I think a Dale Carnegie approach has simply cut loose from the anchor of ethos and shifts in the wind to suit whatever is blowing at the time. I don't think that there is anything in this that reflects on Rogers at all.

AUDIENCE (ED CORBETT). I agree with Dick Young and Maxine's comments on ethos. One of the reasons rhetoric has a bad reputation is the suspicion of the flim-flam. . .

MAXINE HAIRSTON. But a sturdy ethos, a sturdy ethical base to an argument, counteracts that.

AUDIENCE (ED CORBETT). Ethos is the biggest part of it, but the audience has to be able to proceed.

MAXINE HAIRSTON. Audiences are fallible, and often they don't proceed; but sooner or later they will. I guess I'm romantic, too.

3. APPLICATIONS OF ROGERS TO COMPOSING AND PERSUADING

AUDIENCE (woman). I'd like to continue the discussion we were just having and move it from ethos to where Rogers may enter into the composing process. If you apply Rogerian argument as an inventional tool, then it can't be a tactic. If it's an *early* inventional tool, then it's at the point where you're deciding what your own opinion is, and not how to get your opinion adopted by your audience. So if you are really early enough in applying Rogers, and if you're in a problematic situation (as posed in Young et al., 1970), you'd have to be in a situation in which you were willing to consider both sides of the question, or even consider giving up your initial point of view. Rogerian argument seems to be most valuable at this early point. To go back to Richard Young's early comment on the possible situations in which Rogers is useful, it's getting people before they become steadfast, before they've hardened into some position.

LISA EDE. But why call it Rogerian argument? Why not call that common sense?

AUDIENCE (same woman). Because it's a particular kind of common sense; it's taking the other side.

LISA EDE. If I could add that I think it is important to remember that Perelman [1982] cites epideictic discourse, ceremonial discourse, as one of the most essential forms of rhetorical communication. I think that this connects to the relationship between the rhetor and the audience, and to the kind of social base of communication that has to be assumed.

AUDIENCE (BOB CONNORS). I'd like to ask Maxine, given the fact that Kenneth Burke says that, wherever there's meaning, there's persuasion, why don't you teach argument any more?

MAXINE HAIRSTON. I don't feel any need to focus one part of the class on argument. I teach writing, and I have my students write. Some of you may have read my recent article, "Different Products, Different Processes" [Hairston, 1986]. I'm trying to move students through different processes rather than saying: write a persuasive paper, write a narrative, etc. What I'm calling Class III writing—reflective, open writing—often is persuasive. I just found that trying to teach a separate unit on argument seemed to be artificial.

Jim Kinneavy and I have argued about this ever since I've known him. He really does separate referential discourse and persuasive discourse. He really does believe (I think, in his heart) that emotional discourse is not as good as rational discourse, and that you can separate them. I just don't think you can do it. A piece of technical writing is persuasive, just as much as epideictic discourse is persuasive. So I find the classification of argument no longer useful. I outgrew it.

LISA EDE. And that's a very Burkean perspective.

AUDIENCE (woman). I want to reiterate something Toby Fulwiler said a little while ago about Rogers' ultimate respect for language and ultimate respect for the communication act. Professor Ede, I'm still distressed by your comment that you respect Rogers but you don't respect the notion of Rogerian rhetoric, Rogerian argument. Could you speak to that, to qualify your notion of what rhetoric is and why you do not consider Carl Rogers' work as a rhetoric?

LISA EDE. It's not that I would exclude from rhetoric some of the principles that have been articulated in what we have called "Rogerian rhetoric." Many of them are embodied in classical and contemporary rhetorics. Burke [1969] and Perelman [1982] both articulated many of the notions of how one persuades another person: the kind of identification that is necessary in Burke's terms, the kind of enthymemic common ground in Perelman's. What I'm arguing against is an unnecessary naming and proliferation of theories, unnecessarily going outside our field, not looking at Burke and Perelman. They are much richer; they speak more directly to us in their view of language. Take the question John Bean raised. I think they have a much more sophisticated, much more theoretically complex view of language. So that I see Rogerian theory as an unnecessary and weak construct that, in its worst form, reinforces the notion that there is something called rational argument and that we can somehow in language have logical demonstration. And then our alternative to this is Rogerian rhetoric.

Now I share Maxine's view that all language inherently persuades. This view is, as I said, characteristic of Burke and Perelman. I do believe that Rogers is suspicious of the evaluative, persuasive aspect of language and does seek in his therapy to get beyond it and into some kind of self-moving self. I do perceive Rogers to have an arhetorical view of language, not the most promising of theories to construct another kind of rhetoric. But why do we need it when we've got wonderful Kenneth Burke still alive and kicking around, saying great things in really complex ways about language, as Perelman does. Is that an answer?

AUDIENCE (same woman). Yes, but can't you consider, in light of these wonderful rhetoricians still alive and kicking, that Carl Rogers has something to contribute toward developing multiple perspectives toward the discipline called rhetoric?

LISA EDE. I don't, really, if by that you mean what we have called Rogerian rhetoric. If you're referring to discussions of what we as teachers can learn from Rogers, I think that's quite a lot. But in terms of theorizing, it seems to me not parsimonious to create something called Rogerian rhetoric to understand the kinds of ideas in question. I'm not persuaded of its usefulness. I think when you call something a particular theory and put it in stages, you're likely to have students respond to it as they do to comparison–contrast, to cause–effect, to the five-paragraph essay. There is a danger of really missing the richness, of reducing what is valuable—as the useful things Richard says to students in his book.

RICHARD YOUNG. On the notion of parsimony in theorizing, I think you ought not to introduce matters that have already been treated elsewhere, but I don't know of any treatment of that peculiar sort of situation which we were describing, and which Corder describes at considerable length. I think Rogers was particularly interested in it when he was thinking of the rhetorical applications of his own work. This is the situation where people are steadfast in violent opposition. I don't think Aristotle, or the Aristotelian tradition, or the classical tradition (whatever we call it) really addresses that situation.

It has been proposed that Rogerian argument is really concerned with the situation prior to the situation that Aristotle is concerned with. That is, Aristotle is very clear that there are only certain situations that he would call rhetorical. There are other situations, characterized by conflict, where we don't do rhetoric. Rhetoric is concerned only with a certain kind of situation where there is a disagreement and where there is the possibility for argument. We [Young, et al., 1970] were asking the question: what about the other situation that we find ourselves in all the while?—when you are arguing with your kids, your husband, or your wife, or when the disagreements go deep and we get upset. What about that kind of situation? It is an entirely human situation, a frequent situation, and when we find ourselves in it, we know it's an important situation.

I maintain we do not have anything in traditional rhetoric that addresses this kind of situation directly. So what we were trying to do was to see whether there was any contribution that might be made to help us address this problem. Well, you might ask, doesn't Aristotelian argument work? I would say, only if the opponents have been brought to the position where they are willing to talk, and it seems to me that's where Rogerian argument can contribute. At least that's what we thought Rogerian argument could do.

REFERENCES

Burke, K. (1969). *A rhetoric of motives*. Berkeley, CA: University of California Press.

Corder, J. W. (1978). Varieties of ethical argument, with some account of the significance of *ethos* in the teaching of composition. *Freshman English News, 6*, 1–23.

Hairston, M. (1986). Different products, different processes: A theory about writing. *College Composition and Communication, 37*, 442–452.

Perelman, C. (1982). *The realm of rhetoric* (W. Klubak, Trans.). Notre Dame, IN: University of Notre Dame Press.

Rogers, C. R. (1969). *Freedom to learn*. Columbus, OH: Merrill.

Young, R. E., Becker, A. L., & Pike, K. L. (1970). *Rhetoric: Discovery and change*. New York: Harcourt, Brace.

CHAPTER 5
Classical and Rogerian Persuasion: An Archaeological/Ecological Explication

Richard M. Coe

Rhetorical structures are pre-pared ways of responding, frozen in synchronicity. They embody our social memory of standard strategies for responding to types of situations we encounter repeatedly. When we see past the uniqueness of a particular situation and recognize it as familiar, we activate (at least provisionally) a structure we have previously decided is generally appropriate to that type of situation. New and radically different types of situations call for new strategies, which may be embodied in new structures (cf. Coe, 1974).

Both Classical and Rogerian persuasion are rhetorical strategies that are commonly taught and remembered as structures. Though the reduction of strategies to structures is convenient and perhaps efficient, it creates an ahistorical abstractness that masks the connection to what the anthropologist Bronislaw Malinowski (1923) called "context of situation" (cf. Burke, 1969, pp. 65, 205–206). It also interrupts the logical flow that should take us from consideration of strategies to consideration of the ends those strategies serve—and hence, from rhetoric to ethics. To understand and explain rhetorical structures we should remember the strategies they embody, the types of enunciative situations to which they cor-respond, and the ends they are structured to serve.

Such an explication makes functional sense of the formal features of a genre. It resolves the false dichotomy between form and process, "transforming a polarity of two terms—process and product—into a dialectic" (Phelps, 1988, pp. 160–161). Text structures are understood as fossil remnants of the process that created the text. Deconstructing the text, we reconstruct the communicative strategy that guided the creative process. Because text structure ("product") is understood by reimagining its creation and function ("process") and explained as strategic adaptation to the "context of situation," such explication may be called archaeological (Foucault, 1972) or ecological (Cooper, 1986).

NARRATIO

Let us begin, mythically at least, at the beginning.

Once upon a time, long, long ago and far, far away—to be more precise, some 466 years before the beginning of the Common Era, in Syracuse, a Greek *polis* on the island of Sicily—the people revolted against Thrasybulus, the last of a series of dictators, and reestablished democracy. Thereafter, the courts were flooded with litigation from citizens claiming property that had allegedly been confiscated by the despots and given to their various followers. In circumstances where proof absolute was often unavailable, hundreds of citizens were faced with the need to present persuasive arguments substantiating their proprietary rights.

Responding to this need, Corax is said to have *form-alized* a strategy for presenting arguments effectively in courts of law—and, thereby, initiated rhetoric as a self-conscious, formal discipline. For the succeeding two-and-a-half millennia, this formal structure, slightly amplified by Corax's Greek and Roman successors, has been taught as the standard way to organize an argument. Most commonly, Classical persuasion is represented as a six-part structure: (1) introduction, (2) narration, (3) proposition and partition, (4) proofs, (5) refutations, and (6) peroration. Even the modern five-paragraph essay is an abridged variation on this structure, with introduction, narration, proposition, and partition collapsed into a single opening paragraph, followed by three proofs, no refutation, and a summary peroration.

More recently—to be precise, 1970 years into the Common Era (which is to say, just past the middle of that historical epoch we call "the sixties")—Young, Becker, and Pike introduced an alternative strategy and structure for persuasion, based on concepts derived from the work of psychologist Carl Rogers.

"The sixties" was a time of extraordinary optimism and exceptional conflict. Unusually large numbers of people believed that they could change both the world and themselves for the better in very basic ways. In part because of their attempts to create these changes, "the sixties" was also a time when the United States seemed to many in danger of tearing itself apart because people could not understand each other's positions on the Vietnam War, sex, work, drugs, capitalism, and other very basic matters (cf. Zappen, 1980, p. 99).

To facilitate change or to reduce conflict (or both), various groups proposed new forms of communication. Humanistic psychologists sponsored "encounter groups" and other means of facilitating interpersonal communication. Feminists and New Left activists proposed new forms of constructive criticism and consensus democracy, including structures that created more openings for the personal within political and intellectual discourses.

Rhetoricians, too, proposed radical new communicative strategies, including honesty, spontaneity, and freewriting (see, for instance, Coe, 1974, Elbow, 1973; Fort, 1971; Macrorie, 1970), some of which were promulgated not as new forms but as anti-forms—and many of which were designed to promote "good writing" by subverting traditional forms of academic discourse (especially, "the essay"). Though innovative and perhaps daring, Young, Becker, and Pike's attempt to introduce a new form of persuasion was in keeping with its times.[1]

Like various Classical rhetoricians (especially Cicero), Young, Becker, and Pike (1970) made it clear that they were presenting a strategy, that the "parts" of the structure represented persuasive functions to be performed. Although presented as a four-item list, their structure, too, has six parts: (1) an introduction that frames the subject as a problem, (2) a fair and accurate statement of the opposing position, (3) an assertion of the contexts in which that position may be valid, (4) a fair statement of the writer's position, (5) an assertion of the contexts in which the writer's position is valid, and (6) an ending that shows how readers would benefit from adopting at least elements of the writer's position (Young, Becker, & Pike, 1970, p. 283).

CONTEXT OF SITUATION

Classical rhetoric was clearly a set of strategies that arose in response to certain types of situations we can sum up with the word *democracy*. Corax's story demonstrates how this rhetoric was a response to a particular sort of legal system that was itself a component of a particular sort of political system. Both in the courts and in the political arena, significant advantage went to those who could argue persuasively.

The Greek courts, like our own, were founded on the principle of adversary advocacy (and mercantile Athens was famous, as is the modern-day United States, for its extraordinarily litigious citizens). In a situation where antagonists have conflicting interests, we seek truth by having an advocate represent each of the antagonistic interests. We appoint a referee to make sure the debate is conducted fairly and a disinterested jury to decide who is right. We expect each advocate to seek not truth, but advantage. We would be shocked if the defense attorney were to announce, "Your Honor, after hearing the plaintiff's case, I am convinced my clients were at fault and should pay damages, so I will say nothing in their defense." By contrast, we expect the judge and jury to be not only neutral but passive: they observe and judge, but they do not actively investigate.

Interestingly and somewhat paradoxically, though the system as a whole is designed to determine truth, no individual in the system is assigned to actively seek the truth. In this, the Greek courts were unusual: magistrates in the ancient world were generally active investigators and mediators, whose task was to seek out the truth and devise a resolution to the conflict. The contrast can be seen most easily in the case of contemporary China, which had a comparable political and cultural sophistication, but where rhetoric did not arise as a significant discipline.

As the contrast with China suggests, Greek political democracy was the situation to which Classical rhetoric was an effective response. Political decisions—even military decisions (e.g., Xenophon's address to the soldiers, reprinted in Corbett, 1971, pp. 203–209)—were made by public discussion and voting. Skill at political debate, therefore, was a means to power. Since higher education served to develop both the ability to think about political issues and the ability to speak persuasively before large audiences, rhetoric was an appropriate core discipline. As rhetoric was central to litigation, politics, and education, it became a much-admired *techne*, hence performed on ceremonial occasions. Thus the four major applications of rhetoric in the Classical world were legal pleading, political debate, educational practice, and ceremonial performance.

What these four situations have in common is that rhetors conflict or compete before public audiences which, however they may be biased or predisposed, are not themselves parties to the debate. That is to say, the situation is tripartite: there is a rhetor, one or more opponents, and an audience; the rhetor argues against the opponent(s) in order to persuade not the opponent(s), but the audience. Legal pleading and political debate, moreover, typically involve real material conflicts of interest, where any resolution is likely to produce both winners and losers.

Since the "old Rhetoric was an offspring of dispute," it is not surprising that its defining metaphor is "the battle of words" and its strategies antagonistic, "dominated by the combative impulse" (Richards, 1936, p. 24). The word *antagonistic* comes from the Greek *agonia*, meaning a "contest," such as a wrestling match, in which athletes contend for a prize, compete against each other in a contest refereed and judged by a disinterested third party. That is essentially the sort of context rhetoricians traditionally assumed when discussing persuasion: *the rhetors who argue are trying to defeat, not to convince each other*. The lawyer for the plaintiff does not expect to convince the defense attorney, just the judge and jury. Debating politicians, similarly, are not trying to change each other's minds; they argue against each other in order to convince the voters. Similarly, when a writer produces an article that takes a position on a controversial issue, perhaps responding to a previous article in the same publication, that writer is usually trying to convince the general readership. The writer may argue overtly against the author of a previous article, but the persuasion is ordinarily aimed at other readers who are, in effect, a third party judging the debate.

Under such circumstances, an essentially antagonistic strategy, which represents the rhetor's position strongly, is generally appropriate.[2] Depending on the nature of the issue, opponents, and audience, this strategy may include criticizing, refuting, or even ridiculing opposing viewpoints and their representatives. Balance resides in the system of oppositions, not in the individual presentation. Though the ultimate purpose of such persuasion may be a social good—such as determining truth or responsibility, choosing an effective course of action or the best candidate—the rhetorical means are "dominated by the combative impulse."

Rogerian rhetoric arises in response to very different situations. Rogers' own expertise is as a therapist, and the model for the crux of Rogerian persuasion is the "restatement rule" he created for group therapy: "you can't state your point until you can restate your opponent's point *to his satisfaction*" (Teich, 1985, emphasis added). In therapy, of course, audience and "opponent" are one (the patient), deeply held feelings are involved, the goal is to facilitate change and, within the therapeutic relationship, there is no ultimate conflict of interests:

therapy is not a zero-sum game; neither the therapist nor the other participants in group therapy ordinarily "lose" if the patient "gets better."

Rogers' rule serves to make empathy a prerequisite to assertion. Rogers invented this rule because he considers empathy—which for him means not just understanding of the other person's perspective but also nonjudgmental acceptance of the other person's feelings—the key to constructive, growth-producing relationships. Like other humanistic psychologists, he tends to see most social and psychological problems as failures of communication; he partakes of the traditional liberal ideology that men of good will should be able to resolve their differences through discussion and mutual understanding.[3] His goal is not to *judge* (i.e., not to decide who is right), but to *mediate* (i.e., to achieve consensus).

For Rogers, the essence of Rogerian rhetoric is its purpose, not its techniques. He defines Rogerian communication in terms of its goals (i.e., ethically), not in terms of its strategies (i.e., not rhetorically). Rogers has stated quite clearly that he regards the use of Rogerian techniques for the purpose of winning an argument or *changing another person's mind* as "a perversion of my thinking." His purpose in "extending sensitive empathy to another person" is to "enable him or her to come forth and gain a better understanding of himself and what direction he's going" (Teich, 1985).

Rogers seems, in effect, to agree with Lisa Ede (1984, p. 44), who suggests that "the non-directive nature of [Rogers'] enterprise" calls into question "the very possibility" of "Rogerian argument." But as Rogers himself recognizes in his discussion of brainwashing, a rhetorical technique can be adapted to various, even contrary ends (Teich, 1985). The strategy Rogers proposes is limited neither to therapeutic situations, nor to Rogerian ends. Indeed, Richard Young reports that he, Becker, and Pike were attracted to Rogers because "he knew something that could be useful in . . . situations in which individuals disagree and judgments must be made" (Teich, 1987).

In current usage and practice, the term *Rogerian rhetoric* refers primarily to what Young, Becker, and Pike created in response to Anatol Rapoport's interpretation of concepts from Rogers' work (cf. Zappen, 1980, p. 100–101). Though we may argue about "whether Rogerian rhetoric, as defined by Young, Becker and Pike . . . really merits the adjective 'Rogerian' " (Ede, 1984, p. 46), the underlying premise of what we call Rogerian rhetoric is "that we are more likely to establish real communication with people, especially on sensitive or controversial issues, if we give up traditional, legalistic kinds of arguments and use a non-threatening approach based on shared concerns and common goals" (Hairston, 1982, p. 50).

Rogers himself is extraordinarily optimistic about what can be accomplished by facilitating "better communication." Even in discussing his experience in Northern Ireland, he clearly assumes the conflict between Catholics and Protestants there is only apparently antagonistic, that the "tensions exist because of failures in communication" (Teich, 1985; cf. Zappen, 1980, pp. 103–104).

Young, Becker, and Pike (1970, p. 278) cite Rapoport, who says that the object in persuasion is "to induce the opponent to admit stimuli which he had not admitted before, in short to enlarge his vision." But should we always assume that those who disagree do so because they are missing certain "stimuli," that if we just manage to communicate the missing information we can resolve the misunderstanding?

Rapoport himself says no, "we cannot, as a rule, expect issues to disappear as a result of semantic analysis and improved communication" (Young, Becker, & Pike, 1970, p. 279). Thus Rogers' strategy is appropriate in Northern Ireland only insofar as he is correct in his assumption that the basis of conflict in Northern Ireland is misunderstanding. And generally, Rogerian persuasion is especially appropriate to conflicts that seem more antagonistic than they really are because the opponents share significant common ground.

What, however, about contexts in which this assumption is clearly false?

Except perhaps as a devious rhetorical trick to sway the court by presenting a falsely reasonable persona, Rogerian persuasion would not have been an appropriate strategy in Corax's situation. Corax's clients, unlike Rogers', were not trying to encourage personal growth or constructive relationships, just to win their property back from those who had allegedly stolen it. The goal was to persuade the jury, not the thief. There was, moreover, no conflict over basic values (such as the propriety of private property); and the conflict was genuinely antagonistic, a zero-sum game in which one person would win and others lose the property.

THE ROGERIAN SITUATION

When a rhetor is arguing with somebody *and trying to convince that same person*, the situation *may* be radically different from the sorts of situations that gave rise to Classical persuasion (Hairston, 1976). Suppose the rhetor is writing a private letter to the author of an article in an attempt to persuade that author to retract (cf. Appendix A). Where the "opponent" and the audience are the same person, an antagonistic strategy may be ineffective, for to present such a case strongly is to strongly attack the position with which the reader(s) identify. When attacked, people often feel threatened, get defensive and "stick to their guns." So if one's purpose—like Rogers'—is to induce people to change (if only in the sense of actualizing potentials), the last thing one wants is to make those people feel defensive. One may win "the battle of words" and still not win over the opponent.

Of course, people do sometimes manage not to take arguments personally, do manage not to react defensively even though their positions are being criticized. Often this is because the particular positions being criticized do not reflect deeply held beliefs, are not positions with which those people identify to the extent that their sense of self is threatened. A shared commitment to reading literature sensitively and interpreting it accurately may enable literary critics to hear without much defensiveness strong arguments against interpretations they have previously espoused. Those same critics, however, may have more difficulty listening to strong arguments that challenge the critical approach within which they have worked for decades.

Classical persuasion, as Aristotle emphasized, is based on the enthymeme. On the level of structure, an enthymeme is an incompletely stated syllogism. On the level of strategy, the syllogism is left incompletely stated because the audience already believes the unstated premise. As Burke (1969, p. 56) said, "the rhetorician may have to change an audience's opinion in one respect; but he can succeed only insofar as he yields to that audience's opinions in other respects." Classical rhetors relied on opinions they shared with their audiences, on a set of basic beliefs from which particular conclusions can be drawn. (Aristotle's *topoi*, for instance, can be interpreted as a catalog of shared beliefs.)

But what about rhetors who must argue against their audience's deeply held beliefs, beliefs that the audience could not give up without changing very basically who they are? "Carefully reasoned logical arguments, Rogers claims, may be totally ineffectual when employed in a rhetorical situation where the audience feels its beliefs or values are being threatened" (Bator, 1980, p. 428). In such situations, the most important audience analysis question becomes, "What does the audience fear?" Classical argument is often not the best response to situations defined by one or more of the following:

1. audience and "opponent" are one,
2. deeply held beliefs are at stake,
3. the rhetor's purpose is to mediate or facilitate,
4. a consensus or win-win solution seems possible.

In such situations it is often both desirable and possible to induce change while avoiding threat.

Explicit disagreements are sometimes founded on very basic value assumptions. In arguments about abortion, for instance, the overt discussion typically turns on such issues as whether a fetus should be considered a person (in which case abortion becomes homicide, legally justifiable only in special cases, such as self-defense), whether the pregnant woman's well-being should take priority over the well-being of the fetus, whether the individual woman or society should make the decision. But the ultimate basis of disagreement is often even more basic, as indicated by research showing that anti-abortion and pro-choice activists have diametrically different beliefs about the purpose of human life, the nature of moral choice, and appropriate gender roles (Luker, 1984, pp. 158–186).[4] Insofar as the pattern of beliefs Luker discovered is indicative of values implicit in typical anti-abortion and pro-choice positions, to change a person's stance on abortion is to change her sub-stance, switch the ground on which she stands, radically revise her conception of herself. To argue against her position on abortion is to attack her sense of who she is. Rogerian persuasion is an attempt to resolve that contradiction by creating a context of demonstrated understanding and respect in which individuals may feel safe to reconsider basic beliefs and values.

ARISTOTLE AND ROGERS

There has been considerable debate about whether Rogerian persuasion is genuinely new or just an application of classical rhetorical principles. Like many discussions of whether there is anything qualitatively new under the sun, this one turns on level of generality. We can make Aristotle's generalizations—beginning with his definition of rhetoric as "the faculty of observing in any given case the available means of persuasion"—encompass the main features of Rogerian persuasion (Lunsford, 1979; cf. also Ede, 1984). Certainly if one starts with Aristotle's list of three basic appeals, one sees Rogerian persuasion as an emphasis on the ethical appeal, which Aristotle bases on a rhetor's ability to project himself (1) as a sensible person who knows the subject, (2) as a good and forthright person who would not lie to the audience, and (3) as an unselfish and benevolent person who has their best interests at heart.

When we move to specifics or examine the actual practice of traditional argumentation, however, Rogerian persuasion becomes a radical innovation. Certainly, student writers produce radically different persuasive texts after being taught Rogerian techniques (see Appendix A and Coe, 1990, pp. 389–390, 399–405). Though as Lunsford (1979, p. 148) suggests, one can see the entire first half of the Rogerian structure as a means for "getting the audience in the right frame of mind" (Aristotle), students who think about it that way tend to be Rogerian only through the first half—then they breathe a sigh of relief, shift to an assertive tone, present their position as strongly as they can, and thus destroy the Rogerian ethos. Considering that traditional female rhetorical practice in our culture is much closer to Rogerian persuasion, and traditional male rhetorical practice is much closer to Classical argument, moreover, it is probably not pure coincidence that those who have argued Rogerian rhetoric falls within their interpretation of Aristotle's rhetoric have been women.

More important, Lunsford and Ede (1984, p. 44) assert that "Aristotle's concept of the goal of rhetoric is as an interactive means of discovering meaning through language. . . . The process may be termed 'persuasion' only in the broad sense that all language is inherently persuasive." This is such a New Rhetorical reading of Aristotle that, in the next sentence, Lunsford and Ede cite Kenneth Burke—in such a way as to imply that Burke is saying Aristotle would agree with Burke's assertion, down the page, that the meanings of the terms "persuasion, identification ('consubstantiality'), and communication" are inseparable.[5] If Lunsford and Ede's reading of Aristotle does not exaggerate the scope of Classical rhetoric, then Rogerian persuasion certainly fits within it.

PEDAGOGICAL IMPLICATIONS

Thus framed, however, their conclusion no longer negates the claims of those who advocate teaching Rogerian as well as Classical persuasion. For the issue is not the correct reading of Classical rhetorical theory, but rather how the social practice of persuasion is influenced by the teaching of Classical argument (or its derivatives) in modern composition courses—and how this social practice might change if students also learned Rogerian persuasion. Rather than analyze or continue the rhetorical debate, it is for this purpose more pertinent to specify the features of Rogerian persuasion that distinguish it from Classical argument (as normally taught and practiced), to define the sorts of situations in which each is likely to be an appropriate strategy, and to demonstrate the distinctive sort of persuasion likely to be produced by students who have studied Rogerian principles.

The most obvious distinction is between the assertive presentation of one's position in Classical argument and the evenhanded, fair-minded presentation used in Rogerian persuasion. Beyond that the distinctive features of Rogerian persuasion are as follows:

1. The subject is introduced as a *problem*, not an issue. Thus it can be treated as something we should work cooperatively to solve, not as something that divides. Though somewhat comparable to the Classical introduction and narration, the Rogerian introduction weaves a very different kind of web.
2. Rogerian writers demonstrate both empathy and respect for opposing views before presenting their own. The same points that might be discussed in a Classical refutation are presented in a radically different tone to serve a radically different purpose. The equivalent of the Classical proposition, partition, and proofs (i.e., the equivalent of the logical appeal) *must* come after this demonstration—which is very different from Cicero's notion that it *may* under exceptional circumstances follow the refutation).
3. Though not much discussed in our textbooks, a crucial structure in Rogerian persuasion is the turning point, the transition to the presentation of the writer's position. If this transition is not handled well, the audience will likely decide that all the preceding fairmindedness was just a devious rhetorical trick.
4. The Rogerian ending is not a reiteration but a *promise*; it explains what the audience/"opponent" has to gain by adopting at least some of what the writer advocates. Though it is founded on *pathos* in George Campbell's sense—it appeals to "some desire or passion in the hearers" and suggests that what the writer advocates will gratify that desire—it does not emphasize what modern textbooks call the "emotional appeal." In effect, it explicitly states the mutual purpose shared by rhetor and readers.

These tactics—presenting the subject as a problem to be solved, maintaining an evenhanded, fairminded tone throughout, demonstrating empathy and respect, moving smoothly from validation of the opposing position to presentation of the writer's position, and ending with a promise of gratification—are features of a strategy that will generally be more effective than Classical argument in the types of situation defined above.[6]

The formal structure of Rogerian persuasion, like any other rhetorical pattern, should be treated as a flexible guide, not as a rigidity. One of my students, for instance, quite effectively used the contrast between contexts in which smoking is fully acceptable and those in which it may not be acceptable as the transition to stating her opinion (i.e., she went from the third to the fifth and then back to the fourth part of the standard structure).

> Thus smokers will wish to have the cigarette they are accustomed to. And when smokers are seated next to patrons who share their preference or when other patrons are seated far enough away that the smoke does not reach them, smoking is fully acceptable because no one is unwillingly subjected to it. When the dining area is crowded, many nonsmokers may feel some degree of discomfort. In this sense, smoking, though a personal preference, is not an individual act that can always be dealt with on an individual basis. As a public act, it sometimes has to be dealt with in the spirit of compromise.

There is also a larger lesson to be learned from the juxtaposition of these two approaches: rhetorical forms matter because they are not just containers; they shape as well as convey ideas. The juxtaposition of Classical and Rogerian persuasion can teach valuable lessons about the relationship between means and ends, form and function, structure, strategy, situation, and goals—about how to teach form as heuristic, not algorithmic, as process, not formula (cf. Christie's and Freadman's responses to Dixon in Reid, n.d.; see also Coe, 1987, esp. pp. 23–24; and Coe, 1988, pp. 5–12, 19–25, 74–76). It can also in various ways validate humanism (e.g., Elbow's discussion of "methodological doubt" and "methodological belief," 1986, pp. 249, 254–300).

And that brings us to the relationship between rhetoric and ethics.

ETHICS

Rogerian persuasion may seem morally superior to Classical persuasion because it is founded on empathy and works toward common ground, while Classical persuasion is founded on conflict and works toward winning. The assertiveness of traditional argument often constitutes verbal violence, lack of empathy, lack of respect and consideration for others. This is part of what is meant by those who suggest that academic discourse is a "male" or patriarchal discourse.

But there is also a sense—and it is almost always a male student who makes this point in my writing classes—in which traditional argument is more honest because it's more direct. Rogerian persuasion does involve what a combative debater might call "pulling your punches." Rogerian persuasion usually means not fully revealing (perhaps even concealing) your own position until after the turning point. And even then you often do not assert it as strongly as you feel it.

As envisioned by Rogers and those who adapted his concept to written communication, Rogerian persuasion means to understand those who oppose you and to work with them toward the best possible resolution. Occasionally, writers using the Rogerian structure actually convince themselves and change their minds while writing the first half. Broadly conceived, Rogerian rhetoric is an application of the ancient ethical principle, "Do unto others as you would have others do unto you"; that is, demonstrate that you have considered and understood their position as carefully as you want them to consider yours. That, not the precise formal structure, is what makes it Rogerian and humanistic. But the Rogerian strategy and structure can also be used deviously by writers who want only to win and only pretend to empathize and respect. Like any rhetorical technique, Rogerian principles can be used or abused.

As there are rhetorical contexts in which Classical persuasion offers a more effective structure, and rhetorical contexts in which Rogerian persuasion offers a more effective structure, so there are contexts in which it seems ethically most important to be direct and out front, contexts in which it seems ethically most important to be gentle and empathetic. There are even extreme contexts in which it seems ethical to lie. Either structure, moreover, can be used or abused. For better and for worse, there is no simple rule. Whether Classical or Rogerian persuasion is superior, ethically or rhetorically, depends on the context. In the tradition of the *paideia* and *humanitas*, students learn important principles from such ethical and rhetorical complexities.

Rhetoric shows us the tools of persuasion and teaches us how to use them effectively. Rhetoric cannot tell us whether a particular use is ethical. The same rhetorical technique that is good in one use may be devious in another. For example, when speaking to someone recently bereaved, it is a kindness to use euphemism and say "passed away" in order to avoid direct reference to death. But the very same rhetorical structure, euphemism, was abused when someone in the U.S. State Department decided to instruct employees not to use the word *kill* in reports on human rights abuse—in State Department reports, death squads no longer kill anybody; officially what happens is the "unlawful or arbitrary deprivation of life." Although they have leanings, rhetorical structures are not intrinsically good or bad.

There is, of course, some relationship between the structure of means and the nature of the ends. A screwdriver is less likely than a machine gun to be used for killing, a machine gun less likely than a screwdriver to be used to take apart a soft drink vending machine (but cf. "Dr. Strangelove"). On the other hand, a bomb that was designed to destroy a city can be used to dig a canal. Marshall McLuhan was partially wrong—the medium is not the whole message; in fact,

McLuhan's later, metaphorical formulation, "the medium is the massage," is more accurate (McLuhan, 1964, 1967; cf. Burke, 1966, pp. 410–418)—but certain rhetorical structures do increase the likelihood of certain sorts of outcomes. The Rogerian structure does tend to induce gentleness and empathy. The Classical structure is more likely to produce directness. Writers who wish to be both ethical and persuasive in various contexts are well advised to master both Classical and Rogerian modes.

Even (or perhaps especially) in Aristotelian terms, substance, purpose, audience, strategy, and form are intertwined concepts. Sterile polarities, such as those between form and content, process and product, are more fruitfully renamed as dialectical distinctions (which imply interrelationship). As Park asserts, the very concept of audience "points to the final cause for which form exists, to the purposefulness—or its lack—that makes a piece of prose shapely and full of possibility, or aimless and empty. . . . Much of the time it is not possible to separate a sense of audience from a sense of genre and convention" (1982, pp. 247, 256). Concretely contextual discussion of Classical and Rogerian strategies for persuasion can lead students to a more sophisticated understanding of how strategy and structure, process and product, context and text, form and substance are interrelated. In my experience, such a discussion almost always leads also to serious pondering of the ethical implications of rhetorical choices.

Rhetoric itself is rhetorical, hence, ethical. By teaching particular rhetorical processes, techniques, genres, conventions—*and not others* (any selection is a deflection)—we encourage particular sorts of texts and processes.

OTHER ROGERIAN STRUCTURES

As presented in composition textbooks, Rogerian rhetoric is the strategy invented by Young, Becker, and Pike, and nothing more. But if we take Rogerian rhetoric to mean all rhetorical strategies that serve Rogerian aims as defined by Rogers, Rapoport, or Young, Becker, and Pike, it should include considerably more. That is, we should define Rogerian rhetoric to include all rhetorical strategies and structures that facilitate empathy, consensus, nonantagonistic communication, mediation of disputes, problem solving, and so on. Thus Hairston (1982, pp. 50–51) says she is "using Rogerian strategies" when she "phrase[s] questions neutrally in order to elicit genuine answers" and when she "withhold[s] my response until people have had a chance to express their views." In this sense, various rhetorical techniques that have been designed to facilitate constructive criticism and consensus thus fall within Rogerian rhetoric (cf. Zappen, 1980, pp. 106–107).

These are, moreover, strategies of very great use to writers. Not only can these strategies be used in certain types of texts, but they are also useful in the processes of writing, editing, and publishing. The ability to give and take constructive criticism is useful to writers in many contexts. So is the ability to achieve consensus, especially when the writing is collaborative or produced to serve a group purpose.

Constructive criticism is a strategy closely related to Rogerian persuasion. It aims not merely to be correct (thereby allowing the criticizer to feel righteous), but to persuade the criticized person or people to construct changes. Especially as developed and articulated by feminists (see Lyons, 1976), constructive criticism is not based on the power of the criticizer; it is appropriate for situations where success depends on persuading the criticized person.

Like Rogerian persuasion, constructive criticism attempts to minimize threat. One way to achieve a reassuring context is by self-criticism: "I can see what's wrong here because I often do (or used to do) the same thing myself." Another way to achieve a reassuring context is to praise before criticizing. (Such praise should, of course, be genuine and specific: hardly anyone is taken in by the formula, "This is basically good, but . . . .")

The threatening nature of criticism can also be reduced if what is being criticized is clearly a particular action (or set of actions), not the person or people who did it. Criticism is also more threatening (hence less constructive) when it is not clear what can be done about it. There is a heuristic formula for constructive criticism that can help keep the criticism specific, make it clear that a particular action (not a person) is being criticized, and constrain the criticizer to indicate what can be done about the criticism. It goes like this:

When you ____________________, *I feel/think* ____________________,
so I wish you would ____________________________, *instead.*

Like Rogerian persuasion, constructive criticism also emphasizes the other person's potential advantage. The third slot in the criticism expresses a desire: the purpose is to encourage the other person to do what is suggested there. As a Rogerian persuasion ends by appealing to the readers' interests, so a constructive criticism should end by indicating what the other person could gain by adopting the suggestion.

It is, of course, not the formula but the strategy that constitutes constructive criticism. It is not hard, if one tries, to subvert the purpose of the formula by filling the slots inappropriately. Nonetheless, the formula works well as a guide, a learning aid, a heuristic to help genuinely motivated people criticize constructively.

The distinction between antagonistic and constructive criticism is parallel to the distinction between traditional and Rogerian persuasion. Antagonistic criticism often plays to an audience. It is righteous. It passes judgment. It demonstrates the superiority of the criticizer and the inferiority of those criticized. Antagonistic criticism often works if the issue is not important enough to be taken personally. It works if the critic really is a "superior" (i.e., has the power to enforce the criticism, hence need not only rely on genuine persuasion). Perhaps most interestingly, it works when those criticized have a certain kind of love and/or respect for the criticizer, for example, when the tough coach (or other father figure) uses the threat of harsh criticism to motivate those who want to please and fear to displease him.

Constructive criticism, by contrast, is addressed to those criticized and often addresses touchy subjects. It relies on genuine suasion and internal motivation, so its strategy is to minimize threat and induce change. (Only a small minority of coaches think it wins more football games than Vince Lombardi.)

It is worth noting that this formula for constructive criticism was invented, shaped, and promulgated within the feminist movement of the 1970s—and that it was inspired by two major sources: humanistic psychology and marxist dialectics, specifically, Mao Zedung's essay on "Criticism/Self-Criticism" (cf. Lyons, 1976).

The Maoist distinction between nonantagonistic and antagonistic relationships is relevant. Where there is an ultimate unity of interests and one cares about the other people involved, there is room for a Rogerian win-win strategy, such as constructive criticism. Where there is a basic conflict of interests and consequently a win-lose situation, a more assertive Classical strategy is often appropriate. The feminist movement, after all, created and promulgated both constructive criticism and assertiveness training.

Consensus is even less discussed in writing texts than constructive criticism. As LeFevre (1986) emphasizes, however, collaborative writing is common, and certain types of texts are actually produced by negotiation. Reaching consensus is a key factor in the success of such writing.

Consensus, it must be emphasized, means everybody (or almost everybody) is in essential agreement. Consensus is not majority rule; it is achieved by extended discussion, not by voting. Indeed, though people who equate democracy with elections do tend to forget this, the need for voting and other such procedures indicates the absence of a consensus. When the goal is a clear and effective piece of writing, consensus is better than majority rule: an early majority may not be right and an unconvinced minority may not cooperate wholeheartedly, so it is better to extend the discussion until issues are resolved. The process of reaching consensus is usually a process of clarifying and improving both the substance and the form of the writing. The advantage of voting (i.e., of democracy defined as the dictatorship of the majority) is that less time is spent discussing.

As the following guidelines for achieving consensus indicate, consensus is in certain essential ways similar to making constructive criticisms and Rogerian persuasion:

> View differences of opinion as helpful, not as hindrances. When the discussion locks, seek alternative solutions that synthesize the best of all the individual suggestions or offer a whole new approach. Keep the group's purpose always in view. Remember the goal is not for any individual member's suggestion to "win," but to make decisions which will best achieve the group's purpose.

In terms of underlying strategies, rhetorical techniques designed to facilitate constructive criticism and consensus by reducing threat to encourage communication and empathy fall within Rogerian rhetoric. Rhetorically, these processes are of the same sort as what we have since 1970 called Rogerian persuasion—and they have particular relevance to recent investigations of collaborative writing and social processes that engender writing (cf. LeFevre, 1986) as well as to recent discussions of "male" and "female" modes of rhetoric (cf., e.g., Taylor, 1978; Farrell, 1979). There are, undoubtedly, other rhetorical strategies that serve similar goals and share the same ethical essence which should be included in Rogerian rhetoric.

CODA

Human society is founded on cooperation. Perhaps the most basic function of language is to induce and facilitate that cooperation. The essential function of language, in which rhetoric is rooted, is its use "as a symbolic means of inducing cooperation in beings that by nature respond to symbols" (Burke, 1969, p. 43). As Burke also notes, however, the counterpart (*antistrophos*) of cooperation is division: we need rhetoric only because people are divided from each other (are, as one schizophrenic put it, "in-divide-you-alls"); to induce cooperation among one group of people is, moreover, to divide them from other people (who don't share the sub-stance which underlies that cooperation).

Though it inevitably creates various levels of division (indeed, values highly the divisions that individualize us), Rogerian strategy emphasizes cooperation (the limits within which there is agreement). Though the Classical strategy does emphasize division—Classical rhetors use both their proofs and their refutations to divide the audience from opposing opinions and those who hold them—it does so also to induce cooperation. If we understand the relationships among rhetorical structures, rhetorical strategies, the types of situations to which they cor-respond, and the ends they are structured to serve, we can use, value, and teach both of these rhetorics effectively and ethically.

APPENDIX A

Here is what happened when one writer tried to write two responses—one Classical, the other Rogerian—to an article on world starvation, which had argued,

> The problem is this: our meat industry uses scarce, rich agricultural land to grow grain for cattle—high quality grain that could be eaten directly by humans. . . . As individuals, we can be part of the solution to feeding the world's hungry and malnourished by reducing the amount of meat we eat and thereby releasing grain for human consumption instead of feed for cattle.

In his Classical persuasion, Dominique Lecasse addresses those who read and were perhaps convinced by the original article; in his Rogerian persuasion he addresses the author of the original article. The tone, of course, shifts radically. In moving from Classical to Rogerian persuasion, Lecasse had to delete such strong (and clever) statements as these:

> Here's the beef. I think JW is full of granola when she says . . . that if we all ate more grain the world would be a fatter place. . . . JW's simplistic solution . . . ignores the far more important political and economic aspects of the problem, and naively proposes to remedy the inequities of the world's complex economic infrastructure with a few granola and soybean recipes for gout-afflicted Westerners.

Certain arguments, moreover, appear in different orders and the fact that the entire piece is essentially a refutation blurs the distinction between the proofs and refutation sections of the Classical version. Note how successfully the Rogerian version ends with a promise rather than a put-down—because the basis of the whole piece is *agreement* that we should do something about world hunger.

To the Editor:

Here's the beef. I think JW is full of granola when she says in her article, "Thought for Food," that if we all ate more grain the world would be a fatter place. Specifically, she claims that meat eaters contribute to world hunger because the animals they eat are fattened on rich grain that could have fed many more people than the meat does. She says, "we can all be part of the solution to feeding the world's hungry and malnourished by reducing the amount of meat we eat and thereby releasing grain for human consumption instead of feed for cattle." Unfortunately, the suggestion is a gross oversimplification of a very complex and difficult problem.

The problem is important, too important to be defined so narrowly. The Ethiopian famine of the summer of '86 illustrates the tragic consequences of food shortages in disadvantaged countries. Thousands died tragically, and perhaps needlessly. Surely, given the choice, we would all want to be "part of the solution." The real difficulty, though, comes in identifying the solution and, perhaps more importantly, in implementing it. JW's simplistic solution—giving up meat, and eating more grain and legumes—ignores the far more important political and economic aspects of the problem, and naively proposes to remedy the inequities of the world's complex economic infrastructure with a few granola and soybean recipes for gout-afflicted Westerners.

In short, JW chooses to ignore the social context of the problem and focuses too narrowly on the simplistic equation that feed cattle must eat twenty pounds of grain to produce one pound of protein. Though there are other flaws in JW's argument, the main criticisms I have are these: (1) she fails to show how the grain would get to the hungry; (2) she ignores the costs that an effective distribution system would entail; and most importantly, (3) she ignored the problem of mustering the necessary political will at home when unemployment is high and people line up for government assistance of every kind.

The first thing to consider then is how more grain at home translate into more food in places like Africa. The answer is that it doesn't. Not unless we are willing to pay the costs of harvesting, shipping, and distribution in the areas of need. More grain at home will help feed the world only if this new supply of food is indeed diverted to the needy. A more likely outcome is that farmers would simply stop producing the crops altogether, unless they were assured a paying market.

The issue is whether or not the developed nations want to accept financial responsibility for feeding the world. Supposing that we did increase the global grain supply through a large-scale change in diet, who would pay for the distribution, and what would the costs be? Indeed, is this not the situation today? Countries like Canada, the USA, and Australia produce grain far in excess of their own requirements, but their first interest is to get it to paying markets. And even if excess grain remains, it is cheaper and simpler too "dump" the surplus output than to attempt a costly distribution program to the scattered and unorganized nations in need. Governments in developed countries have for years been paying farmers *not* to produce crops they could not sell.

This last statement gets to the heart of the problem—political will. For even if the costs and distribution problems were manageable, the problems of the politician's need to satisfy fickle voters at home remains. Yes, we do "give generously" when asked. But for the most part, charity is not a matter of ongoing policy; it is frequently a matter of responding to particular crises, and often motivated by guilt or tax considerations. So in this kind of social environment, and given the political realities of elections and budget deficits, it seems doubtful that many governments could commit the resources required to make JW's "recipe" work, at least on a longterm basis. It is an economic and moral problem, not simply a matter of diet choice, and even this is an oversimplification; after all, would it not be a better use of resources to supply the needy with the means to help themselves?

Are twenty pounds of grain better than one pound of animal protein? Unfortunately, JW's argument cannot be evaluated in a political and economic vacuum. Her assumption that the freed-up grain would automatically flow to the needy is simply untenable. (If everyone in Vancouver were to fast today, would that make anyone in Bangladesh less hungry tomorrow?) As is invariably the case in a "free market" society, resources will typically be allocated on the basis of power or ability to pay, and only a small residual will flow to the less fortunate—and that only given the right political and economic conditions.

Dominique Lecasse

Dear Ms. JW:

I read with interest your recent article, "Thought for Food." The solution to the world food shortage you propose in that article deserves consideration—perhaps we should all try to "do our part" right here by adopting a grain-based diet. This, as you say, would be a more efficient use of agricultural resources than using grain to fatten cattle. You will get no argument from me—the problem of world hunger is serious, and every possible solution should be explored.

You say that our preference for meat over grain as a primary source of protein leads to inefficient food production practices, because it takes twenty pounds of grain to produce one pound of meat, and that this inefficiency contributes to the problem of feeding the world's hungry. It follows then that lowering the demand for meat should free scarce agricultural land for the production of grain for people instead of grain for cattle, and that this arrangement could feed more people.

Your argument, based as it is on the relative efficiencies of these two food sources, certainly holds well in a situation where the grain can readily be passed on to the hungry. For example, if farmers are fattening cattle in a region where the grain supply is inadequate to feed the hungry, say in Ethiopia itself, then it is fairly clear that such a strategy could prove helpful. In such a situation, where the grain source is relatively close to the point of consumption, more grain should translate into less malnutrition and starvation. There would be more food around, and this could conceivably make it more affordable for those of meager means. And this, of course, is another necessary assumption: that those in need have at least the minimal means to compensate the producers and also access to essential implements for food preparation, such as water and containers.

I do agree that meat appears to be a wasteful method for obtaining protein. I wonder, however, if you have considered the other variables that may play an equally important part in the problem. It is not clear that a greater grain supply will necessarily lead to a more equitable distribution of agricultural output. I wonder, for example, who will pay Canadian farmers (who already struggle to meet their own obligations) to ship their wheat across the oceans and continents? And who will build, organize, and pay for the transportation system in the countries that receive the food? It has been widely reported, for example, that the most unfortunate aspect of the Ethiopian relief project was that much of the good donated never reached its destinations within the country for a lack of adequate roads and vehicles. The problem is not really a "world food shortage"; it is an uneven distribution of resources and population. It is a complicated geographic, economic, and political problem that goes well beyond diet management.

The crux of the matter then revolves around the question of physical distances and economic inequalities that separate meat-producing regions and those nations we awkwardly call "underdeveloped." If the physical or economic barriers are great, then finding the economic resources and political will necessary to redistribute the life-giving food is clearly the biggest problem and the most important priority. We must also admit that the "charity begins at home" mentality cannot easily be discounted in periods of high unemployment and huge government deficits. When governments cannot find the resources to solve domestic problems, they may be hard-pressed to maintain, let alone increase, expenditures abroad. In these circumstances, economic and political variables are likely to seriously overshadow the relative efficiencies of diet.

It is an axiom of all problem-solving strategies that the most important step is to identify the problem accurately and completely. For it is only through identifying the relative importance of the various factors involved, while recognizing the complexity of their interrelationships, that we can start toward a usable solution. This holds for finding an equitable solution to global food production and distribution. For though an efficient mix of nutritional sources may be part of the "food solution," it will solve nothing if the economic and political dimensions of the problem are not first recognized and addressed. Yes, we may eventually substitute much grain for a little meat. But first we will have to make financial sacrifices and tough political decisions to move that grain and, ultimately, to help the less fortunate acquire the resources and knowledge necessary to feed themselves. For now, though, the question is not really what food do we eat, but rather who should eat it? That is where the solution lies—not so much in a change of diet as in a more equitably "balanced diet."

Dominique Lecasse

NOTES

1. Perhaps it is not surprising that "the eighties" were less friendly to Rogerian persuasion. In the United States, at least, "the eighties" was a less optimistic time. Many people were more concerned with adapting to the status quo than with changing it, with feeling good about themselves and "America" than with qualitatively improving either. Those who did work for change were more likely than in "the sixties" to be working within (or at least with) the system. With some notable exceptions (especially among feminists), rhetoricians and composition specialists put more emphasis on teaching academic discourse (perhaps critically) than on subverting it. (n.b., despite the formal tyranny of our decimal system, I take "the sixties" to end about 1974–75 and "the eighties" to begin not long thereafter.)
2. For somewhat different reasons, the same remains true when rhetoric merges with dialectic, understood in the traditional sense as argumentative discussion aimed at determining the truth (or the best policy). In such discussions, often over dinner or wine (the etymological meaning of *symposium*), some commonality ordinarily encompasses the divisions; the discussion, however heated, remains ultimately friendly. This consubstantiality may be an agreement on basic values that predominate over the relatively minor specific disagreement, a strong common interest in the correct conclusion, or even joy in the play of debate (especially when nothing that truly matters is at stake).

   In evaluating a persuasive strategy, one should also remember that a defensive reaction does not necessarily mean a failed argument. People often change later, when the threat is gone—perhaps without even remembering when or by whom they were persuaded.
3. Cf. Ede's assertion (1984, p. 40) that "Rogers' ontological and epistemological assumptions imply an arhetorical view of language, one in which language functions ideally as a transparent means of self-expression." Such positivistic misunderstandings of language are part of this same liberal tradition.
4. I use the term *anti-abortion* (rather than *pro-life*) and *pro-choice* (rather than *pro-abortion*) because the evidence indicates that anti-abortion activists are actually opposed to abortions while pro-choice activists tend to see abortions as an essentially undesirable last resort and favor only the individual woman's right to choose. Thus, *anti-abortion* and *pro-choice* seem to be the most specific and accurate terms.

   Anti-abortion activists generally believe: (1) that the availability of abortion (like the availability of highly effective contraception) worsens women's position by allowing men to be irresponsible and to treat women as sexual objects, (2) that men and women have different vocations in life (and that what makes women special is their natural ability to nurture), and (3) that the universe is guided by a greater purpose to which human beings should subordinate themselves (Luker, 1984, pp. 158–175). Pro-choice arguments are based on very different assumptions: (1) that women should not try to better their position within the "battle of the sexes" by holding men more responsible but by taking more responsibility for themselves; (2) that one's vocation in life should not be determined by gender (and that *involuntary* motherhood oppresses women); and (3) that the ultimate social purpose is to enable human beings to actualize their potential (Luker, 1984, pp. 175–186). Anti-abortion activists, moreover, are moral absolutists who presume clear rules, an absolute moral code, by which human conduct can be judged; pro-choice activists, by contrast, believe people must use moral judgment because the concrete implications of basic ethical principles vary with particular situations (Cf. Faludi, 1989.)

No verbal persuasion, Classical or Rogerian, is likely to sway the activists Luker investigated. But if the pattern of beliefs she discovered underlies typical anti-abortion and pro-choice positions, then those values constitute the unstated propositions of the enthymemes upon which an effective Classical argument would rest. If an audience is not yet firmly committed and shares the appropriate values, a Classical strategy may well persuade. But if an audience, however uncommitted, does not share the rhetor's assumptions about the purpose of human life, the nature of moral choice, and appropriate gender roles, there is an apparent contradiction between the rhetor's need to avoid threatening and her need to explain and justify her position.

5. The context for these assertions is Lunsford and Ede's refutation of a view of Classical rhetoric as assuming:
   1. Man is a rational animal living in a society marked by social cohesion and agreed-upon values.
   2. Emphasis is on logical (or rational) proofs.
   3. Rhetor–audience relationship is antagonistic.
   4. Goal is persuasion (not communication).

   In suggesting Lunsford and Ede may be overstating their conclusion, I do not mean to imply agreement with the view they criticize. The view of Classical rhetoric implicit in my contrast between Classical and Rogerian persuasion does assume that the Classical goal is persuasion, that is, more limited than what either Burke or Rogers mean by communication. But I am explicitly asserting that the Classical rhetor–audience relationship is not especially or necessarily antagonistic. And, though I certainly do not agree with the first two assumptions Lunsford and Ede refute, the extent to which rhetor, audience, or proofs are rational is not crucial or even particularly pertinent to the distinction I am making.
6. I do not mean to suggest that such tactics cannot be used within a Classical strategy. Both Corbett (1971) and Horner (1988) treat such tactics, albeit briefly, in composition textbooks explicitly based on Classical rhetoric. Both authors do so under the heading of *ethos* (specifically *eunoia*, "good

will" or "benevolence"). In his discussion of types of introductions, Corbett includes *insinuatio*, "ingratiating oneself with the audience," and asserts that, in "counteracting prejudices" writers must "proceed with the utmost subtlety" (p. 308). Horner includes in her guide, "ways of establishing credibility," four questions that could encourage Rogerian tactics:

> Have I acknowledged and given careful consideration to the audience's viewpoint?
> Have I reviewed our points of agreement?
> Have I reminded my audience of our common interests and concerns?
> Have I demonstrated that I respect and acknowledge my audience's intelligence, sincerity, and common sense? (p. 55)

But there is a qualitative difference between using some Rogerian tactics within a Classical strategy and using a Rogerian approach to define one's whole persuasive strategy. Though a Classical strategy may not exclude a Rogerian approach, it certainly is not structured to encourage it. Neither Corbett's nor Horner's discussion of *refutatio* suggests the sort of refutation one would have to write to validate Lunsford's assertion that Rogerian persuasion should be understood as a kind of Classical argument where the refutation comes near the beginning.

REFERENCES

Bator, P. (1980). Aristotelian and Rogerian rhetoric. *College Composition and Communication, 31*, 427–432.

Burke, K. (1966). *Language as symbolic action.* Berkeley: University of California Press.

Burke, K. (1969). *A rhetoric of motives.* Berkeley: University of California Press.

Coe, R. M. (1974). Rhetoric 2001. *Freshman English News, 3*, 1–13.

Coe, R. (1987). An apology for form; or, who took the form out of the process. *College English, 49*, 13–28.

Coe, R. (1988). *Toward a grammar of passages.* Carbondale, IL: Southern Illinois University Press.

Coe, R. (1990). *Process, form, and substance.* Englewood Cliffs, NJ: Prentice-Hall.

Cooper, M. (1986). The ecology of writing. *College English, 48*, 364–375.

Corbett, E. P. J. (1971). *Classical rhetoric for the modern student* (2nd ed.). New York: Oxford.

Ede, L. (1984). Is Rogerian rhetoric really Rogerian? *Rhetoric Review, 3*, 40–48.

Elbow, P. (1973). *Writing without teachers.* New York: Oxford.

Elbow, P. (1986). *Embracing contraries.* New York: Oxford.

Faludi, S. (1989). Where did Randy go wrong? *Mother Jones, 14*, 22–28, 61–64.

Farrell, T. J. (1979). The male and female modes of rhetoric. *College English, 40*, 909–921.

Fort, K. (1971). Form, authority, and the critical essay. *College English, 33*, 629–639.

Foucault, M. (1972). *The archaeology of knowledge & the discourse on language*, (Trans. A. M. S. Smith). New York: Pantheon.

Hairston, M. (1976). Carl Rogers' alternative to traditional rhetoric. *College Composition and Communication, 27*, 373–377.

Hairston, M. (1982). Using Carl Rogers' communication theories in the composition classroom. *Rhetoric Review, 1*, 50–55.

Horner, W. B. (1988). *Rhetoric in the classical tradition*. New York: St. Martin's.

LeFevre, K. B. (1986). *Invention as a social act*. Carbondale, IL: Southern Illinois University Press.

Luker, K. (1984), *Abortion and the politics of motherhood*. Berkeley: University of California Press.

Lunsford, A. (1979). Aristotelian vs. Rogerian argument: A reassessment. *College Composition and Communication, 30*, 146–151.

Lunsford, A. A., & Ede, L. S. (1984). On distinctions between classical and modern rhetoric. In R. J. Connors, L. S. Ede, & A. A. Lunsford (Eds.), *Essays on classical rhetoric and modern discourse* (pp. 37–49). Carbondale, IL: Southern Illinois University Press.

Lyons, G. (1976). *Constructive criticism*. Oakland, CA: Inkwords. [Reprinted by Wingbow, 1988.]

Macrorie, K. (1970). *Telling writing*. New York: Hayden.

Malinowski, B. (1923). The problem of meaning in primitive languages. In C. K. Ogden & I. A. Richards (Eds.), *The meaning of meaning* (Supp. 1). London: Kegan Paul.

McLuhan, M. (1964). *Understanding Media*. New York: Signet.

McLuhan, M. (1967). *The medium is the massage*. New York: Bantam.

Park, D. B. (1982). The meanings of 'audience.' *College English, 44*, 247–257.

Phelps, L. W. (1988). *Composition as a human science*. New York: Oxford.

Reid, I. (Ed.). (n.d.). *The place of genre in learning: Current debates*. Victoria, Australia: Deakin University Centre for Studies in Literary Education, Typereader Publication, no. 1.

Richards, I. A. (1936). *The philosophy of rhetoric*. London: Oxford.

Taylor, S. O. (1978). Women in a double bind: Hazards of the argumentative edge. *College Composition and Communication, 29*, 385–389.

Teich, N. (1985). Conversation with Carl Rogers. (Reprinted as Chapter 3, this volume.)

Teich, N. (1987). Forum: Reassessing Carl Rogers' principles in composition instruction. (Reprinted as Chapter 4, this volume.)

Young, R. L., Becker, A. L., & Pike, K. L. (1970). *Rhetoric: Discovery and change*. New York: Harcourt, Brace.

Zappen, J. P. (1980). Carl R. Rogers and political rhetoric. *PRE/TEXT, 1*, 95–113.

CHAPTER 6
Rogerian Argument and the Context of Situation: Taking a Closer Look

Richard E. Young

I

In his "Argument as Emergence, Rhetoric as Love," Jim Corder remarks that "the arguments most significant to us are just where threat occurs and continues, just where emotions and differences do not get calmly talked away," where "contention generates that flushed, feverish, quaky, shaky, angry, scared, hurt, shocked, disappointed, alarmed, outraged, even terrified condition" that characterizes value-laden dispute (1985, p. 25). I quote Professor Corder's description because I want to make clear at the start what kind of experiences are at issue in the discussion that follows and, by implication, what kinds are not. Whatever other features instances of such conflicts may have, all are dyadic (that is, they involve two people or two groups of people), and, in all, strongly held values are at issue, values that are perceived by the participants as essential to their well-being, so much so that often the primary goal of the participants is the defense of these values.

Twenty years ago, conflicts of this kind prompted Alton Becker, Kenneth Pike, and me to develop a suggestion by Carl Rogers in his "Communication: Its Blocking and Its Facilitation" (1951)[1] and introduce it into modern rhetorical theory and pedagogy. Since then what we called *Rogerian argument* has prompted a surprisingly wide range of reactions: it has been seen as a promising basis for a modern rhetoric

(Bator, 1980)—a much more expansive function than the one we had proposed; as aiding real-world problem solving (Teich, 1987); as impairing our ability to deal effectively with the socioeconomic dimensions of conflict (Pounds, 1987); as an extension of, or at least consistent with, Aristotelian rhetoric (Lunsford, 1979); as fundamentally inconsistent with Aristotelian rhetoric (Mader, 1980); as inappropriate for written communication (Ede, 1984); as appropriate for written communication and its teaching (Hairston, 1982); as not really a kind of argument at all (Mader, 1980); and as a misguided and potentially harmful innovation (Ede, 1984). The diversity and incompatibility of the reactions alone suggest the need to take a closer look, not only at how we presented Rogerian argument at the time, but at the possibilities that we saw as well, since it would be a mistake to reject the idea because our effort to realize it may have been flawed. In taking a closer look here, I hope I can persuade others to do the same. Until we have looked more closely, we ought, I think, to defer making claims about what Rogerian argument can and cannot do, or for that matter what it could do if it were modified in the light of what we know now. A more tentative, inquiring stance seems most appropriate to the situation we find ourselves in today.

"Rogerian argument," we said, "rests on the assumption that out of a need to preserve the stability of his image [i.e., his system of beliefs], a person will refuse to consider alternatives that he feels are threatening, and hence that changing a person's image depends on eliminating this sense of threat" (Young, Becker, & Pike, 1970, p. 274), thus making it possible to consider another position. Hence, the efforts of this kind of argument are strongly directed toward reducing the opponent's feeling of threat: e.g., by avoiding highly evaluative language, by demonstrating that the opponent's position has been understood in a way that is sensitive to its personal meaning and implications, by indicating that the opponent's position is seen as reasonable, by acting out of an assumption of similarity and identifying shared features that could become possible bases for further interaction. (Such efforts are functions or subgoals of the discourse, not parts of its structure.) *Winning* the argument, if that word can be appropriately used in this context, means making it possible for the opponent to consider alternatives, or establishing and maintaining communication, or creating a willingness to enter into a common effort to solve a common problem—in general expanding the possibilities for cooperation beyond those that had hitherto been available in the dispute.

Even though classical argument does effectively address conflicts in the courts and other public forums, relatively little has been said by classical rhetoricians about conflicts of the sort I have described, despite their being so intrusive and often so important in our lives. The whole orientation of the great classical tradition has been toward the conduct of public affairs; it is a rhetoric that presupposes communities with widely shared beliefs and conflicts in which opponents are willing and able to communicate. It has not spoken directly to dyadic situations where a sense of threat makes it difficult and at times impossible for one or both of the participants to even consider adopting another position; where fundamental beliefs are often not shared; where there is a greater sense of diversity than of community, indeed, where in some cases, say an Amish pacifist and a Pentagon hawk, the differences are so extreme that one questions whether mutual understanding is possible; where confrontation often veers toward coercion and violence. This is not to say that classical argument is either irrelevant or unimportant in modern society or that Rogerian argument can replace it. They were invented for quite different kinds of situations, and many of their distinctive features derive from the differences in these situations.

In our thinking about value-laden dyadic situations, however, Becker, Pike, and I were preoccupied with how they differed from situations in which traditional argument can be effective.[2] We did not pay enough attention to the considerable variation in actual dyadic situations; and we did not see that both the use and the usefulness of Rogerian argument seem to vary as the situation varies. The peculiarities of the particular situation affect, or should affect, the choices one makes in addressing it; not understanding this leads to inappropriate and ineffective choices.

II

If we examine some of the suggestions for using Rogerian argument, we see several kinds of situations that can be differentiated on the basis of how willing and able the parties are to address their differences. For example, Nathaniel Teich (1987) argues for the use of Rogerian argument in situations that are quite different from the highly conflicted one I have been describing:

> As a prerequisite for achieving Rogers' goal of "real communication," however, the parties must share a common interest in resolving a problem or dispute by a mutually satisfactory solution. (p. 53)

And further,

> All aspects of Rogerian communication—intent, purpose, and product—are governed by the presupposition that the parties are willing to compromise. (p. 55)

In the writing class this assumption affects the students' choice of topic:

> If you cannot adopt Rogers' Rule [that the other's position must be restated satisfactorily before you may state your own] or risk changing your views . . . [Teich cautions his students], then you should reconsider your choice of topic. Consequently, students tend to avoid arguing about such potentially loaded topics as abortion, gun control, nuclear power, world disarmament, religious preferences, and political partisanship, because these problems are usually bound up in categorical issues of belief and value. (pp. 57–58)

Here Rogerian argument is used as a way of encouraging a willingness to communicate and cooperate that already exists. Becker, Pike, and I were interested in quite a different kind of situation, the very sort of situation that Teich excludes, that characterized by defensiveness and antagonism on the part of one or both the parties, where communication is impaired and as yet no common desire to cooperate exists. In noting this difference, I do not mean to imply that Teich is wrong; Rogerian methods are quite likely to be useful in the situation he describes. And it is easier to address the situation Teich describes, certainly easier in the classroom, than the situation we were interested in.

A very different sort of situation is apparent in Maxine Hairston's proposal that Rogerian argument can be helpful in creating a classroom atmosphere that is low-risk, nonthreatening, and hence encouraging to the novice writer. Hairston remarks that "*few students write well out of fear*. They do not do their best work or develop as writers as long as they feel they are in a high risk situation, and all too often they perceive the writing classroom as an extremely high risk situation" (1982, p. 51, emphasis in original). The relation between the teacher and the students is obviously dyadic and, no doubt from many students' point of view, often laden with strong emotions. Notice, though, that the situation is not a conflict; the situation is much more like that between therapist and patient. Like the therapist with a patient, the teacher does not feel threatened or antagonistic and has an understanding of the situation and a control over it that the student lacks.

In contrast to Hairston's proposal, Jim Corder's "Argument as

Emergence" does address powerful dyadic conflicts. He states that in this sort of situation, "the arguer must, with no assurance, go out, inviting the other to enter a world that the arguer tries to make commodious, inviting the other to emerge as well, but with no assurance of kind or even thoughtful response." "How," he asks, "does this happen? Better, how can it happen?" His answer is that "it can happen if we learn to love before we disagree. Usually," he says, "it's the other way around: if we learn to love, it is only after silence or conflict or both" (1985, p. 26). If I understand what Corder is saying, one of the opponents is not wholly captured by the conflict, but has, rather, in some sense transcended it, or at least has enough control over his own feelings that he can reach out to the other and try to understand. Although a participant in a dispute in which the stakes are perceived as being very high, he, also, is different from the shocked, disappointed, alarmed, outraged combatant Corder described earlier.

III

Consider now still another form that value-laden dyadic conflict can take, one in which *both* of the arguers are zealous in the preservation of their own values and unbending in the pursuit of their own goals. "We have not," Corder says with considerable understatement, "fully considered what happens in argument when the arguers are steadfast" (1985, p. 23). That is probably reason enough to take a closer look, even though at first glance its extremeness makes the situation appear to be an unpromising subject for inquiry. But it is at least possible that the situation only appears to be unpromising because we approach it with fixed assumptions.

If our goal is the resolution of conflict, the great difficulty when both arguers are steadfast is that neither is very interested in reducing the other's sense of threat or in controlling antagonistic feelings. Self-control and conciliation are not what we desire when we find ourselves in such situations, though they appear to be what is necessary if the conflict is to be resolved. We may well know what we could do to quiet the conflict and transform it into something more constructive: Rogerian argument certainly offers a way of proceeding that is both ethically and pragmatically attractive. But we may not be wiling or, at that time, even able to make the effort necessary to understand the other's position in any but the most superficial sense—just enough understanding of the position, that is, to give us something to attack. Carl Rogers describes the usual outcome of such arguments when he remarks that "the stronger our feelings the more likely it is that there will be no mutual element in the communication. There will be just two ideas, two feelings, two judgments, missing each other in psychological space" (1951, p. 331). The threats and commands that erupt in such conflicts—Henry Johnstone calls them "degenerate" forms of argument (1978, p. 108)—tend to replace more conventional forms. One peculiar, and disheartening, feature of Rogerian argument, then, is that when we need it most, we are least inclined to use it. In the situation in which both parties are steadfast, it can be a method for reaching a goal that, at the appropriate moment, we as often as not have no desire to reach. In fact, in this particular situation, we often seek contrary goals: i.e., not to conciliate but to attack, not to understand another but to protect ourselves, not to cooperate but to dominate—or, in Corder's more general terms, not to love but to oppose.

In this kind of situation, as Corder has pointed out (1985, p. 21), the strategy Becker, Pike, and I outlined seems inappropriate, because it presupposes that at least one of the antagonists has the courage and the desire to use it. We did not attend to that inconsistency, nor have others since then, and the result has been proposals for instructional methods which in *that particular kind of situation* are unlikely to be effective. The methods may well be effective in other situations, such as those described earlier by Teich (1987) and Hairston (1982), but not when both arguers are steadfast in their own positions.

One important question to ask, before we consider any further the situation in which both arguers are steadfast, is whether we, as students of rhetoric, *should* consider it. It certainly occurs frequently, we may feel that it is important in our lives, and as Corder says, it is unexplored territory. But is it a situation that can be characterized as rhetorical? Of necessity, any discipline draws a line around itself, deciding what sorts of issues are appropriate for it to examine and what sorts are beyond its interest. So we can reasonably ask whether what happens when opponents are steadfast is an issue that falls within the domain of rhetoric.

In his "Functional Communication: A Situational Perspective," Lloyd Bitzer argues that certain problems though real are beyond our control (e.g., a friend dying of an untreatable disease); other problems do not require communication with someone else in order to be solved (e.g., finding a way of reconciling a contradiction in one's own thinking). Some problems, however, require or invite communication addressed to audiences whose actions can bring about the desired change; such problems, Bitzer says, are rhetorical (1980, pp. 26–27). Unless such a problem is present, Bitzer argues, a rhetorical situation never develops, and, hence, a rhetorical act never occurs. Something else may happen, but not a rhetorical something.

Value-laden dyadic conflict appears to fall within the category of rhetorical problems, as Bitzer conceives of them, i.e., problems that arise out of human difference, the solution to which requires a change in belief or behavior on the part of at least one of the parties in the dispute. But suppose the parties are steadfast in their beliefs. Is the problem still rhetorical? Bitzer observes that "the person who speaks in order to modify a nonrhetorical exigence—one which discourse cannot possibly change—is engaged in a futile venture" (1980, p. 27). With steadfast opponents, communication would certainly appear to be futile. But does it follow that the problem is nonrhetorical? Does at least one of the two antagonists initially have to be willing to change before change is possible and hence before a rhetorical situation can develop? If so, the situations of the sort that Teich and Hairston discuss and the situation with steadfast opponents are not variant forms of the same concept but are, instead, different in nature; and the latter would appear to be immune to argument, Rogerian or otherwise.

There are, however, reasons to pause before saying that the apparently intractable situation we are examining lies outside the domain of rhetoric. Rogers himself offers one reason: the case in which a third party, using Rogerian methods, mediates the conflict. As Rogers says, the movement toward understanding "can . . . be initiated by a neutral third person, providing he can gain a minimum of cooperation from one of the parties" (1951, p. 336). In discussing the role of facilitator in groups where conflict runs high, James Zappen observes that "the movement from often bitter expression of personal feelings toward collective consideration of issues, collective decision making, and constructive action is documented in Rogers' own and others' experiences, not only with oppressed minorities but with other groups as well, including even such bitter opponents as Catholics and Protestants in Northern Ireland" (1980, p. 104).

Or consider disputes in which the antagonists not only refuse to communicate, but literally or figuratively walk away from the confrontation. Is walking away the end of the dispute? Corder shrewdly observes that "we must pile time into argumentative discourse . . . in our most grievous and disturbing conflicts, we need time to accept, to understand, to love the other. At crisis points in adversarial relationships, we do not, however, have time; we are already in opposition and confrontation" (1985, p. 31). But is walking away, at least sometimes, a very undemanding kind of rhetorical act, and, precisely because it is undemanding, a valuable one? It requires no great courage or generosity, and it can pile time into argument. In doing so, it perhaps holds out some hope that change may eventually become possible.

Even though inconsistent with the common view of an argument as a polished performance (a finished piece of writing or a carefully constructed speech), is it unreasonable to think of a single argument as a groping, intermittent effort—whether written or spoken or both—made up of several utterances and extending over what might turn out to be a substantial span of time? Though we can no doubt find instances in our own experience, our art ignores the possibility of argument as a continuing though discontinuous dialogue in which the emphasis is on the intent and effects of the statements rather than on features of the statement itself (its truth or falsity, its stylistic distinction). If in actuality some arguments are of this unconventional sort, then simply holding open the possibility of change becomes an important rhetorical goal.

The effectiveness of Rogerian argument seems to depend much more heavily than Becker, Pike, and I had assumed not only on timeliness, but on duration of time. It has been only in the last generation that the ancient notion of *kairos* and such related notions as situational context and rhetorical situation have begun to play a significant role once again in rhetorical theory and pedagogy (Kinneavy, 1986). In the contexts we have been exploring, knowing when not to try to communicate would appear to be as important as knowing when to try; however, time and timeliness have seldom been subjects for sustained discussion in composition texts.

Or, again, consider disputes that erupt into actual violence of some sort: getting into a shouting match, for example, and then suddenly realizing what one is doing and apologizing; the fist fight you had with the neighbor kid and the subsequent friendship; the reconciliation between husband and wife after a bitter fight; Corder's example of the memorial service for American and German troops at the Remagen Bridge in 1985 (1985, p. 27); the moving ending to the recent film "Children of a Lesser God," where the pattern I am describing is in fact the plot of the film. All dyadic, all freighted with powerful values, all full of language. We can, of course, also come up with plenty of examples of violence that do not evolve into their opposites. But that does not negate the point I am trying to make. Somehow the dynamics of conflict can at times alter the willingness of the participants to come to new understanding and reach some sort of accommodation.

Henry Johnstone has remarked that "in general the risk a person takes by listening to an argument is that he may have to change himself. It is the self, not any specific belief or mode of conduct, that the arguer's respondent wishes to maintain. But his interest in maintaining it cannot be absolute, for if it were he would be presenting a closed mind to the argument" (1978, pp. 109–110). There is always a tension in the participants in an argument between the desire to maintain themselves and their worlds and the necessity of exposing themselves to the risk of change implicit in the argument. However, suppose both are steadfast out of conviction and fear change. Out of a desire to preserve the stability of their images, they resist opening themselves to alternatives that they feel threaten fundamental beliefs. When opponents are steadfast and fear change, neither permits himself any choice or, more accurately, has any choice, at least at the moment, except to persist in his beliefs. And, as Edward Corbett points out, "where the choices are arbitrarily pared down or eliminated, rhetoric begins to disappear" (1969, p. 293).

Change as a psychological goal is clearly central to any conception of rhetoric. But in order to be considered rhetorical, must the change always entail persuasion, in the sense of a significant alteration or abandonment of the audience's position as the result of argument? We can, I think, accept Johnstone's observation that the absolutely closed mind is beyond rhetoric (assuming that there is such a thing as an absolutely closed mind) and still acknowledge the possibility of modest though nonetheless important changes in the situation where the opponents hold steadfastly to their beliefs. For example, we might consider extending our notion of rhetorical change to include dialogical exchanges in which the opposing positions retain their integrity while being strengthened and deepened by the opposition. Since our beliefs are fully revealed and understood only in contrast to other beliefs, a possible outcome of a dispute in which the arguers are steadfast can be greater understanding of one's own position and perhaps, at least gradually, the opponent's as well. Dialogical exchanges of the sort I have in mind might result in altered conceptions of the world in which both disputants have a place, though not the same place; or perhaps a heightened awareness of each other as *Thous*, to borrow Buber's term; or an emerging mutual respect and, as a consequence, a willingness to continue the dialogue. Such growth of understanding need not mean abandoning beliefs regarded as important, though it may well qualify them and introduce new complexities; and it might soften harsh attitudes toward those who believe something else. Resisting change and a deepening of commitment may well be desirable, since to change a position is not necessarily to make it more adequate (Pike, 1961, pp. 272–273). Unfortunately, beyond discussions of fallacious reasoning, the rhetorical tradition has had little to say about resisting change and what the effort of resisting change in order to preserve one's own system of beliefs does to thinking, argument, and conduct.[3]

It appears, then, that the situation in which the opponents are steadfast constitutes some sort of boundary condition. In talking about it, are we still talking about rhetoric? I have tried to suggest reasons for thinking that we are, though traditional conceptions of rhetoric, certainly those that have been dominant in English departments, would have to change to accommodate them. The intractable situation I have been exploring is a very general description of innumerable concrete situations that, in the past, would have been considered unrhetorical or, perhaps more accurately, prerhetorical, because, traditionally, a rhetorical situation presupposes a sense of community and shared values and a tacit agreement to enter into an exchange that may significantly alter beliefs. But conflicts in which the opponents are steadfast are so common and unavoidable, so characteristic of a diverse and rapidly changing society, and world, that we must learn to address them. Aristotle observed that it is easy to praise Athenians to Athenians. But it is very hard to praise Greeks to Turks, or Israelis to Arabs, or Irish Catholics to Irish Protestants, or prochoice advocates to prolife advocates. . . .

If serious investigation of Rogerian argument and its situations can open up new questions for rhetorical study, it can also reintroduce, in a particularly insistent way, questions that have been neglected in the rhetoric that has dominated English departments for the last century. As we have seen, it raises questions about the scope of rhetoric, rhetorical situations, and appropriate action. It also encourages us to think again about *logos, ethos*, and *pathos* as persuasive appeals. For generations, the rhetoric taught in the schools, particularly in composition classes, has tended to valorize the logical appeal, treating issues of personal authority and the emotions as, relatively speaking, peripheral. What were originally conceived of as mutually reinforcing appeals have been sharply separated in this tradition, with *ethos* and *pathos* being for the most part relegated to the margin of our attention.[4] The effort by Becker, Pike, and me, and by others since then, to extend Rogers' suggestions into rhetorical theory and practice can be seen, in part at least, as an effort to breathe new life into the ancient concepts of *ethos* and *pathos* and to position them within an enriched conception of rhetoric, which, like its ancient counterpart, addresses the question of how one invents arguments under the constraints of actual situations.

Rogerian argument, in so far as it is an effort to respond to intense dyadic conflict, seems to offer a means for reasserting the dialogic character of rhetorical argument in its long slide toward dialectics. "Take a dialogue," M.M. Bahktin remarks, "and remove the voices (the partitioning of voices), remove the intonations (emotional and individualizing ones), carve out abstract concepts and judgments from living words and responses, cram everything into one abstract consciousness—and that's how you get dialectics" (1986, p. 147). The artificial and highly questionable separation of the study of writing from the study of speaking in academic institutions has encouraged a view of written argument as *logos*; as presented in our writing texts, rhetorical argument has moved very close, too close I think, to logic. Rogerian argument might well be one means of reintroducing a notion of rhetorical argument as addressed by someone in particular to particular individuals at particular times in particular places and for particular purposes.

NOTES

1. "Can we," Rogers asked, "take this small scale answer [to conflict and breakdowns in communication], investigate it further, refine it, develop it and apply it to the tragic and well-nigh fatal failures of communication which threaten the very existence of our modern world" (1951, p. 337).
2. For example, we noted three kinds of situations that classical rhetoric addresses effectively: (1) low-value dyadic situations (i.e., two-party conflicts in which differences are not perceived as fundamental or threatening and hence are resolvable by traditional means, which presuppose that the possibility of communication and change already exists), (2) low-value triadic situations (i.e., conflicts in which the argument is directed to a third party who is not a participant in the conflict but who decides the outcome of the argument, e.g., two lawyers arguing a routine case before a judge); and (3) high-value triadic situations (e.g., two lawyers in a court case that involves issues perceived as fundamental to the welfare of the participants). A fourth kind of situation contrasts with these, i.e., high-value dyadic situations. This very general set of situations, contrasted in a two-by-two matrix, was a convenient way of explaining the differences in distribution of classical and Rogerian argument: in retrospect, however, it seems a bit too tidy.
3. James Baumlin (1987) discusses some of the rhetorical implications of steadfastness in "Persuasion, Rogerian Rhetoric, and Imaginative Play."
4. Making a similar point about the emphasis on critical thought, Alice Brand (1987) has sought to raise the issue of emotion as a counterpart to cognitive activity in the process of writing, linking it to the writer's motivation; it is interesting to see this as an effort to expand the meaning of *pathos* to include a concern with the psychology of the writer as well as the reader. Recent work on *ethos*, particularly that of Jim Corder (1978), Michael Halloran (1982), and Nan Johnson (1984), demonstrates the value of scholarly inquiry into the notion of *ethos* and the complexity of the task. For a discussion of this work, see my article entitled "Recent Developments in Rhetorical Invention" (Young, 1987), especially pages 18–20.

REFERENCES

Bakhtin, M. M. (1986). *Speech genres and other late essays.* (V. McGee, Trans.; C. Emerson & M. Holquist, Eds.). Austin, TX: University of Texas Press.

Bator, P. (1980). Aristotelian and Rogerian rhetoric. *College Composition and Communication, 31*, 427–432.

Baumlin, J. S. (1987). Persuasion, Rogerian rhetoric, and imaginative play. *Rhetoric Society Quarterly, 17*, 33–43.

Bitzer, L. (1980). Functional communication: A situational perspective. In E. White (Ed.), *Rhetoric in transition: Studies in the nature and uses of rhetoric* (pp. 21–38). University Park, PA: Pennsylvania State University Press.

Brand, A. (1987). The why of cognition: Emotion and the writing process: *College Composition and Communication, 38*, 436–443.

Corbett, E. (1969). The rhetoric of the open hand and the rhetoric of the closed fist. *College Composition and Communication, 20*, 288–296.

Corder, J. W. (1978). Varieties of ethical argument, with some account of the significance of *ethos* in the teaching of composition. *Freshman English News, 6*, 1–23.

Corder, J. W. (1985). Argument as emergence, rhetoric as love. *Rhetoric Review, 4*, 16–32.

Ede, L. (1984). Is Rogerian rhetoric really Rogerian? *Rhetoric Review, 3*, 40–48.

Hairston, M. (1976). Carl Rogers' alternative to traditional rhetoric. *College Composition and Communication, 27*, 373–377.

Hairston, M. (1982). Using Carl Rogers' communication theories in the composition classroom. *Rhetoric Review, 1*, 50–55.

Halloran, M. (1982). Aristotle's concept of ethos, or if not his somebody else's. *Rhetoric Review, 1*, 58–63.

Johnson, N. (1984). Ethos and the aims of rhetoric. In R. Connors, L. Ede, & A. Lunsford (Eds.), *Essays on classical rhetoric and modern discourse* (pp. 98–114). Carbondale, IL: Southern Illinois University Press.

Johnstone, H. (1978). *Validity and rhetoric in philosophical argument: An outlook in transition.* University Park, PA: Dialogue Press.

Kinneavy, J. (1986). Kairos: A neglected concept in classical rhetoric. In J. Moss (Ed.), *Rhetoric and praxis: The contribution of classical rhetoric to practical reasoning* (pp. 79–105). Washington, DC: Catholic University of America Press.

Lunsford, A. (1979). Aristotelian vs. Rogerian argument: A reassessment. *College Composition and Communication, 30,* 146–151.

Mader, D. (1980). What are they doing to Carl Rogers? *ETC.: A Review of General Semantics, 37*, 314–320.

Pike, K. L. (1961). Stimulating and resisting change. *Practical Anthropology, 8*, 267–274.

Pounds, W. (1987). The context of no context: A Burkean critique of Rogerian argument. *Rhetoric Society Quarterly, 17*, 45–59.

Rogers, C. R. (1951). Communication: Its blocking and its facilitation. In C. R. Rogers, *On becoming a person* (pp. 329–337). Boston, MA: Houghton Mifflin.

Teich, N. (1987). Rogerian problem-solving and the rhetoric of argumentation. *Journal of Advanced Composition, 7*, 52–61.

Young, R. (1987). Recent development in rhetorical invention. In G. Tate (Ed.), *Teaching composition: Twelve bibliographic essays* (pp. 1–38). Fort Worth, TX: Texas Christian University Press.

Young, R. E., Becker, A. L., & Pike, K. L. (1970). *Rhetoric: Discovery and change*. New York: Harcourt, Brace.

Zappen, J. P. (1980). Carl R. Rogers and political rhetoric. *PRE/TEXT, 1*, 95–113.

CHAPTER 7
Rogerian and Platonic Dialogue in—and Beyond—the Writing Classroom

James S. Baumlin
Tita French Baumlin

A majority of the early, indeed seminal, articles on Carl Rogers sought to demonstrate, or else deny, the possible connections between Aristotelian and what has become Rogerian rhetoric (Hairston, 1976; Lunsford, 1979; Bator, 1980; Mader, 1980). Theorists searching for a collaborative mode of argument found in Rogers a useful complement to Aristotle and a means of reassessing the role of speaker/audience cooperation in traditional theory; others found simply the antithesis of Aristotle and an attitude perilously ignorant of the putatively adversarial nature of public argument. In either case the comparison has proven unfortunate. Rogers aims at something more fundamental than persuasion (which is always the focus of Aristotelian theory); he aims, rather, at mutual *understanding*—a Romantic rather than classical concept, one that attempts to unify thought and feeling in communication (to join *Verständnis* to *Verstand*), attempts literally to dwell within the mental life of another human being. There is of course much psychology in the *Rhetorica,* but it does not take this sort of turn. We should, in a word, scrap the project of making Rogers an Aristotelian, or Aristotle a Rogerian. For Rogerianism is no less valid a theory for being un-Aristotelian—and, perhaps, no less grounded in tradition.

We may well be risking the same embarrassment in suggesting *any* classical source or analogue to Rogerianism (and surely we do not imply that Rogers is at all influenced by a specific classical author). In an earlier paper (Baumlin, 1987) one of us explored the pre-Socratic or Gorgianic elements in Rogerian rhetoric; we would like here to explore a final—and, perhaps, the closest—classical model to Rogerianism, the Platonic "rhetoric of dialogue." Itself both a psychology and a rhetoric of intimate interpersonal relation, Platonic theory provides striking comparisons to Rogers' own therapeutic/rhetorical methods. The following, then, outlines briefly the thematic relations between their theories, ending with an example of classroom practice.

1. THEORY

> I am no politician, Polus, and last year when I became a member of the Council and my tribe was presiding and it was my duty to put the question to vote, I raised a laugh because I did not know how to. And so do not on this occasion either bid me to put the question to those present, but if you can contrive no better refutation than this, then leave it to me in my turn, as I suggested just now, and try out what I consider the proper form of refutation. For I know how to produce one witness to the truth of what I say, the man with whom I am debating, but the others I ignore. I know how to secure one man's vote, but with the many I will not even enter into discussion.
>
> —Socrates, in the *Gorgias* (p. 256)

What is this *elenchus* or "refutation" which Plato's Socrates seeks throughout the dialogues? Is it the defeat of an opposing argument, as in Aristotle's *rhetorica?* Or is it something more *healing*—literally, a cleansing or righting of the speaker's soul? Though Platonic truth has its origins in a divine idealism, this truth never remains impersonal but becomes *incarnate in the individual (Meno,* p. 364)—and must be so, if it is to have any entry into or influence upon the material world. *The human soul brings truth into the world.* Humankind becomes, therefore, the embodiment and repository of truth, though the soul, born into a world of flesh, puts on thereby the "cloak of forgetfulness": from the moment of birth, then, knowledge involves *anamnesis (Meno,* p. 371), a continuous need to remember or reawaken the soul to its own self-knowledge. Of course the modern philosopher/psychologist would relativize knowledge, reducing truth to the mechanisms of reality testing; indeed, if the word continues to have any meaning at all, it must derive from an individual's lived experience rather than a spirit's prelife dwelling in a World of Forms. The point, though, is that truth and reality—regardless of their status or origins—are not *above* so much as *within* the individual. And each individual, when in harmony with the truth, achieves his or her own moral/spiritual/emotional health. The healthy soul—the soul possessed of its own self-knowledge—exercises the capacity to repudiate illusions, fears, and the false opinions that parade as knowledge. For this, indeed, forms at least a part of Socrates's definition of truth: more than an ideal, it is the healthy state of the soul, of the soul's own self-harmony.

Now ignorance, opinion, and moral weakness, as Socrates asserts continuously throughout the dialogues, are frailties or sicknesses of the soul. There is, in addition, a sickness *of discourse,* which Socrates terms sophism: a mode of discourse addressed to the masses, one that seeks victory or approval at all cost, one that remains ignorant of or subverts the true needs of soul. Ethics and psychology—and the "rhetoric" of dialogue—are thus inseparable: the truth that Socrates awakens in the soul of an interlocutor, the opinion and error he strips away, the arguments he utters in dialogue, are all intended to heal the soul and restore harmony. Socratic dialogue is inherently therapeutic, then, and structured as a psychotherapy—a healing of the soul through language. Of course there are ground-rules to the therapy of dialogue. The interlocutor must submit willingly to the Socratic philosopher/therapist's interrogation. In the *Gorgias,* for example, Socrates complains of the sophist Callicles's lack of faith, his repudiation of genuine dialogue for a mere war of words: Callicles's is a combative rhetoric, a rhetoric that seeks victory over (the speaker's own) health. The interlocutor's words must also respond genuinely and sensitively to the interrogation/discussion. Thus in the *Protagoras* Socrates chides the sophist for seeking to persuade rather than open himself up to interrogation. "Personally," Socrates quips, "I thought that companionable talk was one thing, and public speaking another" (*Progatoras,* p. 331). And Protagoras, likewise, states his position: "Frankly, Socrates,"

> I have fought many a contest of words, and if I had done as you bid me, that is, adopted the method chosen by my opponent, I should have proved no better than anyone else. (p. 330)

To be "no better than anyone else" may be anathema to the sophist, but it defines, perhaps ironically, the ideal relationship of discussants in dialogue. Healing discourse must aim to be "companionable" and interrogative, not combative. More importantly, though, an openness to Socrates's interrogations would involve Protagoras in a risk of refutation. This, again, may be anathema to the sophist; to Socrates, however, the discovery and banishment of error from the soul is the highest aim of discourse—as he suggests to Callicles in the *Gorgias*: for "if you leave this unrefuted,"

> then, by the dog that is god in Egypt, Callicles himself will not agree with you, Callicles, but will be at variance with you throughout your life. And yet I think it is better, my good friend, that my lyre should be discordant and out of tune . . . and that the majority of mankind should disagree with and oppose me, rather than that I, who am but one man, should be out of tune with and contradict myself. (p. 265)

Finally, then, the interlocutor—particularly the philosopher/therapist—must have intimate knowledge of the soul of his or her addressee, its needs, its powers, its limitations. For it is to the soul, ultimately, and to the health of soul that the philosopher/therapist directs his or her words. As Socrates states in the *Phaedrus,*

> if we are to address people scientifically, we shall show them precisely what is the real and true nature of that object on which our discourse is brought to bear. And that object, I take it, is the soul. (p. 516)

But let us conclude this detour into Platonism. How do the dialogues in any way anticipate Rogerian therapy, particularly in its guise as Rogerian rhetoric? Similarly to the Socratic method, the therapeutic situation described by Carl Rogers finds two people, therapist and client, in an intimate dialogical relationship. Typically the client *seeks out* the therapist's healing, opens himself or herself to the therapist's healing, allowing the therapist entry into his or her own mental life—an approximate if demystified equivalent of the Platonic soul—for the purpose of *changing* the contours and orientations of that life. And language becomes the means of this healing. Client and therapist together share worlds and experiences—test them, disarm them, validate them, enable them—by means of words. *Knowledge,* precise knowledge of the client's world, sympathetic *understanding* of that world, and *sensitivity* towards its limitations and potentials are essential to the therapeutic session: without these the therapy becomes a sham art, an art of platitude and flattery—much like Socrates's description of sophistic rhetoric in the *Gorgias.*

By the same token, then, Rogerianism *cannot be broadcast,* cannot be conducted anonymously. For in a rhetoric of mass appeal one can no longer "know the soul" of each member of an audience—nor, indeed, can one even *know* or control who the audience shall be. "For I know how to produce one witness to the truth," as Socrates observes in the *Gorgias,* "but with the many I will not even enter into discussion" (p. 256). And like Platonism, Rogerianism asks participants to personalize or *embody* their truths: not simply to argue for what is right in some abstract or absolute, impersonal sense—though one could do this, and Socrates at times *seems* to do just this—but rather to argue for the truth that dwells within and gives shape to the self. It is not enough, therefore, to adduce some external authority, some impersonal statistic, some abstract reasoning in support of a belief; Rogerianism must always ask the question, what is this belief *to you, to me, to us?* And like the Socratic dialogue, Rogerianism must therefore reject impersonal communication and any notion of victory-at-all-costs; indeed, there can be no victory sought in Rogerianism outside of the health and growth of individual participants.

For there is otherwise a danger that the collaboration will become merely manipulative. Granted, only fools and cowards refuse medicine when their bodies are in a state of sickness; even minds and emotions are subject to illness and cure. And one can, perhaps, speak of the health/illness of entire communities or groups within a community. But what makes a person (or group) culturally, politically, or intellectually "ill" and in need of cure? Patients typically—though again, not always—seek cure voluntarily, placing themselves in a therapist's hands; but how does one bring a group or community to a "cure" or to health when they stand unaware of their collective "illness" in thought or belief? What speaker shall be given the right to diagnose a community's collective "illness"? How shall any audience know when to open itself to the curative of another's world-view? Some world-views, fascism, for instance, are infectious rather than curative—some speakers, as Socrates observes, turn rhetoric into a "cookery" rather than a medicine for the soul, and do so by aiming "at what is pleasant, ignoring the good," that is, what is best for the audience's moral health (*Gorgias,* p. 247). There will always be quacks in health, and people who abuse the drug of persuasive language. Like other rhetorics, then, Rogerianism is incapable of regulating itself from the standpoint of ethics. And like other rhetorics, the crucial problem of Rogerianism is that it must assume both the good intentions of a speaker and the active, uncoerced participation of an audience. And even should the speaker's intentions be assured, there lurks a further danger in Rogerianism—as in Platonism: the danger of authoritarianism, where the therapist/speaker's views become absolute, inviolate, to be swallowed wholesale.

So we must ask whether Rogerianism can thrive where only one side risks change. The family situation provides an analogy: though parents and children enjoy common interests and mutual good will, a parent's peculiar sense of right too often turns harmony and health into simple coercion and an abuse of the child's openness, trust, dependence. Let the physician (or parent, or politician) then heal himself or herself in the manner of Socrates, who speaks to all as he speaks here to Polus: "if you have any interest in what has been said and wish to set it right, then, as I said just now, retract whatever you please, question and answer in turn . . . and refute me and be refuted" (*Gorgias,* p. 244). *And refute me:* change me: show a better way: in true Rogerianism, as in Platonism, even the therapist must be at risk. Indeed, the vocabulary and the roles of "therapist" and "client" must ultimately be scrapped for some other, more egalitarian vocabulary, whether this be of lovers, as Jim W. Corder suggests (1985), communicants, or, simply, discussants. And Rogerianism must also, therefore, proceed by means of dialogue, sharing and risking world-views, seeking responsibility for one's beliefs, *owning* and embodying one's beliefs, and at the same time opening oneself to the beliefs of the other, trying these new beliefs on, valuing them as alternatives, *understanding* them as valid, vital, enabling perspectives, and, ultimately, exercising one's freedom to choose a world and way of belief.

Let us ask, then: shall we aim at a Rogerian *rhetoric,* meaning a rhetoric of mass appeal? Or shall we aim at a Rogerian *dialogic,* a mode of discourse that seeks to generate, and not merely simulate, genuine interpersonal communication, *genuine understanding* between two individuals—a genuine sharing of worlds through words? This is the crucial point: there can be no claim of "understanding" outside of an *actual dialogic encounter* between individuals. Written texts can surely mediate this dialogue, but we must emphasize that Rogerian discourse, when successful, will always rise above monologism. For Rogerianism finds its destination and, indeed, its fulfillment in the response of an interlocutor; Rogerian argument remains *incomplete* until there is a meeting and intermingling of words and worlds. And thus classroom instruction in Rogerian argument must attempt to turn discourse—particularly written discourse—from a monologic to a dialogic art. The writing we teach our students must become the occasion for, and enactment of, interrogation and interpersonal communication. Writing may begin as monologue. But Rogerianism will teach that writing—like conversation, like the Socratic method—yearns to be dialogue: the writer must learn to *anticipate* an answer, *invite* an answer, and, indeed, sometimes *become* an answer. Understanding, then, which lies at the heart of Rogerian therapy, becomes nothing less than the fostering of sympathetic questioning and *response,* which are both inherently dialogic. If we can remind our students, further, that we write or speak to *heal* each other, to *help* each other, to "lend our minds out," as Browning's Fra Lippo Lippi so eloquently puts it, then we shall have done something as teachers.

2. PRACTICE

And in the naked light I saw
Ten thousand people maybe more,
People talking without speaking,
People hearing without listening,
People writing songs that voices never share
And no one dares disturb the sound of silence.
—Paul Simon, "The Sound of Silence" (1964)

It is through language that ideas touch and shape us, change our beliefs, and thereby change our selves. A world devoid of language sincerely given and deeply shared becomes a nightmare realm, a realm of silence; yet do not we all know from experience the eerie "naked" world of Simon's song, where speech is divorced from personal meaning through the disjunction of the individuals in the discourse? We talk without truly speaking; we hear without truly listening; we create discourse that no one shares. And nowhere is this malaise more truly feared, perhaps, than in the composition classroom.

We—students and teachers alike—fear that our works, our papers and discussions, become artifacts entirely useless outside the classroom and, indeed, that some of our rhetoric may have little if any significance *inside* our classrooms. And yet the alternative is equally unsettling: if we share our selves, our beliefs and dearest values, the discourse too often dissolves into combat—an aggressive fighting for our beliefs and values as if our lives were at stake. And indeed, since we define ourselves, our very identities, in accordance with those beliefs, in this real sense our lives *are* at stake. But we fight in this arena—in this sharing of selves—because we have forgotten that we can *change* ourselves, change each other, grow towards each other rather than apart. We engage in verbal combat because we have not considered the deepest meaning of "victory" in our personal lives: each of us knows the sad irony of having won an argument but lost a friend, for in the realm of interpersonal relationships, there are no "winners" in arguments (see Hartman, 1981; Corder, 1985). If we are to produce true "victory" in interpersonal discourse, we must reevaluate persuasion to find a rhetoric which truly *functions* in a Platonic/Rogerian manner. We must find the means to escape the realm of the "sound of silence" and truly share ourselves with an audience who truly listens: we must seek, together, to recreate and heal each other. So if we wish to employ Rogerian methods in the composition classroom, we must awaken our students to a radically different form of persuasion, one which will embrace the world in a dialogic manner, one which will bear actual consequences in their lives.

Do such methods already exist in classroom practice? We think not, though there are useful antecedents. One handbook offers a means for instituting "Rogerian listening" in classroom discussions (Simon, Howe, & Kirschenbaum, 1972, pp. 295–298). Howard Kirschenbaum's strategy here, to teach students to listen well, requires discussion participants to abide by one general rule: Before one may offer any point of view, one must first "summarize the essence of the previous speaker's statement, so that the previous speaker honestly feels his statement has been understood" (p. 296). To insure that the discussants listen well, a monitor (a rotating role among the group members) is assigned to halt the discussants whenever they do not follow the prescribed process. This exercise, it seems, does much to teach listening skills, particularly when students are urged to "empathiz[e] with the speaker," to feel his or her feelings and to see the world "through the speaker's eyes" (p. 295). But while the discussion fosters empathy and fairplay among students in an oral discussion, this Rogerian exercise stops short of developing strategies for writing. To this end, James E. Miller, Jr. offers two interesting assignments: the student is asked to "write a letter to yourself from your father (or mother) giving you advice on how to get along in an uncertain, dangerous, and cruel world" and afterward to "write a letter from yourself to your father (or mother) explaining how all the advice he has given you has not (or has) prepared you for the world you have met" (Miller, 1972, p. 16). Indeed, this assignment *simulates* dialogue by asking the student to assume the voice of a parent and then to respond to it. But while the exercise may well prove valuable in imaginative role playing, there emerges no means by which the student's role playing can be verified and adjusted, no means for enlarging or enriching his or her own perception of parental role, of student self, of the *actual* relationship between himself or herself and the parent. Such an assignment (though admittedly not offered as a Rogerian sequence) cannot lead the student into that sharing and risking of world views that represent Rogerianism at its best. As noted earlier, Rogerian dialogic *requires* the opening of the self to the world view and values of the other; the *understanding* of these values enables the healing reassessment and *revision* of self for those who commit themselves to intimate dialogue.

Perhaps, then, a writing assignment more explicitly Rogerian in conception would ask students to engage in actual dialogue, though in written form. While it might be useful to ask students to write to one another in a class, presenting points of view on issues significant to their lives, it may still be difficult to produce the intimate, collaborative dialogue that is intrinsic to the Rogerian process: students may not know each other well enough, nor may there be enough time in the assignment sequence to produce this necessary intimacy. Worst of all, instructors could find themselves in a position of needing to *manufacture* disagreement among the students in order to push them toward dialogic interaction. We will describe, then, a writing assignment which incorporates aspects of both described above, but which focuses on intimate dialogue in the world outside the classroom: students are asked to write actual letters to their parents and to request written responses in kind, all in an effort to create an authentic dialogic encounter between individuals who, characteristically, do not inhabit precisely the same worlds, but would wish to reach some *genuine understanding* of the other's world and values. Typically, by this time in their lives, the interpersonal relationships of college students and parents have reached a crucial point: seldom before have these parties so clearly realized that each inhabits a world—a reality—so radically different from the other. And while the "generation gap" is a ready-made field of risk and conflict—and potential pain—in the students' lives, it is also a rich field of potential growth in the emotions, and verbal skills, of *both* parties. In a classroom experiment at a Texas university this assignment proved to open wide the doors of our composition classrooms—to touch the lives as well as the minds of our students, to let in actual readers for, and responses to, their writing.

First, we concocted a class handout in the guise of a "Letter to the Editor" written to the campus newspaper by a "Dr. Random," supposedly a university official. Our Dr. Random, in fine anti-Rogerian form, complains with great vehemence about the materialism and self-centeredness that he finds in this current freshman class:

Dear Editor:

In my professional position as admissions officer at our university, I have had the occasion to meet and interview thousands of college students every year; and with each incoming class, I form a fairly detailed image of the characteristics of the current generation. I have seen many classes of students, have watched them from orientation to graduation, have laughed with them, applauded with them, wept with them as they confronted the joys, challenges, and disasters that the ages have produced. And I have felt my share of disappointment, even rage, when students have expressed their growing pains in public: I was here when there were anti-war demonstrations on the mall lawn and draft-card burnings in the student center; I was a committee member during the days of the bitter strife between students and administration, when open rioting—not curriculum changes—was our greatest fear. I have seen students sit-in, sit-out, sit-around, and generally do anything but sit down. And yet I have respected, and often admired, these passing generations of young people, for their passions were genuine and their causes—if only in their own minds, even—were just.

However, as the times have swiftly changed, so have the students at this university, and it is in this concern that I write this open letter regarding the incoming freshman class. For the past two or three years, I have found myself increasingly alarmed at the general nature and character of the current generation of youths—those who are beginning their university study and who will, someday soon, take up their positions of professional authority for which they are now preparing. These young people, unlike their radical and passionate predecessors, seem to care passionately for nothing; the only dedication I can see in this generation is a dedication to Self, to selfishly obtaining all the material goods that this world can possibly offer. It is often said of this generation that they are a "career-minded" group of people, and I would agree, but I am distressed to add that it appears to me that this generation is "career-minded" *not* in planning toward their future contributions to our society and to our culture, but in planning toward their own amassing of money, for it is that—money, always money, and only money—which seems their deepest motivation in life. The desire for status symbols—wearing the most expensive fashions, driving the finest sports cars—is more prevalent in this generation than in any I have ever seen. And these youths' propensity for self-indulgence, whether in the realm of avoiding study in favor of drinking and "partying" as they call it (whatever besides drinking that ominous "partying" entails), or in avoiding study in total absorption and fascination with their own bodies' athletic prowess, is rampant and, in fact, alarming. I used to believe that labels were useless at best, reductive at worst; however, I have seen nothing in the past three years that leads me to oppose calling this generation the "Me Generation." And this realization distresses me a great deal, partially because I want to believe in the future growth of our culture toward enlightenment, but also because I, myself, have a son who belongs—in every sense of the word—to this group.

The truth, as I see it, is that my son and his peers *have* no future, not in the human sense, as long as they persist in this blind, mad rush toward self-aggrandizement and gross materialism. And that, sadly, means that there is no future for our culture, either, for in their heedless flight into pleasure and wealth, they are leaving behind them a rich cultural heritage—the likes of Shakespeare and Bach, of Gödel and Heidegger, of Socrates and Cicero—of which they have no knowledge and no thirst for knowing. They do not want education, neither in the historical, cultural sense, nor in the sense of the enlightenment of the soul; they want only money and the leisure in which to spend money to pleasure the body, to adorn it with bought tans and designer clothing, to surround it with the finest objects, to pump through it the most expensive chemicals, to create an appearance of beauty for which there is no inner substance or support.

I am, in short, appalled at what this generation has shown me, and what it continues to show. It is not that I wish to persist in my current estimation of these young people, for I would like to understand them and to find reason to hope in the future of us all. But I have, as yet, found no one who could help me understand their world or find meaning or humanity in this generation.

Yours sincerely,

Dr. T. W. Random

In short, the letter presented a frontal assault upon the students' generation and, from the evidence of class discussion, it seemed that our Dr. Random had challenged many students' senses of identity. Students were asked to freewrite in class to facilitate discussion, and they displayed in their vocal and written responses that we had clearly struck a nerve. Consider this student's response: "He doesn't have any right to make us sound so awful! I guess he's right, though, about most of the things he says, but how can he blame us for it? It's our parents' fault because they've always given us everything we wanted—just like it's Dr. Random's fault if he has raised a son he's ashamed of." Several students wanted Dr. Random's phone number so that they could register their angry complaints, but when pressed to discuss their own lives, they eventually saw this assault to be evidence of the clichéd "Generation Gap" which they admitted to have witnessed in their own lives from time to time: they had all heard these charges before.

At this point, they were asked to look at the third page of the handout which asked them to freewrite in response to these questions: "Would it help you understand Dr. Random's position if you knew that he was born in the Depression Era, grew up in South Philadelphia, and obtained his education only through the ability to carry three jobs while he studied? What if Dr. Random's son were to respond to this letter by writing a letter of his own? What sorts of details would you want him to include in this attempt to create *understanding* between himself (as a representative of his generation) and his father?" Some students replied simply, "I think this Dr. Random is just jealous that we've having so much fun in college," but others remembered their own parents' frequent statements, "I want to you have it better than I did when I was growing up." They discovered deeper complexities of the issue: parents' intentions versus the effects of their parenting. How, then, should Dr. Random and his son go about healing their own obvious gap in communication? In classroom discussion, students were urged to discover that the son would benefit more fully if he did *not* seek to refute his father or to "win" the argument; the greatest benefit would reside in finding the details which would help his father *enter his world* and thus understand the human beings who live there. The students then took additional freewriting time to sketch out possible approaches or details which could be included in such a reply letter from Dr. Random's son or daughter.

The formal writing assignment, then, involved each student's incorporation of the predicament into his or her own personal life, into the family situation itself. The written assignment sheet read as follows:

> Dr. Random's predicament is, one might think, not unusual. The term "generation gap" has been in use for some time now, but we might suspect that the concept—unnamed—has *always* been with us. What is involved when we seek not to "win" the ever-present arguments but instead to eradicate the generation gap? True communication, it seems, involves *sharing* each other's worlds, finding the *language* which allows us to share each other and each other's world, and thereby finding true understanding of each other. We might all agree that your reality is radically different from your parents' reality (or your children's if you, yourself, are a parent); how does one go about communicating that differing reality?
>
> Your writing assignment is intended to be both playful and serious, for it will be both an assignment (for fulfillment of a grade) *and* a document that functions in your world outside the classroom. You are to choose a person in your own family who is not of your generation (parent, grandparent, aunt, uncle, perhaps your own child if you are a parent); choose someone who is able to and likely to respond (in writing) to your quest. Next, you will write a letter to that person, describing your own generation in such a way as to heal the Dr. Random Syndrome (the "generation gap") and to create understanding in your audience. This letter will go through many drafts and many workshops, like our other major papers; when you finalize it, however, you will create *two* copies—one to turn in and one to *send* to the letter's addressee. In your letter, you will be careful to urge your addressee to reply in kind with a return letter to *you,* responding in whatever way he/she finds appropriate. Your goal—your quest—is to share your world and yourself with your addressee in such a way that you create understanding and that you invite him/her to *share* his/her world with you. Be vivid; be playful, be humorous, if you wish; above all, be sincere in attempting to communicate something important about your generation.
>
> If and when you receive a reply letter, please bring it to us; we can eventually create a class in which we can share those replies together.

Every face registered the creeping realization: "Someone *else* is going to read this?" Of course, in terms of classroom procedure "someone else" had always been an explicit part of the reading audience of their papers—themselves, their own peers. But this time the "someone else" would be a someone *outside* the sanctuary of the classroom, someone who would likely be so engaged in the topic as to read every word of the letter and to respond—at length! No simple, clean letter grades or terminal epideictic comments they had come to expect from us: this letter would receive an actual response. It was a frightening proposition, that writing would have an element of *real* risk, that their assignments would not be mere "student exercises," that they thus would need actually to communicate something intelligent, that the mere grade assigned by the teacher might not be, in the end, the greatest sign of achievement or failure for this piece of writing. In short, if even for a moment, the instructor's judgment ceased to be the goal (the scourge, the reward) and the need to communicate in the world outside of academia took over.

But Dr. Random's letter had provoked such initial outrage that many students found it difficult to appropriate Rogerian techniques into their persuasion: they were already angry, even threatened, by the charges made against their generation. We spent a class period reviewing principles of Rogerian dialogue and some appropriate details about the background of Rogers's work, and we spoke at length of the effects of combative persuasion in interpersonal relations, that is, anywhere outside academia: in the "real" world, the "winning" of an argument often means the loss of a friend, the wounding of trust, the obscuring of some deeper wound in need of healing. In fact, *Dr. Random's letter now served as a useful tool for discussing aggression and combative language,* for it functions well as an example of "failed" Rogerian rhetoric: although Random desires that someone help him understand, his plea comes only after he has thoroughly evoked the hostility of his young audience through accusations, an aggressive tone, and an authoritarian voice. Students themselves were urged to point out elements in Random's language that may have contributed to the lack of communication between himself and his son. Dr. Random's infuriating letter had, indeed, been a necessary foundation for the writing sequence for two reasons: first, the letter itself provided students with a graphic example of what Rogerian rhetoric *isn't* and what pain such a combative rhetoric can cause; second, and perhaps more important, the students' anger was a most realistic basis for their careful composition of their own letters, for seldom in life do we find the need to heal a schism when there is no engagement of our own vulnerable egos or wounded pride. These students were actually grappling with the frustrations of learning, as adults, a new language to speak of, and attempt to heal, old wounds.

* * *

The final letters, like any papers in composition class, varied in their achievements of the principal goal at hand—the "healing" language of Rogerian theory. However, these "essays" were typically at least twice as long as the students' previous papers and reached for more direct, concrete language, more wit, charm, and heartfelt sincerity than ever before. Here are three very different excerpts from student papers:

> Dear Grandpa,
>
> Do you remember when Uncle Bob had long hair, didn't own a suit, and needed a job? You told him that he should get a haircut and buy a suit. He wouldn't take your advice and three months later he was *still* unemployed. Finally, when he cut his hair, *you* bought him the suit. And he got the job. You are probably wondering why I am reminding you of a story we often joke about. I am trying to bring together the way two great minds—yours and mine—think. While I know I am not nearly as perfect as some people—like a certain Grandpa I know!—I am coming to know that I am ultimately the one responsible for my own actions. . . .

> I am a prime example of the changes in generations, Mom. I'm unhappy here at college and, as a result, I'm certain that I will be leaving at the end of next semester. Back in the sixties, instead of simply leaving, you would have led sit-ins and walk-outs and demonstrations against the *de facto* segregation of this university and this community. But this is now, and I shall leave quietly. If you're angry, I can understand your anger: your generation didn't go through all that strife for your children to end up as passive, hedonistic conduits of pleasure. I also know that you've always wanted the best for your children, but you did not intend for it to be at the expense of social awareness and concern for the way in which the actions of the individual affect society as a whole. You didn't work so hard for me to come here and, upon my finding an environment hostile to my growth and identity, to see me leave without a fight. But the difference, now, is that we don't feel we have anything to prove. We are and forever will be in the shadow of your generation, for we can never recreate the sentiment and activism which flourished during the sixties. . . .

> Dad, do you remember how many times we confronted each other over the genre of music for the stereo? I demanded to listen to Billy Squier,

while you preferred a Bach chorale. Somehow, we always managed to listen to Bach! But then you struck a magic chord in my soul one day when you played "Pictures at an Exhibition" for me and for the first time in my life, I understood how a person could enjoy classical music. You took an aspect of your generation and your culture and showed that aspect to me in a way that I could comprehend it. But how do I explain rock and roll to you? How should I show you myself and my generation in a manner that you will understand? . . .

What seemed to be the most surprising to these writers were their parents' reactions to the letters; many students received long distance phone calls immediately when the mail arrived at home. Students were shocked to find that Mom or Dad—that same parent who had once been so inattentive to their chattering about rock music or fashion—was already busily drafting a letter of reply. They were shocked to find that they didn't *really* know as much about Mom or Dad as they had thought.

And perhaps the most interesting aspect of the assignment was the proof that Rogerian approach to dialogue *could,* indeed, produce an open, sharing, nonthreatened reply from the older generation. Consider this response which one student had the pleasure and privilege to receive from her grandmother, Ida Mae Marsh:

Dear Carrie,

It seemed quite ironic to me to have received your letter on the same day as the "Almost" Wall Street Crash of the 1980s. You speak of your generation's concern with wealth and status, yet those of us who were children of the Great Depression in the thirties find it hard to comprehend the extravagance and waste of the eighties.

I remember my father walking ten blocks to save a dime on a sack of turnip greens. The greens cost a quarter and, with buttermilk and cornbread, helped feed a family over the whole weekend. The dime he saved bought two cigars which were smoked during Amos 'n Andy. On Sundays we splurged and spent fifty cents for a hen, but about half the time my father was too "chicken" to kill it. We were never hungry, but a dollar was hard to come by, and you appreciated one hundred cents of it.

In defense of my generation, here is something I have never figured out—when I was a child, the grown-ups ate first; when I grew up, the children ate first.

One might well ask, "When do I get mine?"

But more important questions center on why this shift occurred in our attitude toward children and child-raising, and more significantly, what such a shift has meant to our mental and economic health. The day came when child-rearing became the obsession of a nation. It had not escaped notice that a baby boom had created a huge new market of small people who, if their needs were adequately exploited, could be translated into big money. And so it became very important to raise a child right. Adults were led into competitive child-raising. From educational toys to fashion clothes to the best schools, your kid needed the best of everything if he were to become "the best." The money rolled. Educators jumped on the bandwagon. And new and old theories of "best" ways to educate children vied for time and dollar. Soon methodologies drew battle lines, and the common sense of teaching children took a back seat to professional ambitions.

And soon followed grief. All this effort. All this money. And kids, being kids, were no better than before. Frustration turned to guilt; guilt to rage. And rage searched for escape. We blamed society, the schools, television, the government, the bad influence of the kids next door. Ourselves. Finally, we blamed the kid.

Where are we now? We have gone from a time when children were obligated to please their elders to a time when adults are expected to serve the children. But it has also been a shift to a time when children are perceived as little gods, yet exploited both as merchandising devices and as the fodder for social upheaval.

In your letter, Carrie, you state that in today's society, "the sign of success is money." I somehow feel that we are all emerging into an era of *dubious* distinction where all of us—young and old—wind up less but somehow equal, unsure of our roles but determined to do our utmost to right them.

The grown-ups no longer eat first; but the children don't, either. I think we are all sitting together in front of the TV with a sack of Big Macs.

This is not exactly progress.

But we are learning to cope, now, with the eighties. And coping means to handle, to confront, to stand up to, to deal with, to keep going. You can cope with anything; you really can. But this matter of having to cope must be learned early in life. And it is only as one develops this skill that ultimate and final victory comes to a person. I would remind you of a subtle and sound comment by William Feather: "Success is seldom achieved by people who contemplate the possibility of failure." So, Carrie, hold the thought; hold it tenaciously as you make the important choices in your life.

Love,
Grandma Marsh

Carrie's reactions to her Grandma's letter were a mixture of admiration and sheepishness: "This letter really makes me feel embarrassed about the things I said in my letter—all about the importance of money and status, and how we can't be blamed for materialism when our parents have given us everything. Gee, I wish I could have written it like *she* did, instead of sounding like a silly student!"

"Carrie," her instructor replied, "I couldn't have written this, either."

Somehow, a bridge had been crossed—a bridge between generations, but also a bridge between student and teacher—when distinctions of authority ceased to exist.

This is not to report that these students *felt* particularly successful in their struggles to express complex and difficult emotions, nor that most of the final products were more than the imperfect records of struggle and frustration. Most students, in fact, emerged from the assignment like Carrie—a bit embarrassed to have sent such "studenty" prose to someone who took every word to heart (and may remind them of it from time to time), but many expressed a sense of accomplishment that their addressees had truly listened and responded. We set aside a class period during which students brought in reply letters and read them aloud, sharing the older generation's responses with enthusiasm and pride. The entire experience itself—from the initial attack and outrage, through the frustration of trying to communicate sincerely and noncombatively, to the final realization that their writing could touch someone in their world and could evoke unexpected and, likewise, touching responses—this experience may well represent one of the few moments when the borderline between academic and "real" life ceases to exist and the students' words give shape to their worlds, allowing both participants in the dialogue to embrace change and to recreate the self anew.

> The Sufi Bayazid says this about himself: "I was a revolutionary when I was young and all my prayer to God was 'Lord, give me the energy to change the world.' As I approached middle age and realized that half of my life was gone without my changing a single soul, I changed my prayer to 'Lord, give me the grace to change all those who come in contact with me. Just my family and friends, and I shall be satisfied.'
>
> "Now that I am an old man and my days are numbered, my one prayer is, 'Lord, give me the grace to change myself.' If I had prayed for this right from the start I should not have wasted my life."
>
> —Anthony de Mello, *Song of the Bird* (1984, p. 153)

REFERENCES

Bator, P. (1980). Aristotelian and Rogerian rhetoric. *College Composition and Communication, 31,* 427–432.

Baumlin, J. S. (1987). Persuasion, Rogerian rhetoric, and imaginative play. *Rhetoric Society Quarterly, 18,* 33–43.

Corder, J. W. (1985). Argument as emergence, rhetoric as love. *Rhetoric Review, 4,* 16–32.

de Mello, A. (1984). *The song of the bird.* New York: Image Books.

Hairston, M. (1976). Carl Rogers' alternative to traditional rhetoric. *College Composition and Communication, 27,* 373–377.

Hartman, G. H. (1981). *Saving the text.* Baltimore, MD: Johns Hopkins University Press.

Lunsford, A. (1979). Aristotelian vs. Rogerian argument: A reassessment. *College Composition and Communication, 30,* 146–151.

Mader, D. C. (1980). What are they doing to Carl Rogers? *ETC: A Review of General Semantics. 37,* 314–320.

Miller, J. E., Jr. (1972). *Word, self, reality: The rhetoric of imagination.* New York: Dodd, Mead & Company.

Plato. (1961). Gorgias, Phaedrus, Protagoras, Meno. In E. Hamilton & H. Cairns (Eds.), *The collected dialogues.* Princeton, NJ: Princeton University Press.

Simon, P. (1964). *The sound of silence.* New York: Charing Cross Music.

Simon, S. B., Howe, L. W., & Kirschenbaum, H. (Eds.). (1972). *Values clarification: A handbook of practical strategies for teachers and students.* New York: Dodd, Mead & Company.

CHAPTER 8
The Fully Functioning Person, the Fully Functioning Writer: Carl Rogers and Expressive Pedagogy

Kay Halasek

As I sat down to compose this chapter, I began as I usually do. I ordered a pizza for delivery, warmed up the morning's coffee, and arranged my source materials: in one pile, Rogers' texts; in another, the articles that make up the previous decade's commentary on Rogerian argument; in a third, Young, Becker, and Pike (1970) and Hairston (1974)—the two texts from which all the debate sprouted; finally, in the last stack, numerous articles and texts of composition theorists labeled "expressionists" by such historians as Berlin (1987) and Faigley (1986). Only then did the misdirection of these years of controversy become spatially clear to me. Bator, Lunsford, Ede, et al., discussed only Young, Becker, and Pike, and Hairston, and one another, yet never mentioned expressivist practitioners—Elbow, Macrorie, Murray, and Stewart. I became more puzzled. Ede (1984, p. 41) noted the paucity of Rogerian pedagogy in Young, Becker, and Pike—a mere 17 pages, and Hairston's text offered only a general summary of four pages. Do these 21 pages merit the attention they've received when compared to the fuller incorporation of Rogers' theory and philosophy in the work of the expressivists?

Before I sat down to write my first draft I had answered that question negatively. I won't proclaim, "Epiphany!" But I did visually prove to myself my own hypothesis: until Elbow's references (1986) to

Rogers, discussions of Rogers' work in composition studies neglected his influence on those teachers who—in philosophy, practice, and spirit—most fully characterized his basic principles of the self.[1] Ede (1984) may justifiably have decried our advocacy of a psychotherapeutic model for composition studies while we overlook work in our own field, but we cannot ignore our own pedagogical history and the importance of Rogers' theory in that history.

However, Bator (1980) provided material to redirect the discussion. He pointed out that the dichotomy of Aristotelian and Rogerian argument rests in the relationship between speaker and audience and in the aim of the rhetor, not in the process and structure of the argument, as Lunsford (1979) argued. Aristotelian argument, Bator suggested, "presupposes . . . an antagonistic speaker/audience relationship; its aim is to *win advantage* through discovery of psychological weaknesses in the audience" (1980, p. 428; emphasis added). It aims to persuade. On the other hand, in Rogerian argument, "the goal of the writer becomes one of facilitating change by striving for *mutual understanding and cooperation* with the audience" (Bator, 1980, p. 429; emphasis added). As Jim Corder (1985, p. 22) rightly suggested, Bator underscored Rogerian methodology as an aid to "building bridges" between writer and reader. Rogerian principles take on a pedagogical function rather than an argumentative one.

LeFevre's *Invention as a Social Act* (1987) provided a new perspective on the importance of Rogerian principles in the expressivist classroom and on the work of the expressivists themselves. LeFevre extended Mader's (1980) declaration that what has been passed down in composition studies as Rogerian "argument" is not in the least intended as an argumentative form. Instead, Mader suggested, the end of the Rogerian method is effective problem solving. Rogerian argument serves as an internally dialogic means of invention in LeFevre's heuristic continuum, and she suggested that Rogerian argument also serves as "an invention procedure that takes into account the ideas and values of others as the writer imagines them to be" (1987, pp. 59, 52–53). LeFevre's heuristic continuum ranges from the monologic Platonic through the internally dialogic and collaborative to the collective and social. While Berlin (1987) described expressive heuristics as monologic and individualistic, LeFevre (1987) granted them a much broader range of inventive strategies. Many of Stewart, Macrorie, Murray, and Elbow's heuristics remain in the most subjective category, but the "internalized other" of Murray and Elbow reaches into the more socially oriented category. The Rogerian strategies of Macrorie, Murray, and Elbow fall in the collaborative realm of invention, thereby allowing for a socially oriented expressivism not wholly recognized by Berlin.

Expressivist philosophies and methodologies promote facilitative attitudes, a principle also employed by Rogers but ignored by previous debates. The similarities between Rogers' client-centered therapy and expressivist theory and practice are perhaps most notable in the very late 1960s and early 1970s in Macrorie's *Writing to be Read* (1968),[2] Murray's *A Writer Teaches Writing* (1968), Stewart's *The Authentic Voice* (1972), and Elbow's *Writing Without Teachers* (1973). In this chapter I present the shared assumptions of Rogers and expressivist theorists of composition and examine the pedagogical strategies by which expressivists develop these assumptions. Finally, I explore Elbow's adaptations of Aristotelian and Rogerian methodologies in his doubting and believing game. Like Mikhail Bakhtin, Elbow has developed an intraindividual dialogue that recognizes the inherently social nature of language, reality, and the individual.

I am not claiming that the psychotherapeutic methods of Carl Rogers made possible an expressivist theory of writing, but rather that the Rogerian psychology and expressivist rhetoric share common methods and goals. If I were to claim a direct influence, rhetorical history alone will prove me wrong. As others have noted (e.g., Berlin, 1987), educators in the early part of our century advocated the student-centered classroom and other expressivist methods of writing pedagogy. Dorothea Brande's *On Becoming a Writer* (1934) recommended freewriting (Halasek, 1987, p. 3). Berlin cited the University of Denver general education program (1939–1946) and its writing courses, which were "built upon the foundation of Rogerian nondirective counseling." The portrait of the Denver project was anything but flattering, however, as the excessive emphasis on life adjustment overshadowed other elements of educational development (Berlin, 1987, pp. 99–104). In more recent years, theorists and practitioners whose work has been associated with Rogers have been accused not only of attempting to conform the self, but also of escapism, self-indulgence, and solipsism.

THE SELF EXPLORED THROUGH WRITING

The expressivist theorists discussed here reflect the Rogerian principles of selfhood and listening with understanding. A fully functioning writer who epitomizes these principles is one who is open, self-dependent, autonomous, and responsible. Like the fully functioning person who grows in self-assurance through therapy, the writer achieves self-awareness through writing. And like the therapist who assists her client in achieving independence, the writing teacher listens with understanding, listens from a nonadversarial position without evaluating or passing judgment. Expressivist theorists and teachers, according to Faigley (1986, pp. 527, 529), may also be described as " 'authentic-voice' proponents" for whom "integrity, spontaneity, and originality" are the most important characteristics of good writing.

According to the expressivists, writers' highest priorities are to represent their beliefs honestly and to express those beliefs uniquely. Stewart (1969, pp. 224, 225) referred to these concepts as "the fundamental integrity of words and their users." It is understandable, then, that expressivists attack insincerity in writing as authorial selling out, going with the popular consensus at the expense of personal beliefs. For these theorists—and particularly for Donald Stewart (1969)—sincere, expressive writing most often speaks against prevalent cultural, social, or political perspectives.

Integrity, spontaneity, and originality aid the writer in reaching one of the primary goals of expressivist rhetoric: improving the ability to judge one's own writing (Elbow, 1973), and thus to become—to adopt Rogers' term—a "fully functioning" writer. Ideally, both Rogers' self-directive therapy and self-expressive writing lead to a person who depends on himself or herself, one who is open to himself or herself and the world, one who experiences and absorbs the world in the "process of being and becoming" (Rogers, 1961, p. 192). For such people, experiences and perceptions of those experiences become increasingly more "congruent" (Evans, 1981, p. 19). Moreover, such people are not asocial. Expressivists encouraged writers to develop characteristics much like those of Rogers' fully functioning person who

> would not necessarily be "adjusted" to his culture, and . . . would almost certainly not be a conformist. But at any time and in any culture he would live constructively, in as much harmony with his culture as a balanced satisfaction of needs demanded. (Rogers, 1961, pp. 193–194)

Like Thoreau's home-cosmographer, the fully functioning person—and the fully functioning writer—is one who "advances confidently in the direction of his dreams, and endeavors to live the life which he has imagined" (1981, p. 294). Furthermore, the fully functioning person is increasingly "more openly aware of his own feelings and attitudes" and the complexity and diversity of the world around him. He or she is more tolerant of the ambiguities of a reality that is constantly in flux (Rogers, 1961, p. 115). As a result, he or she gains a stronger sense of self-trust, a sense of control over the world, becoming increasingly autonomous and seeking from others neither approval nor standards. He or she becomes a decisionmaker, willing to take responsibility for decisions, leaving behind false or deceptive masks, and asking instead, "Am I living in a way which is deeply satisfying to me, and which truly expresses me?" (Rogers, 1961, pp. 118, 170, 167, 119; 1969, pp. 282–288). Rogers' quotation of Søren Kierkegaard aptly described the intended goal of the fully functioning person: "to be that self which one truly is" (in Rogers, 1961, p. 166).

Berlin, then, was correct when he commented that the expressivists (including Rohman & Wlecke, 1964) "relied on the 'self-actualizing' psychology of Rollo May, Abraham Maslow, and Carl Rogers, seeing writing as an act that authenticates and affirms the self" (Berlin, 1987, p. 147). While few claim that writing classes can achieve great alterations in personality and self-actualization, similar goals have been proposed as the desired ends of the writing process. Among the earliest proponents of the student-centered classroom in the 1960s were Donald Murray and Donald Stewart, both of whom promoted self-exploration and self-affirmation as the goals of the writing course (Murray, 1968; Stewart, 1972). *The Authentic Voice* of Stewart (1972), particularly, promoted self-actualization by insisting that the writer use a genuine, authentic "voice" that distinguishes the writer. He contended that the "most visible indication of . . . self-discovery is the appearance, in the student's writing, of an authentic voice. . . . The techniques of pre-writing, developed in the 1960s, will best help the student develop this authentic voice" (1972, p. xii). Even Stewart's more recent work (1988) heralded the expressivists' goal to "encourage students to find their own voices, to escape from the pasteurized and pedestrian prose they had been conditioned to produce in the traditional classroom" (p. 66).

Stewart's characterization of the writer echoed Rogers' fully functioning person:

> self-discovery . . . means the process of acquiring both a more objective and a psychologically deeper sense of the person you are. It is a kind of revelation in which you not only begin to see yourself through the eyes of others, but acquire a fundamental sense of individuality beyond the complex roles you play in life. (Stewart, 1972, p. 1)

Self-discovery demands the dropping of facades, rigorous exploration and critique of personal beliefs, and honest inquiry into the self (Stewart, 1972). This is risky business for the client or the student. As Rogers (1961) also conceded, courage is imperative, for the client is not only opening up to himself, but also to others and can often be threatened by the prospect of having his beliefs questioned and perhaps changed.

Writing involves similar risk-taking because, as Stewart (1972, p. 3) told his readers, "writing is something inseparable from your total personality and behavior, and your essential concern is with an honest representation of the person you are." Lou Kelly (1973), like Stewart, saw writing as a means of self-discovery. Indeed, for Kelly, the student was the center of the classroom, for the entire "content for composition is the writer—as he reveals his self, thoughtfully and feelingly, in his own language, with his own voice" (1973, p. 645). In their position statement "Writing as a Liberating Activity," Richard Gebhardt and Barbara Smith (1976, p. 21) also advocated teaching "from the perspective of student self-awareness" and characterized writing as "a liberating, liberalizing, humanizing activity, which should be made to connect with the student's development as a human being and with the whole process of education." The end of writing, they contended, is to open a student's experiences to analysis to help her gain insight into present living. The writer must communicate to a reader insight, ideas, and information, objectifying the self as subject. According to Murray,

> the writer is on a search for himself. If he finds himself he will find an audience, because all of us have the same common core. And when he digs deeply into himself and is able to define himself, he will find others who will read with a shock of recognition what he has written. (1968, p. 4)

I cannot help but admire these theorists' goals. Self-searching, it seems to me, is imperative for each of us. However, as many critics have noted, we have no way of knowing which is the true self, which facade is the last, which voice is the most authentic, which writing is the most honest, which truth is the most truthful. I can simply concede that this criticism is in part accurate, noting at the same time LeFevre's contention that not all expressivist pedagogy and heuristics aim solely for self-knowledge. It remains, however, that many of those who criticize expressivist rhetoric discard only the subjective epistemology and retain its process methodology and inventive heuristics.

THE "HELPING" CLASSROOM AND THE TEACHER AS FACILITATOR

For Rogers, the most productive therapeutic or interpersonal relationship was a "helping relationship . . . in which at least one of the parties has the intent of promoting the growth, development, maturity, improved functioning, improved coping with life of the other" (Rogers, 1961, p. 39). Successful learning depends on a successful relationship between facilitator and learner (Rogers, 1969). The successful facilitator must be trustworthy, dependable, consistent, communicative, positive, accepting, strong, respectful, secure, sensitive, understanding, nonthreatening, congruent, and most important, confirming of the other's "process of becoming" (Rogers, 1961).

Most teachers have aspired to such qualities in their teaching, and such an open humanism has informed much of modern educational psychology and philosophy. We teach more effectively, just as we write more effectively, if we establish mutual respect with our students and readers. The relationship between therapist and client and between teacher and student, as Rogers and Young, Becker, and Pike have noted, closely resembles Martin Buber's "I-Thou" relationship in which one unconditionally accepts and affirms the existence of another (Rogers, 1961; Young, Becker, & Pike, 1970). The expressivists fully incorporated these characteristics in their classrooms, sometimes to the point of surrendering authority by participating in the writing workshop, as in Peter Elbow's "teacherless writing class" (1973, pp. 76–146).

Rogers, Elbow, and Murray recognized the teacher's tenuous position and teaching's fragility and dependence on the learner. Students can learn without teachers, but teachers require students to teach. Teachers, in fact, "learn to be more *useful* when it is clearer that they are not *necessary*" (Elbow, 1973, p. x). Rogers went so far as to suggest that *"the only learning which significantly influences behavior is self-discovered, self-appropriated learning"* (1961, p. 276). Murray (1968) echoed these observations when he insisted that a teacher's success can be measured by students' ability to teach themselves and one another. The implications of such observations are most likely threatening to the traditional teacher. In the student-centered class, learning is no longer dependent on the teacher teaching and often is hindered by her (Rogers, 1961). The teacher no longer imparts wisdom but stimulates her students' "desire to learn, to enrich, to grow, to create" (Evans, 1981, p. 12) and leads her pupils to "self-initiated" learning (Rogers, 1969, p. 130).

Four notable examples of the helping classroom appeared in the late 1960s and early 1970s. Ken Macrorie's "helping circle," Donald Murray's writing laboratory, Lou Kelly's Iowa Writing Lab and Open-Class Project, and Peter Elbow's "teacherless writing class" established supportive relationships among students by casting aside the teacher's traditional role as an omniscient and dogmatic authority. More than any other practitioner, Murray addressed the teacher's new role.

Murray (1968) likened the teacher to a coach who works individually with athletes and to a doctor who diagnoses patients' illnesses and pays closest attention to the most severe threats to their health. In the writing laboratory, the teacher acts as a reference tool for his or her students rather than as a primary source. This alternative role can unsettle many teachers, even causing guilt in those who are used to complete control and involvement in their classrooms. Leaving the course to the students may, in fact, be the most difficult task a traditional teacher faces (Murray, 1968). Murray did not stop with this abdication of power. He suggested that teachers write with their students, showing them that writing is a craft that must be practiced. This dramatizes that all writers encounter difficulty when writing, but this practice may meet with resistance from teachers and students. As Murray (1968) and Hairston (1982, p. 53) contended, however, teachers facilitate learning by letting their students know that teachers are people, and struggling writers, too. As in other writing workshops,[3] in Murray's, the students maintained control. In Elbow's teacherless writing class,

> [e]ach person comes to the writing group with two commitments. One, he exposes his own writing—which he has written as well as he can—to the other individuals in the group so they can help him make it a better piece of writing. Two, he has a responsibility to help the other participants improve their writing. Each group has a common goal—to improve the writing of its members by evaluation time at the end of the course. (1973, p. 132)

In *Writing to be Read,* Ken Macrorie (1984) described his version of the writing workshop in terms nearly identical to Rogers' description of the helping relationship. The helping relationship simply becomes the "helping circle." This circle is more than an editorial or revision group, however; it is also a cyclical writing and reading process in which the writer garners comments from three different and progressively more social sources: the writer, a close acquaintance or family member, and the circle of writers. In Macrorie's final helping circle, writers first comment positively or ask questions; only later, and after members of the group have become more familiar with one another, are negative comments added to the sessions. Macrorie (like Murray [1968] in *A Writer Teaches Writing* and Elbow [1973] a few years later in *Writing without Teachers*) insisted upon the social and contractual nature of the circle: "If only a few members respond and the others remain silent, there is no circle. If one person dominates, soon others will not listen, no matter how wise the comments" (1984, p. 91). Moreover, the more a writer works as a member of an audience, the better his powers of self-criticism will become.

Elbow made more of psychotherapeutic practices when he established the supportive methods of encounter groups as one of the "past forms" of the teacherless writing class (1973, p. 188). Similarly, Kelly noted that the teacher's relationship to the student is to "help him extend his language, his ideas, and his self" (Kelly, 1973, p. 646). Like the therapist, however, the teacher cannot completely shed his or her traditional role. As Elbow indicated in his text, the successful teacher contributes to the interchange in much the same manner Kelly described:

> I can set up a teacherless writing class in my own class as long as I follow all the same procedures as everyone else: I too must put in my piece of writing each week; I too must get everyone's responses and reactions to it; I too must give my own reactions to other pieces of writing. . . . I can only set up something like the teacherless class in my own class if I adopt more the role of a learner and less the role of a teacher. (Kelly, 1973, p. ix)

These four authors differ somewhat in their conceptions of teacher/student interaction; nevertheless, each clearly viewed the teacher as a facilitator. In addition, each emphasized the social nature of the inventing and revising processes while staunchly maintaining each writer's personal responsibility for his or her writing. Writing workshops similar to these were not peculiar to the expressivist classrooms of the 1960s and 1970s. Composition methodologies that promote Rogerian principles have continued to inform writing classes. Many practitioners, regardless of philosophical or epistemological orientations, have used similar instructional strategies in their classrooms. Kenneth Bruffee's collaborative learning groups, for example, depend upon student interaction and response.[4]

ELBOW'S VARIATION ON THE ROGERIAN THEME

Rogers (1961) established the shortcomings of the traditional persuasive appeal in his 1951 paper, "Communication: Its Blocking and Its Facilitation"; "the major barrier . . . is our very natural tendency to judge, to evaluate, to approve or disapprove, the statement of the other person, or the other group" (330). Our judgmental nature, claimed Rogers (1961), is the primary deterrent to effective communication and effective problem solving. Unfortunately, evaluative tendencies usually increase proportionally with the emotional pitch of a discussion; therefore, the more emotionally charged an interchange, the less likely the participants are to reach even mutual understanding, much less agreement. Rogerian problem solving results in "a decrease in defensiveness, in exaggerated statements, in evaluative and critical behavior" and results in a deceptively simple solution: "Real communication occurs, and this evaluative tendency is avoided, when we listen with understanding" (Rogers, 1961, pp. 334, 331). Rogers' statement of the problem (a tendency to evaluate and judge) and the solution (listening with understanding) formed the rationale and foundation for problem solving that "practically guarantee[s] that some reasonable solution would be reached" (Rogers, 1961, p. 333).

Peter Elbow's *Writing without Teachers* (1973) incorporated theories and methodologies similar to Rogers'. Elbow emphasized listening with understanding to achieve a negotiated solution, and the distinctions he made between the two forms of problem solving (doubting and believing) resembled the distinctions between Aristotelian and Rogerian argument made by Young, Becker, and Pike. Elbow's teacherless writing class was based on a helping relationship. The teacher in this class casts off the garb of dogmatist and puts on the clothing of explorer. The vestiges of authority—evaluation and grading—remain. However, listening and understanding inform the writing process and class discussion of students' work. Writers and readers reach consensus on the issues of writing, but more important, they use a nonevaluative, nonjudgmental approach to learning in their peer responses. The setting in the teacherless class is an ideal one in which to promote this listening with understanding, for the function of the class is mutual improvement. The relationships among peers are not (or should not be) adversarial. Corder (1985) was correct in pointing out that this sort of dynamic does not often exist in interpersonal relationships, but students in a sharing, supportive environment approximate the Rogerian therapist/client relationship and do offer one another the opportunity for personal and authorial growth. As I mentioned earlier, Bator viewed the distinction between Aristotelian and Rogerian argument as determined by the relationship between speaker and audience and by the aim of the rhetor. In the teacherless writing class, as in the "helping circle," the relationship is not oppositional because the writer strives for a Rogerian "mutual understanding and cooperation with the audience" (Bator, 1980, p. 429) to achieve their mutual goal of improved writing. Like the Rogerian methodology, Elbow's served in "building bridges" between writer and reader (Corder, 1985, p. 22).

The "believing game" was the key to Elbow's (1973) first articulation of the teacherless writing class. In discussing peer responses, Elbow emphasized the importance of believing a writer's assertions rather than searching for the error in those assertions. According to Elbow, "the majority spends all its time not merely not-arguing against the individual, not merely listening to him, but actually trying to believe him" (1973, p. 182). In the believing game, negotiation must take place between the writer and the reader, among participants. The meaning of words, interpretations of passages, and other aspects of revision are negotiated within the community of writers. The believing game serves as a tool for peer criticism and textual interpretation, and the role of the student as critic "is not to discredit a bad reading but to make better readings more available. . . . Incorrect readings are never disproven or even undermined. They merely fall into disuse because they don't 'resolve' the text so well" (Elbow, 1973, p. 166).

For Elbow, "the function of . . . the believing game is for people to help each other believe more things, experience more things, and thereby move away from the lowest-common-denominator tendency in a majority conclusion" (1973, p. 170). The end of the believing game is not persuasion; in fact, participants in a teacherless writing class, just as in a Rogerian helping relationship, reach a negotiated truth only by leaving off with argument and taking up collaboration, agreement, and cooperation. As in Rogers' nonthreatening negotiation, Elbow's believing game included cooperation, risk-taking, openness, exploration, listening, and "the acceptance of uncertainty and ambiguity" (1973, p. 179). This believing game, however, will be played effectively only after

> you build its use into an orderly game and follow the rules: never argue; believe everything, particularly what seems strange or unpleasant; try to put yourself into the skin of people with other perceptions. . . . Most important of all, you must get other people to do it with you, and do it for a long time. (Elbow, 1973, p. 170)

Elbow was not blind to the necessity of a dialectic between the doubting and believing games, but he did admit his preference for the believing game in *Writing without Teachers,* "not just because it is nice or sociable, not even just because the doubting game doesn't work everywhere, but because the believing game yields the truth" (1973, p. 176). In defining "truth," however, Elbow admitted that the believing game often settles for a "dirtier" sort negotiated through a speech community (1973, p. 177).

While Elbow (1973) insisted on any community of writers reaching a negotiated truth, he also recognized the "monopoly of the doubting game" in Western thought. Writers and speakers have been conditioned to win or gain acceptance of their points of view, not to compromise. The doubting game rewards powerful rhetorical skill, not truth. The writer/reader relationship is neither congenial nor cooperative, but antagonistic. The writer—whose aim is to persuade, "to win advantage through discovery of psychological weaknesses in the audience"—

engages the reader in an Aristotelian argument (Bator, 1980, p. 428). As a result the doubting game never attains the negotiated truth of the believing game; instead, the writer essentially bullies the reader into compliance or alienation (Elbow, 1973, p. 163). The doubting game, claimed Elbow, is useful, but only when "you work out the rules of logic, transform assertions logically into as many forms as possible, extricate the self, doubt particularly those assertions that seem reasonable, and get opposing propositions to fight each other" (1973, p. 169). The distinction between doubting and believing resembled one that Aristotle made between logic and rhetoric: logic (the doubting game) has concerned itself with questions of certainty and rhetoric (the believing game) with questions of probability.

Elbow's approach to interpretation and inquiry and his understanding of doubting and believing changed from 1973 to 1986. In *Writing with Power* (Elbow, 1981) doubting and believing maintained their functions as critiquing tools, but Elbow no longer conceived the doubting game as less desirable. It can be, he argued, "equally powerful if everyone is up for it. Wrestling can lead to the truth" (1981, p. 271). Elbow's more recent variation in *Embracing Contraries* engaged Rogers' listening with understanding—along with the Aristotelian doubting—as a dialogic means of personal inquiry, effective problem solving, self-exploration, and social interaction.

Elbow moved away from the earlier assumption of the greater inherent worth of the believing game and constructed a new framework for future discussions of the doubting and believing games. In *Embracing Contraries,* doubting and believing are no longer simply means of persuasion. They are methods of inquiry—"artificial, systematic, and disciplined uses of the mind" (Elbow, 1986, p. 258). This combined doubting and believing game exemplifies the internal dialogue in which an individual undertakes a debate or dialogue with an "internalized other" (LeFevre, 1987, pp. 58–62).

In *Embracing Contraries,* Elbow established a *dialogic* between doubting and believing, treating them as "equally necessary" contraries in literary interpretation, the writing process, and the search for truths (1986, p. 258). He maintained distinctions between the two methods, using them constructively by neither denying their individuality nor claiming one or the other as the privileged method of inquiry. He accomplished what others involved in the debates over Aristotelian and Rogerian argument have not—a symbiotic relationship between the two methods of inquiry.

Regarding Elbow's doubting and believing games as a dialogic rather than a dialectic makes a fine, yet crucial, distinction in his development of this concept. I agree with Berlin (1987, p. 153) who commented that Elbow emphasizes in his earlier texts the " 'I' . . . , the self [and] . . . an authentic identity and voice." Yet, in the final chapter of *Embracing Contraries,* Elbow developed a dialogue between the self and the other, between doubting and believing, that did not appear in *Writing without Teachers.* This dialogue resembled LeFevre's internally dialogized invention. In this socially oriented category of invention she placed Rogerian argument, as well as other heuristics influenced by Vygotsky, whose "theory that thought is a form of inner speech internalized from social speech also stresses a development of inner cognitive processes from social patterns and practices" (LeFevre, 1987, p. 58).

Vygotsky's linguistic theory also informed the linguistic theories of Mikhail Bakhtin (1895–1975), the Russian literary theorist whose work has been applied to composition and rhetoric studies.[5] Bakhtin's texts described and only partially defined several versions of dialogue, one of which is an internal, temporal dialogue that takes place "between an earlier and a later self" (Holquist, in Bakhtin, 1981, p. 427). Dialogue, in Bakhtin's system, was the elemental speech activity in which the diversity of cultural voices moves. A muting of the dialogue is a muting of meaning, for only through the give and take of competing voices is meaning achieved. In this, wrote Bakhtin, "we make meaning"; meaning takes place on "interindividual territory" (Volosinov, 1973, p. 12). In the doubting and believing game, the "interindividual territory" is internalized; meaning is reached through an inner dialogue of doubting and believing. The two, together, become knowledge-generating, epistemic activities. Believing affirms established thought on a particular topic; doubting questions and denies it. As methods of inquiry, doubting and believing represent varying perspectives on a subject. As such, they are not solely the position of an individual, but rather are influenced by the prevailing positions within the individual's culture.

Doubting and believing become more than methods of inquiry or means of testing and rejecting or affirming hypotheses; they become ideological stances. Elbow included in the characteristics of doubting and believing the following:

> Doubting is the act of separating or differentiating and thus correlates with individualism; it permits the loner to hold out against the crowd or even—with logic—to conquer. Belief involves merging and participating in a community; indeed a community is created by—and creates—shared beliefs.
>
> Doubting correlates with resisting authority; believing with acquiescence. . . . (Elbow, 1986, p. 264)[6]

Doubting and believing began as two alternatives to giving feedback in the classroom, but in *Embracing Contraries,* Elbow depicted them as more political and ideological by suggesting their powers of consensus and dissensus. This politicized doubting and believing game leads me to compare the dialogue proposed by Elbow to that of Mikhail Bakhtin. Such a comparison affirms the increasingly social nature of Elbow's method and, by extension, of Rogers' therapeutic model.

According to Bakhtin, every discourse is constructed from a multiplicity of voices that interact dialogically. Every utterance is accented with the intentions of previous speakers and must work against the domination of these other accents to reach its own meaning. This dialogism, for Bakhtin, is informed by battling centripetal, unifying, dominant forces and centrifugal, disunifying, subversive forces (Bakhtin, 1981)—those that struggle to maintain a conservative hegemony and those that struggle to topple that hegemony. Centripetal and centrifugal forces, like believing and doubting, represent the forces of consensus and dissensus. Doubting and believing, when reconsidered as centripetal and centrifugal forces, take on epistemological and ideological significance not previously granted them.

Redefining Elbow's dialectic of doubting and believing as a dialogue effectively places him in Bakhtin's preferred sociological-linguistic category in which an individual speaks in unison, harmony, or dissonance with others. Whatever the case, he or she responds to the discourses that preceded, believing and accepting the validity and persuasiveness of some, doubting and rejecting the claims of others. The listeners at whom he or she directs discourse are also instrumental in the construction of that discourse. They will, in turn, believe or doubt—acquiesce to or resist—that discourse and with it his or her ideological position. Meaning (and with it, truths) and the transmission of that meaning are dependent upon the speaker and listeners both as individuals and as members of their communities. The individual is not subordinate to the social in Bakhtin's scheme, but that individual is the social and ideological (Volosinov, 1973). Each person is (to alter slightly a behaviorist tenet) a product of a social, cultural, and ideological environment.

CONCLUSION

The work of Carl Rogers and expressivist composition theorists offers composition studies a more generous view of both Rogerian principles and expressivist rhetoric. Rogerian principles allow one to develop a confident and explored self, an active communicator and contributor to the society, not a self-enveloped seeker of self-truth. The writer strives to find and express perceptions of the world and share them with others (Stewart, 1969). Knowing that an objective reality, if it exists, is not attainable, an individual relies on his or her own perception of reality as one version of truth and respects others (Evans, 1981). In addition, some critics have mistakenly suggested that because it privileges the personal and values the individual, "the expressionist argument ignores the social dimension of language" (Knoblauch, 1988, p. 133).

Resisting a reductive definition of expressivist rhetoric, questioning the concept that all expressivists seek an objective truth within the individual, and broadening the ends of expressivism will save it from condemnation as merely a "quest for 'psychic redemption' and 'personal growth' " (Giroux, in Fiagley, 1986, p. 531) and from criticism as an idiosyncratic "journey into the 'self' [blind] towards those larger social forces that promote economic and cultural disintegration" (Giroux, 1983, p. 220).

Expressivists must reply to critics who condemn subjectivity of self-exploration by emphasizing, as Rogers did, the inherently social nature of the helping relationship (Gebhardt & Smith, 1976). Rogers himself defined the goal of communication as an attempt to resolve differences between therapist and client through the awareness, development, and presentation of the client's own world view, reaching self-understanding, social cooperation, and negotiated solution. Similarly, "the writer's goal is to engage in some sort of cooperative activity with the reader" (Young, Becker, & Pike, 1970, p. 171). The incorporation of Rogerian principles in expressivist rhetoric was far more extensive than the adaptation of Rogerian argument by Young, Becker, and Pike and Hairston. Murray, Stewart, Macrorie, and especially Elbow preserved the psychologist's aims of a congruent self and effective communication. Finally, Elbow, in *Embracing Contraries* (1986), established a new forum for future discussions of Rogerian and Aristotelian approaches by uniting, in a dialogic relationship, the activities of doubting and believing.

In this last form, Rogerian argument becomes part of the dialogic of which LeFevre and Bakhtin wrote. Taken by itself, Rogerian argument offered a nonconfrontational approach to problem solving through mutual understanding. In relation to the more antagonistic Aristotelian argument that strives to persuade, Rogerian argument seeks cooperation. But because the two offer such oppositional strategies and perceptions of the world, they work best in dialogue with one another. The give and take, the struggle of competing views, meanings, and political stances meet and are worked out in the arena of doubting and believing, of centripetal and centrifugal forces. Believing, without doubting, provides only a conservative and hegemonic mode of inquiry that does not disrupt or contend with established understanding, but merges with and reaffirms it. Doubting, without believing, is no better. It resists indiscriminately and may become unconstructive—even anarchistic—because of its excessive antagonism. It becomes clear, as Bakhtin argued, that the two are dependent upon one another, for meaning is constructed out of dialogue and difference. As Elbow suggested, believing and doubting together offer a more complete picture of the truths that are being sought.

NOTES

1. There are, of course, references to Rogers in Young, Becker, and Pike (1970), Hairston (1974), and the others involved in the argument over Rogerian argument, but none makes reference to expressivist pedagogy. LeFevre (1987) cites Charles Yarnoff's discussion (1980) of Young, Becker, and Pike's tagmemic heuristic. Yarnoff, however, neither discusses Rogers at length nor mentions any expressivist theorists in conjunction with Rogers.
2. Macrorie's text originally appeared in 1968; unfortunately, I must work from the third edition of *Writing to be Read* that appeared in 1984. All references to *Writing to be Read* are to the 1984 edition.
3. It is interesting to note that Murray's writing laboratory resembles that described by Francis Ingold Walker of New Trier Township High School in Kenilworth, Illinois. Walker describes her writing laboratory in a 1917 article entitled "The Laboratory System In English."
4. See Bruffee's *A Short Course in Writing: Practical Rhetoric for Teaching Composition through Collaborative Learning* (1985) for a description of his collaborative method.
5. Charles Schuster's *College English* article entitled "Mikhail Bakhtin as Rhetorical Theorist" (1985) offers the first articulation of Bakhtin's worth to composition studies. For further information on Bakhtin, see Clark and Holquist's biography, *Mikhail Bakhtin* (1984). This text also summarizes the Bakhtinian and disputed texts of Volosinov and Medvedev. For continuity, I will refer to Bakhtin as the author of *Marxism and the Philosophy of Language* while citing Volosinov in parenthetical notation to avoid confusion between texts. The debate over this text's authorship continues.
6. Doubting is not an activity reserved for the individual, as Elbow notes. Groups are just as capable as individuals of voicing doubt and striking out against a dominant or hegemonic community. While an individual may be capable of swaying the opinions of her fellow citizens, believing always entails community consensus (Elbow, 1986, p. 264).

REFERENCES

Bakhtin, M. (1981). *The dialogic imagination: Four essays by M. M. Bakhtin* (C. Emerson & M. Holquist, Trans.). (University of Texas Press Slavic Series. 1.) Austin, TX: University of Texas Press.

Bator, P. (1980). Aristotelian and Rogerian rhetoric. *College Composition and Communication, 31,* 427–432.

Berlin, J. (1987). *Rhetoric and reality: Writing instruction in American colleges, 1900–1975.* Carbondale, IL: Southern Illinois University Press.

Brande, D. (1934). *On Becoming a Writer.* New York: Harcourt, Brace.

Bruffee, K. (1985). *A short course in writing: Practical rhetoric for teaching composition through collaborative learning* (3rd ed.). Boston, MA: Little, Brown.

Clark, K., & Holquist, M. (1984). *Mikhail Bakhtin.* Cambridge, MA: Harvard University Press.

Corder, J. W. (1985). Argument as emergence, rhetoric as love. *Rhetoric Review, 4,* 16–32.

Ede, L. (1984). Is Rogerian rhetoric really Rogerian? *Rhetoric Review, 3,* 40–48.

Elbow, P. (1973). *Writing without teachers.* New York: Oxford University Press.

Elbow, P. (1981). *Writing with power.* New York: Oxford University Press.

Elbow, P. (1986). *Embracing contraries: Explorations in learning and teaching.* New York: Oxford University Press.

Evans, R. (1981). *Dialogue with Carl Rogers.* New York: Praeger.

Faigley, L. (1986). Competing theories of process: A critique and a proposal. *College English, 48,* 527–542.

Gebhardt, R., & Smith, B. G. (1976). "Liberation" is not "license," the case for self-awareness through writing. *College Composition and Communication, 27,* 21–24.

Giroux, H. (1983). *Theory and resistance in education.* South Hadley, MA: Bergin.

Halasek, K. (1987). *The politics of expressive rhetoric.* Paper delivered at the Conference on College Composition and Communication, Atlanta, GA.

Hairston, M. (1974). *A contemporary rhetoric.* Boston, MA: Houghton Mifflin.

Hairston, M. (1982). Using Carl Rogers' communication theories in the composition classroom. *Rhetoric Review, 1,* 50–55.

Kelly, L. (1973). Toward competence and creativity in an open class. *College English, 34,* 644–660.

Knoblauch, C. H. (1988). Rhetorical constructions: Dialogue and commitment. *College English, 50,* 125–40.

LeFevre, K. (1987). *Invention as a social act.* Carbondale, IL: Southern Illinois University Press.

Lunsford, A. (1979). Aristotelian vs. Rogerian argument: A reassessment. *College Composition and Communication, 30,* 146–151.

Macrorie, K. (1984). *Writing to be read* (3rd ed.). Upper Montclair, NJ: Boynton/Cook.

Mader, D. (1980). What are they doing to Carl Rogers? *ETC.: A Review of General Semantics, 37,* 314–320.

Murray, D. (1968). *A writer teaches writing: A practical method of teaching composition.* Boston, MA: Houghton Mifflin.

Rogers, C. (1961). *On becoming a person.* Boston, MA: Houghton Mifflin.

Rogers, C. (1969). *Freedom to learn.* Columbus, OH: Merrill.

Rohman, D. G., & Wlecke, A. O. (1964). *Pre-Writing: The construction and application of models for concept formation in writing* (U. S. Office of Education Cooperative Research Project no. 2174). East Lansing, MI: Michigan State University Press.

Schuster, C. (1985). Mikhail Bakhtin as rhetorical theorist. *College English, 47,* 594–607.

Stewart, D. (1969). Prose with integrity: A primary objective. *College Composition and Communication, 20,* 223–227.

Stewart, D. (1972). *The authentic voice: A pre-writing approach to student writing,* Dubuque, IA: William C. Brown.

Stewart, D. (1988). Collaborative learning and composition: Boon or bane? *Rhetoric Review, 7,* 58–83.

Thoreau, H. (1981). *Walden.* Salt Lake City, UT: Gibbs M. Smith.

Volosinov, V. N. (1973). *Marxism and the philosophy of language* (L. Matejka & I. R. Titunik, Trans.). Cambridge, MA: Harvard University Press.

Walker, F. (1917). The laboratory system in English. *English Journal, 6,* 445–453.

Yarnoff, C. (1980). Contemporary theories of invention in the rhetorical tradition. *College English, 41,* 552–560.

Young, R. E., Becker, A. L., & Pike, K. E. (1970). *Rhetoric: Discovery and change.* New York: Harcourt, Brace.

CHAPTER 9
Rogerian Principles and the Invention Process

Rebecca Stephens

Psychologist Carl Rogers' person-centered approach to problem solving appeals to many writing teachers as solid good sense. Beyond this initial interest, however, lies a substantial controversy over how his principles should best be applied to composition instruction. In recent years, Rogerian concepts have been used in two ways: first, as a comprehensive alternative to traditional argumentation, and, second, as a pedagogical approach to the relationship between the student and the teacher. Another application which merits consideration is the heuristic value of Rogerian principles in the invention process. I will explore this new direction and offer a detailed Rogerian heuristic with examples of its use in the invention process. First, however, it is necessary to locate this new application of Rogerian principles in relation to the previous two approaches of pedagogy and argumentation.

ROGERIAN THEORY AND COMMUNICATION

Although at times he criticized the distortion of his principles, Rogers himself began in the 1950s to speculate that the techniques he used in therapy situations might have broader implications in the areas of education, interpersonal communication, and creativity. He explored the potential applications of his principles in detail in a series of essays and lectures compiled in *On Becoming a Person* (1961).

For example, in "Significant Learning: In Therapy and in Education," Rogers drew a series of parallels between therapeutic and educational situations. Common to both environments is the need to recognize a specific problem to be solved. In the classroom, this problem must have relevance to the lives of the students. And like the therapist, the teacher facilitates learning by conveying a unity of experience and awareness known as *congruence*. In other words, the teacher must be accepting and aware of the thoughts and feelings he or she expresses, thus presenting a "real-ness" which frees the student from inhibiting defenses (1961, p. 282).

Also crucial to both therapeutic and learning situations are the qualities which Rogers terms *unconditional positive regard* and *empathic understanding*. These qualities, when displayed by the therapist/teacher, assure the clients/students of their self-worth, and encourage them to consider the attitudinal changes necessary for "significant learning" (1961, p. 281).

Rogers also applied these principles to interpersonal communications. In a 1951 paper entitled "Communication: Its Blocking and Its Facilitation," he cited two barriers to successful communication. First is "our very natural tendency to judge, to evaluate, to approve or disapprove, the statement of the other person, the other group" (1961, p. 330). In other words, people communicate—always subjectively—within the context of their own frame of reference or point of view. We respond, for instance, to judgments with judgments of our own. Second is the impact of a person's feelings and emotions upon his or her perceptions of and responses to communication. The most difficult communication situations, according to Rogers, are those involving intense emotions, values, and beliefs (1961, p. 331). Although Rogers' own attempts to remove these barriers were limited to therapy and small group situations, he hypothesizes that even major international misunderstandings might be avoided or resolved with similar efforts to objectify, clarify, and make reasonable compromises in one's position on an issue.

It was perhaps this optimism which led Young, Becker, and Pike (1970) and Maxine Hairston (1976, p. 373) to recognize in Rogers' principles "profound implications for rhetoric." In *Rhetoric: Discovery and Change,* Young, et al. established Rogerian argument as an alternative to traditional patterns of argumention, which they maintained are often ineffective and threat-producing in areas involving strong values and beliefs. Young et al. based Rogerian argument upon the assumption that "out of a need to preserve the stability of his image, a person will refuse to consider alternatives that he feels are threatening" (1970, p. 274). Accordingly, they developed the following strategy of arrangement. First, the writer establishes the reader's trust by summarizing the opponent's position objectively. The writer then delimits the contexts in which each perspective is valid. In conclusion, the writer demonstrates the benefits that the opponent will gain "if he were to adopt elements of the writer's position" (1970, p. 283). The goal of this approach is to "induce changes in an opponent's mind in order to make mutually advantageous cooperation possible" (p. 283).

Following Young et al., modified versions of Rogerian argument have appeared in numerous articles and textbooks. For example, Coe (1981) introduced "Rogerian persuasion" as a means of achieving a nonantagonistic rhetorical context, with the writer's objectives including "truth, not victory" (p. 341). Most versions of Rogerian argument follow Young et al. by avoiding formulaic structures of arrangement and stressing flexibility, not only in the arrangement of the argument, but also in the writer's position. A truly Rogerian argument, Young et al. stated, "may well involve changes in *both* your opponent's image and your own" (1970, p. 282).

Despite their emphasis upon cooperation and mutual change, the application of Rogerian principles has been criticized as a rigid, potentially manipulative persuasion technique. Ede (1984) maintained that "Rogerian rhetoric represents a distortion of Carl Rogers' own principles" (p. 40). She argued that Young et al.'s emphasis upon changing the mind of the "opponent" reduced Rogers' facilitative philosophy to a severely structured, potentially self-serving technique.

Such was the status of the Rogerian controversy when panelists Richard Young, Maxine Hairston, Paul Bator, Lisa Ede, and Nathaniel Teich gathered at the 1987 Conference on College Composition and Communication to reassess the use of Carl Rogers' principles in composition instruction. As the membership of the panel might indicate, this discussion featured the full spectrum of endorsement and condemnation of Rogerian argument. However, there emerged a new focus which shifted Rogerian principles away from the polarity of the writer–reader relationship and toward a broader Rogerian view of the writing process. (See excerpts from the forum, this volume, Chapter 4).

Hairston, for example, conceded that her views on Rogerian rhetoric have changed since the publication of her 1976 article. She no longer teaches argument as a type of writing; instead, she emphasizes the situational aspects of writing which call for a deeper understanding of audience and purpose. Rogerian principles, she says, are applied indirectly in the writing classroom. First, the teacher facilitates writing by reducing the potential threat of "highly structured, rule-bound situations." She does this by exposing her own attitudes to the risk of change. Second, as writers become aware of writing as a process and conscious of the complexities of their subject, audience, and purpose, they engage in the internal process of "becoming a fully functioning person and writer." These remarks are indicative of the general movement away from the context of persuasion and towards Rogers' stance on education and "significant learning."

ROGERIAN PRINCIPLES AND THE WRITING PROCESS

Now it is time to end the excessive preoccupation with the controversy over Rogerian argumentation, because it ignores other potentially valuable uses of Rogers' concepts in writing instruction. One application, in particular, which has largely been ignored involves the use of a Rogerian-based heuristic for invention.

Applied to the invention process, Rogerian principles provide a workable combination of flexibility and structure not possible in the later stages of arrangement. A concrete, specifically worded heuristic, employed at an early stage of the writing process, can serve as a powerful persuasive tool for student writers in investigating their topics.

In contrast to the previous attention on Rogerian strategies of arrangement, teaching Rogerian invention strategies provides writers with the means to relate to their subject matter in a nonthreatening manner. A Rogerian approach to invention does not assume that students can easily find suitable topics and express their positions without difficulty. Often student writers may be less than certain of their opinions on an issue. The exploratory nature of invention heuristics can help them become familiar with various perspectives on an issue and allow them to develop informed opinions.

Rogerian principles are necessarily vague and abstract in the arrangement approaches of Young et al., Hairston, and Coe. In keeping with the need for conciliation and change, these frameworks refrain from providing a firm structure for the argument. Coe, for example, instructs students to "choose an appropriate thesis, imagine an appropriate rhetorical context, and write a Rogerian persuasion that follows the Rogerian format" (1981, p. 348). But the specified format is not defined.

Assignments of this type do not conjure the image of a living, breathing opponent with emotions and feelings as powerful as the writers'. The concrete and detailed questions of the following heuristic, however, can produce the depth of perception needed to bring about true empathic understanding. The sheer volume of information elicited will enable students to enrich their arguments with descriptive details.

A ROGERIAN-BASED INVENTION HEURISTIC

While a Rogerian-based heuristic can facilitate the broad, multi-perspectival insights, empathic understanding, and internal modification of views which encourage honest communication, its use must be monitored closely by the writing teacher. Like any heuristic, it presumes sincerity and involvement of the students. Its value will be severely limited if it is approached with the detachment often afforded the short-answer quiz it resembles.

One approach, which has yielded success in freshman writing classes at the University of South Florida, is to engage the whole class in the analysis of a single issue. In one session the class investigated several perspectives on the issue of English as an official language. Their efforts illustrate the use of the heuristic provided below.

Because change of perspective is expected and encouraged in a Rogerian-based writing assignment, students' initial selection of a topic is less rigid than in a traditional writing project. To get started, Teich (1987) recommended that students choose a topic which affects their lives directly. Or they simply may be asked to think of a controversial issue for which they think no solution exists. For initial Rogerian assignments, the best subjects are those in which students have a rational—not a deeply emotional—interest. Also for initial writing assignments, it is important that topics have no more than two (possibly three) opposing sides, so that compromise can be satisfactory. Additional perspectives will be confusing to understand and difficult to bring to a compromise. Issues dealing with drug use, for example, have proven to be diffuse and difficult to define, whereas gun control, ownership of pit bull terriers, and abortion are more polarized.

The USF class was initially divided in its choice of a topic. Other suggestions included gun control and legalization of drugs. (They argued unanimously against any topics related to the ongoing presidential election campaign, insisting that it did not affect their lives.) Eventually the strongly voiced and polarized opinions of the Floridians convinced the others that the state-wide issue of English as an official language was worth exploring.

After reaching an agreement on the topic, students worked in pairs to respond to the following questions:

ROGERIAN INVENTION HEURISTIC

1. What is the nature of the issue, in general terms?
2. Whose lives are affected by the issue?
3. In what way are they affected?

4. What are the major points of view, or perspectives, on the issue? (At this point the student should establish a set of two or more perspectives, perhaps setting up a separate page for each.)
5. What kinds of people or groups hold these views?
6. Do these people take an active or passive role in the issue? If active, what do they do to promote their views? If passive, why do they not act?
7. What kinds of people or groups have no interest in this issue? Are their lives affected by the issue in any way?
8. What beliefs and values motivate each of the interested groups?
9. What other things influence their beliefs? For example, are there economic, social, political, legal, or religious reasons which contribute to their perspectives? Name and describe the reason for these influences.
10. What kind of publicity do the various perspectives receive?
11. Are the media biased or unbiased in presenting these views?
12. List the basic terminology used by each group to define the issue and their position.
13. Define each of these terms objectively.
14. Are there any differences in the terms and their definitions among the opposing points of view?
15. When arguing the issue, what would each side probably mention first? Second? Third?
16. When arguing the issue, what fact(s) would each side be likely to ignore or exclude? Why?
17. Under what conditions is each group's position valid?
18. Under what conditions is each group's position invalid?
19. Is any group illogical in its assumptions? If so, explain?
20. What part of each group's opinion is the most important; in other words, what aspect of their beliefs will they refuse to change?
21. What aspect of each group's beliefs might be changed or modified in order to reach a solution?
22. What would have to happen in order to eliminate the disagreement among the opposing groups?
23. What are the chances that this will occur?

The instructor assisted with the first question by asking students to state the issue in terms of a question. They agreed on, "Should English be ruled as the official language of the United States?" She then suggested that they define *official language,* modifying their definition as they worked through the questions.

It may seem useful to encourage students to do some research on the topic before beginning the heuristic. This approach, however, has not proven beneficial. Students may be easily swayed by opinions found in a newspaper or magazine. One article is often enough to prevent the free thinking needed to consider many different perspectives. The instructor, however, must be versed on the issue, and he or she must present—neutrally—as many questions as possible in the topic-search discussion. For this reason, it is best to have students select the topic during the class period prior to the heuristic session.

While writing on the language issue, one student remarked, "These questions all ask the same thing." The instructor asked the class to share their responses to questions defining the groups who comprised the opposing perspectives on the issue. When she received vague answers, such as "people who escaped Cuba" or "legislators," she asked them to create profiles of a "typical" person for and against the issue. At this point students who lived in bilingual and multicultural areas shared their experiences, bringing the issue to life and making it more pertinent to those who had previously viewed it abstractly.

Students working independently on the heuristic have often expressed dramatic shifts in their opinions. In the class which chose the language issue, however, none of the students admitted to a change in opinion. When working in pairs, they may already have compromised their opinions somewhat in order to reach a response to which their partners agreed. For this reason, it would be useful to ask students to summarize their opinions on the topic before answering the questions.

Occasionally, a student will want to abandon his or her issue entirely. These shifts are in keeping with Rogerian principles and should be supported. It is also helpful if students monitor the course of their thoughts on a separate paper, noting important changes in perception and opinion. Some, however, will have difficulty assuming a metaconceptual role.

Once the information is gathered and synthesized, it may be arranged according to Young et al. or another Rogerian framework, or even a traditional Aristotelian approach. Students also should be encouraged to experiment with arrangement patterns of their own which best accommodate their purpose.

Students writing on the language issue, for example, found clarification of the topic a more interesting purpose than pure persuasion. Confirming Maxine Hairston's view that all writing is persuasive, they wrote stimulating essays contemplating the definition of *official language,* dramatic dialogues between opposing viewpoints, and narrative "features" on people directly affected by the issue. All were as persuasive as a deliberately structured argumentative essay.

CONCLUSION

The above heuristic represents a blending of the pedagogical and argumentative aspects of Rogerian problem-solving concepts. It provides students with nonthreatening flexibility in defining the writing project, as well as structure in exploring views of the "opponent."

On a broader scale, the heuristic is a clear example of the value of writing as a process. The exercise itself elicits valuable information in the early stages of writing, thus demonstrating to students the importance of invention and prewriting. And as an experiment in exploring multiple, potentially conflicting perspectives on a particular topic, it can enrich students' analytical and critical thinking abilities, and bring them one step closer to the self-actualization upon which Carl Rogers' principles were originally founded.

REFERENCES

Coe, R. (1981). *Form and substance: An advance rhetoric.* Glenview, IL: Scott, Foresman.

Ede, L. (1984). Is Rogerian rhetoric really Rogerian? *Rhetoric Review, 3,* 40–48.

Hairston, M. (1976). Carl Rogers' alternative to traditional rhetoric. *College Composition and Communication, 27,* 373–377.

Rogers, C. R. (1961). *On becoming a person.* Boston, MA: Houghton Mifflin.

Teich, N. (1987). Rogerian problem-solving and the rhetoric of argumentation. *Journal of Advanced Composition, 7,* 52–61.

Young, R. E., Becker, A. L., & Pike, K. L. (1970). *Rhetoric: Discovery and change.* New York: Harcourt, Brace.

CHAPTER 10
Dewey, Kilpatrick, and Rogers on Expert Communication

James P. Zappen

In the context of Carl R. Rogers' writings, the phrase *expert communication* is paradoxical. In this context, communication, genuine communication, is always communication among persons as persons, never as experts or professionals, hence the paradox or seeming contradiction. However, in this context also, experts are always persons first, their expertise deriving from their attitudes toward themselves and toward other persons rather than from any specialized knowledge or skills. They are not *experts* in the traditional sense of the term. Rogers' views on experts and on expert communication contrast with his view of science and, especially, of technology. Nonetheless, these views constitute a novel perspective on the theory and practice of expert communication. In particular, they suggest the possibility that scientists and engineers might in some situations function productively as providers of information and as participants in group discussion and problem solving. Rogers' views provide an alternative to conventional views of expert communication, particularly scientific and technical communication, views that identify scientists and engineers and their usual types of communication with their traditional roles as technical problem solvers in organizations.

Rogers' views on expert communication derive from the tradition of progressive education in America, in particular from the educational philosophy of John Dewey and William Heard Kilpatrick. Dewey was the major and most influential figure in progressive education in America in the early 20th century (Gutek, 1970, pp. 191–198, 200). Kilpatrick was a student of Dewey and a popular teacher of his educational philosophy at Teachers College, Columbia University (1970, pp. 198–199). Rogers was a student in Kilpatrick's course in the Philosophy of Education at Columbia (Kirschenbaum, 1979, pp. 48–52, 364–380). In this chapter, I trace the development of Rogers' views on expert communication from Dewey through Kilpatrick to Rogers himself, provide some examples of expert communication in environmental science and engineering illustrative of Rogers' views, and finally explain how these views might help to broaden the definition of scientific and technical communication that appears in the theoretical literature and in the textbooks.

JOHN DEWEY ON EXPERIMENTAL METHOD AND ITS ORGANIZATION

In his exposition of his educational philosophy, Dewey emphasizes the experience of the individual learner, an emphasis characteristic of progressive education in general, and he adopts the cooperative experimental method of the physical sciences as a method of inquiry and communication. In a discussion of the role of the social sciences in political affairs, he describes *expertise* as the specialized technical knowledge of particular organized groups and *expert communication* as the dissemination of that knowledge. Dewey's views on experimental method and its characteristic forms of organization still hold within the sciences and engineering and scientific and technical communication.

The experience of the individual learner rather than the experience or knowledge of the teacher, for Dewey as for the other proponents of progressive education, is the basis of all education. This experience is both active and passive, both trying or doing something and undergoing the consequences of that trying (1980, pp. 146–151). Thinking is the conscious discernment of the relation between trying and what happens in consequence of trying (1980, pp. 151–158). And thinking, by its nature and definition, is always individual and as such cannot be imposed from without, even by an experienced teacher (1980, pp. 310–314).

But experience is cooperative as well as individual, for in Dewey's conception it is synonymous with the experimental method of inquiry and communication, which achieved its greatest success as a cooperative method in the physical sciences. For Dewey, experience is simply the experimental method carried on under conditions of deliberate control (1980, pp. 280–284). The experimental method is a five-phase response to a problematic situation: suggesting possible solutions; locating and defining the problem; developing a hypothesis; reasoning, or elaborating the hypothesis; and testing the hypothesis (1980, pp. 159–170; 1986, pp. 196–209). It is both a method of inquiry and a method of communication, both process and product, both a method of thinking and of setting forth the results of thinking (1986, pp. 171–186). The experimental method achieved its greatest success as a cooperative method, "the procedure of organized cooperative inquiry which has won the triumphs of science in the field of physical nature" (1987, pp. 50–51). As such, Dewey insists, this method has nothing in common with popular modes of public discussion, which ignore the organized knowledge of various occupational groups (1987, pp. 50–52). The experimental method, as Dewey describes it, became widely popular in textbooks in speech communication (Ehninger, Monroe, & Gronbeck, 1978, pp. 142–163; Simons, 1986, pp. 164–165), and, in one variation or another, under a variety of names, it still appears in textbooks on scientific and technical communication.[1]

In a discussion of the role of the social sciences in political affairs, Dewey deplores the isolation of experts from common affairs but nonetheless upholds a view of expertise as the specialized technical knowledge of particular organized groups, and of expert communication as the dissemination of that knowledge. Dewey argues that the public is in an "eclipse," that it does not know itself, its own interest (1984, pp. 313–324). He believes that the social sciences can help to define that interest (1984, pp. 345–350). In this context, expertise is the specialized technical knowledge of particular organized groups, usually divorced from common affairs but, in the social sciences, according to Dewey, responsive to the needs of the masses (1984, pp. 362–365). Expertise in the social sciences is the application of the experimental method to political affairs, a task that necessarily "devolves upon experts" (1984, p. 365). It is specifically the application of the experimental method to political affairs for the purpose of determining the consequences of public opinion and thereby assisting in the formation of an informed public interest (1984, pp. 345–348, 361–362). Expert communication is simply the dissemination or distribution of the results of this application of the experimental method (1984, pp. 348–350, 365). Dewey's views on the role of expertise and expert communication in political affairs are problematic because they suggest that expert communication is characteristically communication by the expert *to* rather than *with* the public. These views, like Dewey's views on experimental method, also appear in textbooks on scientific and technical communication, which identify this kind of communication with organizations and enumerate and explain the types of communication, especially internal communication, produced within these organizations.[2]

WILLIAM HEARD KILPATRICK ON GROUP DISCUSSION

Whereas Dewey identifies a role for the experimental method as a mode of expert inquiry and communication in the social sciences, Kilpatrick, when he mentions science and method at all, explicitly rejects any association of science with "expert thinking" (Kilpatrick, 1933, pp. 258–259, 277–279). In his account of his educational philosophy, Kilpatrick reiterates Dewey's emphasis on the experience of the individual learner but adopts the process of group discussion rather than the experimental method as a method of inquiry and communication. He shares Dewey's view of *expertise* as specialized knowledge but regards *expert communication* as merely one dimension of group discussion. In this way, he separates expert communication from the exercise of the experimental method and from its characteristic forms of organization. Like Dewey, Kilpatrick is concerned with political affairs, in particular with the role of education in economic planning. Writing in the midst of the Great Depression, he believes that the people, and their leadership, are in a state of confusion and that group discussion can provide "a way out" (1932, p. 33). For Kilpatrick, as for Dewey, the experience of the individual learner is the basis of education. Broadly, all thoughtful experience, "all life thoughtfully lived," is education (1932, pp. 44–45). Moreover, group experience is also education (1932, p. 45). For Kilpatrick, however, group experience is not governed by the experimental method but by a process of group sharing and group discussion. This process, like the experimental method, is a process of both inquiry and communication. It is a "shared search" for a solution to a common problem or concern and a shared discussion that issues in a "better plan . . . than the best man acting alone could have produced" (1932, pp. 33–34). As such, it belongs among the popular modes of public discussion that Dewey rejects in favor of the experimental method.

Kilpatrick includes experts among the participants in the process of group discussion. However, he regards expertise as specialized knowledge of any kind and regards expert knowledge, and expert communication, as only one of several dimensions of group discussion. In the context of group discussion, *expertise* is any specialized knowledge of any person in the group, and it differs from topic to topic just as it does from person to person (1932, pp. 35–36). Moreover, *expert knowledge* is only one dimension of group discussion, which requires leadership of several kinds, including interest and criticism, statesmanship, and expert knowledge (1932, pp. 34–35). Interest is possible for all members of a group, criticism for most, statesmanship and expert knowledge for the few (1932, pp. 35–36). Nonetheless, for Kilpatrick, expert knowledge differs for different topics and persons and, as a part of the process of group discussion, is mutually educative and democratic (1932, pp. 35–36). For this reason, expert communication is always a part of the process of group discussion and so is always communication *with* rather than *to* other participants in the group. It is not associated with either the experimental method or its characteristic forms of organization.

CARL R. ROGERS ON LARGE-GROUP COMMUNICATION

Rogers follows the tradition of progressive education established by Dewey and Kilpatrick but adds a novel perspective when he explains the attitudes that facilitate communication and introduces these attitudes into the professional education of psychologists and other experts. In his statement of his educational philosophy, he reiterates Dewey's and Kilpatrick's emphasis on the experience of the individual learner and explains how to facilitate experiential learning. In his later writings, he describes the process of learning in large groups in terms similar to Kilpatrick's. But he rejects the view of expertise as specialized knowledge of any kind in favor of a view of *expertise* and of *expert communication* based upon his three characteristic attitudes toward all communication.

Rogers developed his attitudes toward communication in the context of therapist–client relationships and only later brought these attitudes to bear upon the role of the expert in the process of learning in large groups (Zappen, 1980, pp. 102–104). For Rogers, as for Dewey and Kilpatrick, the experience of the individual learner, rather than the experience or knowledge of the teacher, is the basis of education. Experiential learning, in general, is learner-directed rather than teacher-directed. It is personal and pervasive in the learner, self-initiated by the learner, and necessarily evaluated by the learner on the basis of its meaning to the learner (Rogers, 1969, p. 5). Teaching construed in its traditional sense as instructing or imparting knowledge is irrelevant in the context of experiential learning (1969, pp.

103–104, 200). Insofar as it occurs at all, teaching is providing both a climate and resources suitable for experiential learning (1969, pp. 200–201). The attitudes that facilitate experiential learning are Rogers' three characteristic attitudes toward all communication: "realness or genuineness" of the teacher and "prizing, acceptance, trust" and "empathic understanding" of the learner by the teacher (1969, pp. 106–112).

In his later writings, Rogers introduces these attitudes into the process of learning in large groups. For Rogers, as for Kilpatrick, the large-group process is a process of both inquiry and communication. As a process of inquiry, it operates at many levels, as individuals discover new ways of meeting personal needs and develop new understanding and respect for other persons in the group, and as the group as a whole reaches decisions that encompass the views and feelings of every participant in the group (Rogers, 1980, pp. 189–197). Often, it produces outcomes that could not have been predicted at the outset of the process (1980, p. 325). As a process of communication, it is a process of "personal sharing," "honest feedback," and "open confrontation" that belies participants' desire for privacy in their personal lives and confirms their desire to form larger communities (1980, pp. 197–199). And, as such, it depends upon the same facilitative attitudes that Rogers brings to therapist–client and teacher–learner relationships: genuineness, acceptance, and empathy (1980, pp. 114–117, 269–273).

Despite these affinities with the educational philosophy of Dewey and, especially, Kilpatrick, Rogers rejects their view of *expertise* as specialized knowledge in favor of a novel, even radical, view of *expertise* and of *expert communication*. In his observations on the professional education of psychologists, he rejects traditional modes of teaching and certification in psychology and proposes in their place a system of education based upon his concept of experiential learning and a system of certification based upon a kind of "Consumer Protective Service" (Rogers, 1969, pp. 188–202; 1980, pp. 243–248). In such a system, expertise does not derive from any specialized knowledge or mode of certification but upon competence as measured by the effectiveness or quality of work of the therapist or other expert (1980, pp. 243–248). In the context of learning in large groups, expertise is manifested in the exercise of the three attitudes that facilitate all communication, and in this sense it reflects an increasing trend toward participation, as people "demand to take part in choices that affect their lives" and refuse to be told what to do (1980, pp. 323–327, 329–334). Given this meaning of expertise, the phrase *expert communication* is not so much a paradox as a tautology, *expertise* being synonymous with *communication,* in Rogers' sense of both terms.

Rogers frequently uses the terms *science* and *technology* in opposition to his own concept of psychology (1980, pp. 55–59, 139–140, 241, 350). He suggests, for example, that "scientific technology" could be used for military and industrial conquest and that psychological technology could be used to control human behavior (1980, pp. 58–59). Nonetheless, citing Michael Polanyi and others, he asserts that a "human science" is also possible (1980, pp. 236–240, 241–242, 345, 350). The following examples illustrate this possibility in several disciplines within the sciences and engineering that bear upon environmental problems.

EXPERT COMMUNICATION IN ENVIRONMENTAL SCIENCE AND ENGINEERING

Some examples of expert communication and decision making in environmental science and engineering suggest how Rogers' view of expert communication might apply in forums of large-group discussion outside the traditional arena of organizations or, in some instances, between organizations, especially conflicting or competing organizations.[3] The first two examples are *classics* described in published accounts; the last is from my own experience. The first example describes what was at the time a nontraditional forum of large-group discussion and illustrates the possibility of a novel outcome to this discussion. This example is the Snoqualmie dam dispute, which occurred in the State of Washington in the 1960s and 1970s (Cormick & McCarthy, 1974; Cormick & Patton, 1980, pp. 85–90). The dispute arose in 1959 when the Snoqualmie River flooded and the U.S. Army Corps of Engineers proposed to construct a flood-control dam on the Middle Fork of the river. Farmers and townspeople supported the proposal, but environmentalists and citizen groups opposed it on grounds that the dam would open the flood plain to urban sprawl and divert a free-flowing river. The parties on both sides had sufficient legal and political support to hold the project in abeyance until 1974, when the Governor brought in a team of mediators to help to resolve the dispute. Together, the parties redefined the issue as a question that encompassed all of their views: How do we provide flood control, protect the economic viability of the farmers and the town, and establish land-use plans and controls that will preserve the river valley? The project engineer assisted in the process by researching questions, meeting with participants, and in general establishing credibility. The resolution to the dispute, signed by all the parties in the same year, was a complex proposal that included a stipulation that the dam be built on the North Fork rather than the Middle Fork of the river and other stipulations that, as a package, addressed all of the parties' concerns. This resolution was a novel outcome that could not have been achieved had not the views of all of the parties been taken into account.

The second example describes another nontraditional forum of large-group discussion and illustrates both the possibility of novel outcomes and some of the attitudes that facilitate such a discussion. This example is the National Coal Policy Project, which in 1976 brought together 70 prominent industrialists and environmentalists in an effort to develop coal-related energy policies on a wide range of long-standing issues of interest to participants on both sides (Curran, 1978; *Where we agree,* n.d.). Most of the participants were scientific or technical experts on environmental issues (Curran, 1978, pp. 13–14, 20–21). Working in separate task forces, they produced a policy statement on technical and economic issues ranging from mining, transportation, and air pollution to fuel utilization and conservation, energy pricing, and emission charges (*Where we agree,* n.d.). This statement includes numerous innovative policy initiatives such as an "emission charge and rebate plan" that would encourage the development of new pollution abatement technology by penalizing power plants emitting more than an average level of pollutants in relation to production and rewarding those emitting less (*Where we agree,* n.d., p. 11). These initiatives are novel outcomes that reflect the views of participants on both sides.

The guidelines that governed participants' behavior during the project were based upon a principle called *the rule of reason,* which in its original formulation as a principle of corporate litigation called for complete consistency between public statements and corporate discussions and actions (Wessel, 1976, p. 21). This rule, as described by one of the participants, required that all data be shared, that there be no half-truths, that "both sides . . . lay all their cards on the table" (Curran, 1978, p. 13). In practice, it required that both sides "seek an understanding of each other's point of view," which proved to be "the most difficult and the most important part of the whole effort," but which produced "the feeling that the other side was listening and did in fact understand what we were saying" (1978, pp. 13–14). This rule, in principle and in practice, is simply a demand for honesty or genuineness and empathic understanding, two of Rogers' three facilitative attitudes.

The last example introduces the possibility of exercising Rogers' facilitative attitudes in written technical communication between conflicting organizations. This example is the debate between the Environmental Protection Agency and the automotive industry on the issue of gasoline marketing operations (Chrysler, 1984; Environmental Protection Agency [EPA], 1984).[4] The EPA contends that gasoline marketing operations contribute to ambient ozone concentrations and produce known carcinogens such as benzene (EPA, 1984, p. 1–1). It favors vehicle onboard control systems as the best means of controlling emissions (1984, pp. 1–6 to 1–7). The automotive industry counters that no human health risk from gasoline marketing operations has yet been demonstrated, and that onboard control systems would be prohibitively complex and costly (Chrysler, 1984, pp. 1–2). It favors service station systems as the best means of controlling emissions, if such systems should prove to be necessary (1984, p. 2). The automotive industry's response to the EPA claims that the EPA report lacks sufficient data to "accurately" assess the need for controls and "unreasonably" portrays onboard control systems as the best means of control (1984, p. 1). Such a response is certain to generate defensiveness, at best. A response reflecting a more facilitative attitude would at least convey understanding of the values and intentions on the other side, even though it might thoroughly disagree with its conclusions. Such a response goes beyond conventional treatments of audience analysis in scientific and technical communication, for it opens the possibility of understanding not only another person's background or level of education, but that person's or group's values and intentions, and so also opens the possibility of mutual understanding and novel outcomes. However, such a response may only be possible outside the traditional arena of organizational decision making and the traditional types of scientific and technical communication.

As these three examples suggest, Rogers' facilitative attitudes toward communication have a place in scientific and technical as well as other kinds of expert communication, not necessarily in place of, but as a complement to, specialized knowledge. Specifically, these attitudes suggest a role for scientists and engineers as providers of information and participants in group discussion and problem solving in situations, increasingly frequent, in which people disagree about the appropriateness of various technologies, or even the appropriateness of any technology, as a response to complex environmental or social problems. These attitudes may apply in a variety of forums of large-group discussion outside the traditional arena of organizations and may also apply to written technical communication, especially communication between conflicting or competing organizations.

TOWARD A BROADER DEFINITION OF SCIENTIFIC AND TECHNICAL COMMUNICATION

Rogers' views of expert communication suggest the possibility of a broader definition of scientific and technical communication that includes what might be called personal or cultural communication, communication between and among people—designers and users, for example—quite apart from their organizational roles. For at least a decade, the theoretical literature has identified scientific and technical communication with disciplinary and with organizational communities, respectively (Dobrin, 1983, pp. 242–246; Lipson, 1988, pp. 8–10; Miller, 1979, pp. 616–617; Samuels, 1987, p. 64). This literature has sought to delineate the characteristics of particular *discourse communities,* which in practice are organizational communities such as an engineering consulting firm writing for a government agency or a science and engineering R&D division of a large corporation (Miller & Selzer, 1985; Paradis, Dobrin, & Miller, 1985). Despite the prominent place that scientific and technical communication holds in organizations, some recent trends suggest that personal or cultural communication about science and technology may become more important and more frequent. For example, a feminist critique of science calls for a kind of science that is less authoritarian and more democratic, participatory, and humanitarian than traditional science (Harding, 1986, pp. 219–222). And a philosopher of technology points out that technological innovation often occurs outside bureaucratic organizations, and that appropriate technology is more likely to develop through "dialogue" and "interaction" between designers and users within and, especially, across cultural boundaries (Pacey, 1983, pp. 137–159). This same philosopher of technology calls for a better understanding of user attitudes to counteract the "narrowly specialist outlook" of the designer, in effect, a paradigm shift from a bureaucratic to a cultural view of technological innovation, achieved in large measure through fundamental changes in the education of experts (1983, pp. 154, 160–179).

Rogers' views on expert communication are entirely compatible with these trends. Furthermore, Rogers' views—in particular his three facilitative attitudes toward communication—provide a concrete and practical approach to the changes in expert communication that these trends project and demand. Finally, these views suggest the possibility of a broader definition of scientific and technical communication that includes personal or cultural as well as organizational communication —communication that is certainly as complex and as important as the types of organizational communication that typically appear in the textbooks.

NOTES

1. In these textbooks, Dewey's experimental method appears as science and engineering laboratory, research, or test reports (Anderson, 1987, pp. 640–670; Mathes & Stevenson, 1976, pp. 102–107; Olsen & Huckin, 1983, pp. 275–285; Robinson, 1985, pp. 96–98; Roundy, 1985, p. 288; Samuels, 1989, pp. 241–244). In some variations, also attributed to Dewey (Bradley & Baird, 1983, p. 235), it includes problem, criteria or specifications, solution, and/or alternative solutions and so resembles the method of engineering design or feasibility reports (Anderson, 1987, pp. 671–689; Mathes & Stevenson, 1976, pp. 98–102; Olsen & Huckin, 1983, pp. 59–85; Robinson, 1985, pp. 95–96; Roundy, 1985, pp. 287–288; Samuels, 1989, pp. 224–228).
2. The identification of scientific and technical communication with organizations appears, for example, in Anderson, 1987, pp. 2–11; Mathes & Stevenson, 1976, pp. 3–8; Olsen & Huckin, 1983, pp. 3–13; Roundy, 1985, pp. 11–26; Samuels, 1989, p. 6.
3. A recent study suggests how Kenneth Burke's dialectic might be useful in generating productive conflict in collaborative groups, especially within organizations (Karis, 1989, pp. 120–124). In the following examples, I describe situations in which conflict has already led to hostility, defensiveness, and stalemate between groups or organizations, situations in which Rogers' three facilitative attitudes are particularly applicable.
4. I became aware of this issue while teaching at the Engineering Division, Chrysler Corporation, Highland Park, Michigan. I am grateful to officials at Chrysler and the EPA for providing me with statements of their positions.

REFERENCES

Anderson, P. V. (1987). *Technical writing: A reader-centered approach.* San Diego, CA: Harcourt Brace Jovanovich.

Bradley, P. H., & Baird, J. E., Jr. (1983). *Communication for business and the professions* (2nd ed.). Dubuque, IA: Brown.

Chrysler Corporation. (1984, November). *Comments on EPA report 450/3-84-012a "Evaluation of air pollution regulatory strategy for gasoline marketing industry."* (Available from Chrysler Corporation, P.O. Box 1118, Detroit, MI 48288.)

Cormick, G. W., & McCarthy, J. (1974, December). *Environmental mediation: A first dispute: Flood control, recreation and development in the Snoqualmie River Valley.* (Available from Office of Environmental Mediation, Institute for Environmental Studies, University of Washington, Seattle, WA 98195.)

Cormick, G. W., & Patton, L. K. (1980). Environmental mediation: Defining the process through experience. In L. M. Lake (Ed.), *Environmental mediation: The search for consensus* (pp. 76–97). Boulder, CO: Westview Press.

Curran, J. C. (Ed.). (1978). *The National Coal Policy Project: A report of a seminar at the Colorado School of Mines.* Washington, DC: Georgetown University, Center for Strategic and International Studies.

Dewey, J. (1980). *Democracy and education.* In J. A. Boydston (Ed.), *The middle works, 1899–1924* (Vol. 9: 1916, pp. 1–370). Carbondale, IL: Southern Illinois University Press.

Dewey, J. (1984). *The public and its problems.* In J. A. Boydston (Ed.), *The later works, 1925–1953* (Vol. 2: 1925–1927, pp. 235–372). Carbondale, IL: Southern Illinois University Press. (Original work published 1927.)

Dewey, J. (1986). *How we think: A restatement of the relation of reflective thinking to the educative process.* In J. A. Boydston (Ed.), *The later works, 1925–1953* (Vol. 8: 1933, pp. 105–352). Carbondale, IL: Southern Illinois University Press.

Dewey, J. (1987). *Liberalism and social action.* In J. A. Boydston (Ed.), *The later works, 1925–1953* (Vol. 11: 1935–1937, pp. 1–65). Carbondale, IL: Southern Illinois University Press. (Original work published 1935.)

Dobrin, D. N. (1983). What's technical about technical writing? In P. V. Anderson, R. J. Brockmann, & C. R. Miller (Eds.), *New essays in technical and scientific communication: Research, theory, practice* (pp. 227–250). Farmingdale, NY: Baywood.

Ehninger, D., Monroe, A. H., & Gronbeck, B. E. (1978). *Principles and types of speech communication* (8th ed.). Glenview, IL: Scott, Foresman.

Environmental Protection Agency, Office of Air and Radiation. (1984). *Evaluation of air pollution regulatory strategies for gasoline marketing industry* (Report No. EPA-450/3-84-012a). Washington, DC: Author.

Gutek, G. L. (1970). *An historical introduction to American education.* New York: Crowell.

Harding, S. (1986). *The science question in feminism.* Ithaca, NY: Cornell University Press.

Karis, B. (1989). Conflict in collaboration: A Burkean perspective. *Rhetoric Review, 8,* 113–126.

Kilpatrick, W. H. (1932). *Education and the social crisis: A proposed program.* New York: Liveright.

Kilpatrick, W. H. (1933). Professional education from the social point of view. In W. H. Kilpatrick (Ed.), *The educational frontier* (pp. 257–286). New York: Appleton-Century.

Kirschenbaum, H. (1979). *On becoming Carl Rogers.* New York: Dell.

Lipson, C. (1988). A social view of technical writing. *Iowa State Journal of Business and Technical Communication, 2,* 7–20.

Mathes, J. C., & Stevenson, D. W. (1976). *Designing technical reports: Writing for audiences in organizations.* Indianapolis, IN: Bobbs-Merrill.

Miller, C. R. (1979). A humanistic rationale for technical writing. *College English, 40,* 610–617.

Miller, C. R., & Selzer, J. (1985). Special topics of argument in engineering reports. In L. Odell & D. Goswami (Eds.), *Writing in nonacademic settings* (pp. 309–341). New York: Guilford Press.

Olsen, L. A., & Huckin, T. N. (1983). *Principles of communication for science and technology.* New York: McGraw-Hill.

Pacey, A. (1983). *The culture of technology.* Cambridge, MA: MIT Press.

Paradis, J., Dobrin, D., & Miller, R. (1985). Writing at Exxon ITD: Notes on the writing environment of an R&D organization. In L. Odell & D. Goswami (Eds.), *Writing in nonacademic settings* (pp. 281–307). New York: Guilford Press.

Robinson, P. A. (1985). *Fundamentals of technical writing.* Boston, MA: Houghton Mifflin.

Rogers, C. R. (1969). *Freedom to learn: A view of what education might become.* Columbus, OH: Merrill.

Rogers, C. R. (1980). *A way of being.* Boston, MA: Houghton Mifflin.

Roundy, N., with Mair, D. (1985). *Strategies for technical communication.* Boston, MA: Little, Brown.

Samuels, M. S. (1987). Is technical communication "literature"? Current writing scholarship and Vico's cycles of knowledge. *Iowa State Journal of Business and Technical Communication, 1,* 48–67.

Samuels, M. S. (1989). *The technical writing process.* New York: Oxford University Press.

Simons, H. W. (1986). *Persuasion: Understanding, practice, and analysis* (2nd ed.). New York: Random House.

Wessel, M. R. (1976). *The rule of reason: A new approach to corporate litigation.* Reading, MA: Addison-Wesley.

Where we agree: Report of the National Coal Policy Project: Summary and synthesis. (n.d.). Washington, DC: Georgetown University, Center for Strategic and International Studies.

Zappen, J. P. (1980). Carl R. Rogers and political rhetoric. *PRE/TEXT: An Inter-Disciplinary Journal of Rhetoric, 1,* 95–113.

CHAPTER 11
Community Language Learning: Charles Curran's Application of Rogerian Counseling

Wayne Pounds

Collaborative learning, like composition studies in general, can profit from learning its history. Greg Myers (1986) has recently reminded us how far back that history goes in the United States, citing Sterling Andrus Leonard, whose *English Composition as a Social Problem,* a "Dewey inspired textbook" advocating small-group work, appeared in 1917 (p. 154).[1] More recently the work of Kenneth Bruffee (1973, 1984, 1985, 1986b) has moved collaborative learning into the mainstream of English studies, but this movement was preceded by a considerable body of work in foreign language pedagogy, much of it the inspiration and work of a student of Carl Rogers, the late Father Charles Curran. I recently had the discouraging experience of observing at a regional meeting of language teachers that teachers of a major Asian language were re-inventing group learning with no reference to the bodies of existing work in either mainstream English studies or English as a Foreign Language. To avoid similar specialization blindness on the part of English composition teachers, I would like to see wider awareness of Curran's group-learning methods and their application in foreign language and EFL pedagogy.

In what follows I first provide a concrete image of Curran's work by describing its most popular form, *community language learning,* and then contrast it with Bruffee's *collaborative learning*. To suggest the possibilities of Curran's work, I then describe its applications in two distinct EFL settings, one in which the focus of the class is language, the other in which the focus is literary. In the course of this description I emphasize the use of reflection, which I see as Curran's greatest contribution to group pedagogy.

The directly pedagogical phase of Curran's work appeared in the 1970s and was based on research in counseling psychology that goes back to the mid-1940s, when Curran was a graduate student at Ohio State University, where he studied under Rogers and absorbed the latter's notion that therapeutic counseling was a learning process (La Forge, 1975, pp. 1–7, 61; Curran, 1978, pp. xi-xii). Curran's pedagogy, which he called *counseling learning,* was an application of Rogerian counseling to educational contexts.[2] Curran believed that, in the classroom, the "learners" (as he liked to call students, thereby avoiding the usual vertical distance associated with the terms "teacher" and "students") could be blocked by affective factors which a therapeutic turn in pedagogy could relieve, thereby facilitating the learning process. Curran liked to say that "learning is persons," by which he meant that

> it is not merely from books or in response to tests or the threat of failing grades that a person really learns. Rather it is the warm, deep sense of belonging and sharing with another person—the one who knows—and with others engaged with him in the learning enterprise that truly facilitates learning and invests it in with profound personal meaning. (1972, p. 23)

The teacher, Curran believed and in his own teaching effectively demonstrated, can facilitate learning by acting as a counselor to the group. The basic principle is that the learning about oneself that frees the client in therapeutic counseling is as valid and necessary a form of learning as the kind traditionally associated with the classroom.

My discussion so far has been abstract and hard to visualize in classroom practice. To be more concrete, I would like to take up Curran's application of his pedagogy to foreign language teaching, a subject in which he became interested for research purposes. He believed that his pedagogy was readily adaptable to learning a variety of subjects and that foreign language learning was the area in which it was easiest to measure the students' progress (1976, p. 20; 1972, p. 145). Perhaps he had also observed it to be an area in which emotional binds were particularly crippling to the students' efforts. As the research in language learning developed, it became a full-fledged language-teaching method called Community Language Learning (CLL).

For the observer of a CLL class, what was immediately striking was the physical format: a group of students sitting in a circle around a tape recorder, and the teacher, and perhaps a native speaker of the target language, standing outside the circle. (This is not by any means the only format used in CLL exercises, but its striking form and relative popularity came to make it seem representative.) The student speaks—either in his or her own language, if it is an elementary group, or, with an advanced group, in the target language. The teacher gives him or her the same locution again in the target language,—either as a translation, or as an improvement, or as a confirmation. The student records the corrected form on the tape recorder, and then the next student speaks. A conversation is carried on in this way, with the students recording their own voices saying what they choose to say in the target language. The tape of the recorded conversation is then used for study and practice in a variety of ways, listening, speaking, and writing, much as would take place in a conventional class.[3] The advantage of the CLL tape over a textbook is that it is student generated, containing the students' language and reflecting their lives and interests. (This technique of using "student-invested" materials has since been successfully adopted by IBM researchers, who use it to teach reading with the aid of voice-recognition computer systems. Johnny speaks, the words appear on the screen, and he reads what he just said. Recently it has also been used in literacy work: students learned to write by transcribing their own voices from a tape, Holtzman, 1984, p. 235.) In the last stage of the CLL class, after the taped conversation is digested, the teacher (whom Curran labeled the *knower*) calls for a reflection session in which students evaluate their individual and group performances while the teacher acts as group counselor.

Such is CLL as it appears to the observer, but what is going on in this format is more complex than a casual observer may appreciate. The work of Father Paul La Forge is helpful in explicating this scene, for of all scholars working with CLL, La Forge (a former student of Curran's) has made the greatest contribution. La Forge defines CLL as "a supportive language learning contract which consists of group experience and reflection" (1983, p. 27). By *supportive* he means nonthreatening. Curran sees learning occurring within the learner's *space,* the space necessary if one person is to learn from another (1972, p. 91). In traditional language classes, the action of the teacher fills the learner space completely. The learning occurs on a single interpersonal dimension between the teacher and the whole class, and the evaluation is handled by the teacher in the form of tests and exams. This kind of education is called *teacher-centered.* By contrast, the CLL teacher builds communication bridges across the student space on three interpersonal dimensions: the first is between the teacher and the whole group, as in traditional methods, except that, in CLL, this bridge does not monopolize the space. The second dimension is between the teacher and each individual, a bridge that is hard to build in large classes, and here La Forge's innovations can be particularly helpful. The third dimension is the space among the students themselves, a space from which the teacher silently withdraws. The *support* referred to in the definition is the support of individual students for each other in the small groups, and the support of the teacher who reinforces and encourages the small group. La Forge is inclined to emphasize the space and silence, because the students he is working with are Japanese, and *silence* has cultural meanings in Japan that it does not possess in the West.

The next term in La Forge's definition of CLL is *contract learning* (1983, pp. 27–29). In developing his pedagogy, Curran purposely adopted the term *community* as opposed to *group* learning with this distinction in mind: a group is composed of people engaged in a common task; a community is formed around a contract, an agreement by the members to engage in a common task for an agreed-upon purpose. The purpose—language learning in the case of CLL—determines the roles and interactions.

The term *language learning* here seems self-explanatory. The one needed amplification is that Curran's concept of learning is a developmental one (he cites Piaget among others),[4] and CLL pedagogy follows a model which posits learning as developing through five stages from infancy, or total dependence on the teacher, to adulthood and independence (1976, pp. 28–30).

Group reflection is Curran's term for what nowadays is unhappily called *feedback*—unhappily because feedback implies a mechanical model for the processes of introspection and evaluation, whereas the mirror that is the etymological source of *reflection* retains an element of mystery, the mystery of light bending back on itself, and is one of the oldest metaphors our language has for this uniquely human act. Reflection in CLL has two phases: first a minute of silence during which the students review the learning experience to discover its personal significance—a meaning usually given in such plain terms as *good, bad, useful, or boring,* etc.; second, a period of group sharing by way of personal reports. In this second phrase the teacher acts as a Rogerian counselor to the group, listening with "unconditional positive regard" (1972, p. 52) and restating in nonconflictual language the anxieties or other difficulties expressed. The counselor may then resume the role of teacher and direct the group to solutions[5]—exercises or strategies designed to ameliorate the difficulties expressed.

To summarize the description of CLL that emerges from La Forge's definition: its essential rhythm is experience and reflection, experience and reflection, where *experience* means the learning task and *reflection* is the process by which the students make the learning their own.

With this brief sketch of one phase of Curran's work in mind, it should now be possible to distinguish between Bruffee's work with collaborative learning and Curran's with counseling learning. Bruffee's work is more socially oriented—in origins and in theory, at least, if not in practice—than Curran's. Although Curran's work necessarily sees the individual as part of the group, the groups remain artificial, bound to the academic setting, and it might even to be said solipsistic in that they exist only for the purpose of providing membership to the individuals. (This is a frequent weakness of student-centered approaches, including Bruffee's, that too often the communities they create are artificial and confined to the classroom, Harold, 1972, p. 201.) The roots of Bruffee's collaborative learning are in research, such as the 1964 Abercrombie study, *Anatomy of Judgment,* which concluded that medical diagnosis was better learned in small groups; in radical politics, typified in efforts during the Vietnam War era to democratize education and to eliminate destructive authoritarian forms; and in the pressing educational needs of the 1970s, when many students had difficulty adapting to the conventions of the traditional college classroom. As Bruffee writes, what was needed was education "that was not an extension of but an alternative to traditional classroom teaching" (1984, p. 637). Curran's roots, on the other hand, are in the Catholic Church and Rogerian counseling. Curran believed that his faith emphasized "the whole person," an emphasis which is the leitmotif of his work and one that is, of course, congruent with Rogerian counseling.

The personalism of Curran's work, like that of Rogers', should give the socially concerned language teacher pause.[6] Client-centered therapy is concerned with adjusting the alienated citizen to his or her alienation rather than encouraging inquiry into the social determinants of alienation (Jacoby, 1975, pp. 48–49). It is apolitical and thus essentially conservative. Bruffee's work is open to the same charge, though some of his theoretical statements show an awareness of the problem. He has called teaching, for example, "broadly speaking, a political act" (1986a, p. 77) and stated unequivocally that "all of us are committed professionally to change by virtue of our commitment to teaching" (1987, p. 714). Curran too was committed to change, but change for him was personal change in terms of his whole-person model, one which he found congruent with his Catholic faith.

Despite my reservations about the political implications of Curran's work, however, I believe that it is very much worth knowing about, for it provides solutions to practical problems with which collaborative learning is still grappling, particularly the problem of developing the group's self-critical consciousness. Given the ghetto walls of academic specialization, it is perhaps no surprise that neither teachers who work with collaborative learning nor Rogerian rhetoricians seem to know anything about counseling learning (judging at least from the total absence of reference to it),[7] but this situation is regrettable. A well-rounded course for the teacher interested in group work should include all of the main streams: the practical sources in Curran, the Rogerians, and Bruffee, and the theoretical sources in John Dewey and Richard Rorty (not forgetting their critics).[8]

To return to applications of Curran's ideas, I will divide them into two branches and look first at applications to the teaching of language, then to the teaching of literature in a foreign language setting. In both these areas the most interesting work has been done in Japan,[9] exploring cross-cultural complications which are of concern to increasing numbers of educators in the United States, as our own population continues to diversify with the approach of what pundits and futurologists are calling "the Pacific century."

La Forge's work in applying Curran's thinking to foreign language pedagogy is of great interest, particularly for the way he draws on Japanese cultural traditions to advance classroom studies of English.[10] La Forge calls the traditions he uses *social learning mechanisms,* of which he singles out four: silence, age hierarchy, the club camp, and group reflection. Of these *silence* is perhaps the most unexpected, and the only one I will treat in much detail. It is the one which presents the most immediate challenge to the language teacher, an obstacle which La Forge resolves through learning interactions.

1. Silence. Japanese attitudes toward silence are of course an integral part of Japanese culture, but in the classroom they often present an affective bind which hinders progress in acquiring language skills. The attitudes include the following.

A. The aesthetics of silence. This attitude makes a virtue of reticence and a vulgarity of speaking.
B. Separation and belonging. Japanese attitudes toward language are connected with problems of separation from and belonging to the peer group. Japanese groups look for consensus before deciding on a course of action; it is difficult for them to act with part of the group disagreeing.

C. Lack of confidence in language. "Japanese place comparatively light emphasis on overt linguistic expression" (La Forge, 1983, p. 79). The foreign teacher who expects to base his or her class on a lively clash of ideas in discussion is in for a pratfall.
D. Concept of leadership. Whereas a leader in the West is an articulate person who talks even when no one is listening, the leader in Japanese society is often silent. A Japanese leader has very little to say and typically says it with complete lack of eloquence.

How does La Forge deal with these attitudes toward silence? First, he brings silence center stage in the classroom and explores its meaning. Suppose the class has a "contract" for 10 minutes of free conversation in English, and during the 10 minutes nothing is said. La Forge convenes a reflection session in which the students report on their experience of the ten minutes. A common statement would be, "I was silent because I was afraid to speak." The teacher can clarify the motivation here: on the one hand, the student wants the chance to converse in English, for this is the goal of the group; on the other hand, when the chance is given, anxiety prevents conversation. In this way the students become aware of the harmful effects of anxiety and the teacher can suggest remedies. (Sharing the anxiety lessens it, and this is part of the group dynamic in the reflection session.) Another remedy for the teacher would be to appeal to the students for mutual self-help and let them see how the silence may be broken with a simple question to anyone in the group. Students are surprised to find that it is not necessary to say something profound and difficult in a foreign language (1977, pp. 379–380).

Silence has a positive and important meaning in the reflection session. Typically the first minute or two of the allotted time would be taken for silent self-examination and evaluation of the group by all the members. Then the members would report the result of their introspection. La Forge believes that the silence of the first part of the session is important for the process of language learning. Far from being an anxious period at the outset of a new exercise, or a vacuous period after an exercise, the silence of the reflection period is intensively active. In the process of their self- and group-evaluation, the students come to terms with the learning experience and make it their own. Reflection is an exercise which justifies self-expression for the students and helps them handle their anxiety when speaking English in the presence of the teacher.

Silence has a positive meaning in other areas as well. First, an experience of anxious silence is a painful but apparently necessary step for Japanese students exploring English-speaking relationships.

Second, the teacher's silent withdrawal during small-group activities has a positive effect, for it reduces anxiety and allows English-speaking identities to be formed through the group activities. Third, a different kind of silence on the teacher's part is valuable in what La Forge calls *face-to-face practice,* where the class is divided into pairs for short-English conversations and each member, including the teacher, receives a new partner every few minutes. This strategy renders the teacher silent in relation to the group but active with each individual for a limited period of time, and it allows the students to establish relations with the teacher on an individual basis. The time limit, here as elsewhere, is an essential part of the students' security, for even a highly anxious experience can be tolerated if it is known that it will last only a given short time. The face-to-face exercise is the more effective with Japanese students because it is modeled on a familiar tradition, the practice routines of the martial arts like judo and kendo.

To summarize, La Forge's treatment of culturally determined silence shows the rhythm of the CLL class, the movement back and forth from activity to reflection. The time limits keep the demands on the students from becoming overwhelming, and the periodic reflection sessions encourage them to become responsible for their own learning as they evaluate it, hear others' evaluations, and contribute their own notions as to what should be done to promote learning. In each of these activities a place is found for silence—generally the silence of the teacher, except as the students make demands for additional teacher input; but also silence on the part of the students as they introspect or listen to their peers.

The three remaining items on the list of social learning traditions—age hierarchy, social clubs, and reflection—are less problematic and can be treated together.

2. Age hierarchy. Japan is commonly referred to as a vertical society, and chief among its vertical structures is age. Other factors being equal, age always stands above youth, and very frequently, when other factors are not equal, age is still given precedent. The relationship between teacher and student exemplifies the vertical structuring; typically, the age difference is at least a generation, and thus the vertical gap or respect distance is very large. The Japanese word for teacher, *sensei,* means literally *elder* or *earlier born.* Vertical distance may be very small—1 year, for example, between two classes of students—but the difference is still formally recognized and expressed in special terms of address. Within the schools, as throughout the society, where groups are formed for study purposes, the older members pass on their knowledge to the younger ones or organize their study activities (La Forge, 1983, pp. 106–107).

*3. **Club camp-in.*** The age hierarchy also functions in the club life, the extracurricular activities of the school. Recreational activities are informal ways of learning carried on in focused groups usually called (borrowing the English word) *clubs,* including sports, music, traditional arts, special interests, and English speaking. A tradition of most Japanese clubs is the annual or semiannual *gasshuku,* a term which I am translating as *club camp.* The *gasshuku,* however, is in no sense as frivolous an affair as the usual camp in the U.S.; rather it is undertaken as a serious social learning experience structured by a tacit but firm contract, usually as a group response to some upcoming ordeal such as a competition. A comparable institution in the U.S. might be spring training for professional baseball clubs. There is the same round-the-clock dedication to the pursuit of group goals, with a concentration aimed at securing the success of the team effort in the coming season (La Forge, 1983, pp. 107–108). Japanese students studying English during the summer at a university campus represent something like a traveling *gasshuku.* Typically, the students work very hard during the course of their studies, and the usual tourist relaxations are reserved until the course is over.

*4. **Reflection.*** The cultural institution of reflection, made possible by the kind of meaningful silence discussed above, is also part of any Japanese group. In the case of the *gasshuku,* silence and reflection are integral to the activities. Free periods are not times of meaningless play or nonsense. Intellectual or religious pursuits are carried on in a silence which is considered a vital preparation of the mind for the group ordeal. And all Japanese groups, from professional baseball clubs to mandolin societies, practice reflection (Japanese *hansei*) either on a regular basis or as a response to competition or crisis. During a *gasshuku,* typically each evening a period of reflection is held for about an hour, and each activity of the day is reviewed in terms of individual contributions and overall effectiveness (La Forge, 1983, pp. 108–109).

Given these traditional institutions of Japanese culture, it seems likely that La Forge must have reasoned as follows: the customs of age-hierarchy, the *gasshuku,* reflection, and silence are still functional in contemporary Japanese society, but apart from age hierarchy, they are not drawn upon in the classroom. Dominant modern methods of formal education are not based on customs operating in the indigenous society; rather, they are authoritarian cognitive forms which were imported from the West, primarily from Germany, around the turn of the century. Consequently, modern students are left with affective blocks or unresolved frustrations, especially in regard to the study of foreign languages, traditionally thought to be a most difficult challenge. What would happen, then, if we brought cultural forms back into education, coupled with an appropriate language learning methodology? Would it not be possible to provide a learning experience, intimately tied to the social setting, which would occur in groups rather than in isolation from, and in competition with, others?

As an informal experiment, this is precisely what La Forge did. He used a club, an English Speaking Society, composed of 25 boys from junior and senior high school, ages 14 to 17. He set up CLL groups for the normal English-learning activities of the club, and he used CLL to intensify the concentration of the *gasshuku*. He found that "language acquisition took place in a significantly different way from behavioristic teacher-centered learning" (1983, p. 113). Far from being a mere repetition of foreign-language patterns, significant learning took place through cultural traditions. These functioned to transform extrinsic motivation, studying English to make a good grade, into intrinsic motivation, studying English in order to belong to a group.

La Forge believes that the most significant finding of his experiment, which was conducted over a 2-year period, was the connection between silence and learning (1983, p. 114). Apart from the reflection sessions, in which silence functioned overtly, silence had an important role in study periods when it was enforced by the *gasshuku* discipline. A group might maintain silence for an hour working on English speeches, a silence all the more striking since the students were at ease, working and communicating kinesthetically through the rattling of papers, the scratch of writing, and the shifting of body positions—all of which movements conveyed the silent message among the group members that they were busy performing the group activity.

La Forge concludes, "The Japanese case with CLL demonstrates two important conclusions: first, given the right culture-learning mechanisms, the group process leads to social learning centered on values even in extracurricular groups; second, it demonstrates how language and culture interrelate in a specific learning environment" (1983, p. 115). La Forge's experiment not only shows us the pedagogical value of linguistic and cultural interaction, it suggests how existing cultural institutions can be utilized to structure and facilitate collaborative learning.

To turn now to a consideration of how Curran's work may be applied to teaching literature in a foreign language setting, I would like to make the discussion concrete by drawing on my own practice in a particular teaching situation, which I will briefly sketch.[11] Like many Western teachers of literature who go to Japan, I found myself assigned to lecture in English to students whose understanding of spoken

English was not adequate to follow natural speech, even in a somewhat simplified and highly enunciated form. The fourth-year students who made up my class had had 10 years of English study, but almost all of it taught by Japanese teachers using grammar-translation methods, and 1 or 2 years of audiolingual drill in "English conversation" which included 1 hour per week with a native speaker. It was not surprising then, nor a reflection on the students, that they could not follow a lecture in English. What does the teacher do in this kind of situation?

The solution I adopted was to act as the client and ask the class to "counsel" or understand me (Curran, 1972, p. 114). To see what this deceptively simple statement means requires a review of the fundamental concept of roles. In the counseling situation, the two basic roles are the counselor, the person who understands, and the client, the person who asks to be understood. The roles in counseling learning, however, because they are based on a developmental model, are not constant. In terms of Curran's five stages of growth from the complete dependence of the embryo to the independence of adulthood, in the first three stages (embryo, childhood, and early adolescence) the teacher is the counselor and the students are clients. In the fourth and fifth stages (late adolescence and adulthood) the roles are reversed as the students become counselors and the teacher becomes the client (Curran, 1972, pp. 130–135; 1976, pp. 52–54).

The late adolescent stage is characterized by role reversal, for as the students gain in ability they want more independence (Curran, 1972, pp. 133–139; 1976, pp. 3, 54). Use of the native language gradually decreases as the students become more competent in the target language. The beginning of stage four is accompanied by an adolescent crisis, a drive for complete independence from the teacher. If the students are not to stop at this stage, they must begin to understand the teacher's role and the help it can provide. (The alternative would be to terminate prematurely the learning relationship, risking fossilization of language skills at an intermediate stage.)

According to Curran, adolescent and adult learners, by virtue of their strong development of identity and self-consciousness, generally enter a counseling situation in at least a stage-three relationship with the teacher, placing them at the stage when a reversal of roles is appropriate (1972, p. 133). In the foreign-language classroom, this reversal is facilitated if students and teacher share a common language.[12] In an ESL context, the common language would be English; in an EFL context, it is more likely to be the native language of the students. As an adjunct to the target language, this shared common language can be used to create a situation in which adolescent or adult students can become counselors and the teacher can become the client. In this way the students progress beyond the third stage toward greater maturity and independence.

The teacher's first and fundamental task in this situation is to create an atmosphere of trust, and this I try to do by trusting the students, trusting them to understand what I am asking them to do, strange though it may seem to them. I begin by saying something like this: "I want us to have a special kind of class. I want you to understand me. And I want you to show me that you understand by telling me, in your own words, in Japanese, what I have said." Once the class understands and accepts this proposal, I would then ask for a group of three to five students to sit at the front and be counselors (Curran, 1972, p. 115). I pull the appropriate number of chairs out and place them together to suggest a separate and cohesive group, and I give them a time limit. "OK," I say, "we are going to do this for 15 minutes," and, because the time limit makes the students more secure, I write it on the board. Then I return to my original statement, repeat it, and wait for one of the counselors to tell me in Japanese what I said. With this first understanding response, I have a basis upon which to proceed.

I speak one sentence at a time, measured in length and speed to the students' ability to comprehend, and then I stop and wait for their response. At any point in this process, I let them take time to discuss together the meaning of what I have said. I expect confusion, silence, and misunderstanding—not "mistakes." There are no mistakes here, only misunderstandings, and since I overhear the student-counselors' deliberations, it is easy for me to spot the source of the trouble, which typically results from a new word, or a word whose phonological form was not recognized, or blurred word boundaries. If there is too much silence or too many misunderstandings, the fault is mine: the bites I am giving them are too big. "Somewhat as an adult eats food, the learner must have a chance to 'chew' each word or phrase" (Curran, 1972, p. 157). The sentence bite must be the right size for the students' capacity. It takes all the teacher's speaking skill to keep the utterances measured the right length and the diction at the right degree of difficulty.

The size of the group of student-counselors is important, usually 3 to 5. Whether the class is large or small, this small group of counselors sits at the front to represent the entire class. The members of this group are changed at fixed intervals announced in advance. Students should be told that the teacher-client is speaking to the student-counselors only, and that the others in the class are to listen or "overhear" (Curran, 1972, p. 130). This defines very simply the role of the other students—they are "overhearers"—and lets them know that they too have a part in what is happening. (And of course they hear both sides of the exchanges between the client and the counselors.) Even if the class has as few as five or six members, it is better for the class to be divided into two small groups. The small group symbolizes the basic contract by which time and the activity are structured, and the periodic change of members provides a rest from the strain of counseling. The agreement to sit at the front represents the agreement to understand the client-teacher, and the student-counselors in return receive the security of knowing that will be at the front only for the set time.

On this first day and as many class meetings as possible thereafter, the teacher must reserve the last 5 or 10 minutes of the class time for reflection. In reflection the roles change and the teacher becomes the affective counselor to the group (Curran, 1972, pp. 182, 190); the students become clients and report on and evaluate their experience. The systematic use of reflection is the heart of Curran's pedagogy, and his recognition of its centrality in group dynamics is perhaps his greatest contribution to collaborative learning. For the students, reflection is valuable as a moment of self-evaluation, both of what they have learned and what they have contributed to the group effort. It has values also as self-expression: they can express any negative attitudes or emotional binds and, in sharing them with the group and receiving the understanding of the counselor, be released from them. For the teacher, the reflection session has the effect of making the human mass of the group transparent, as needs and desires that may have been only half-guessed at during class become clear and their remedy evident. Finally, above all, the reflection session is important in making the class cohere as a group through the sharing of common frustrations and achievements.

In conclusion, a caveat and an encouragement. The last section describes a procedure for dealing with a difficult situation, but neither here nor in the earlier sections are there any recipes for success in the classroom. I do not believe that such recipes exist anywhere. Certainly there is nothing inherent in any of the procedures described here that, per se, guarantees learning. In any classroom procedure, as every experienced teacher knows, everything depends on the people involved, the teacher and the students, and their unique situation. In the procedures I have described, a great deal depends on the counseling skills of the teacher, though in saying so I do not mean to claim anything particular for myself. Curran puts the matter well:

> In wanting to stress the . . . depth and intensity of the skill of understanding, we do not want to go to the extreme of implying that the reader cannot acquire this skill without long and strenuous effort. Rather, like the analogy of learning a foreign language, sometimes even a small amount of German or French can be quite helpful, especially when there is a need of asking directions, or whatever it might be, in a foreign country. So even a limited knowledge of the real skill of affective-cognitive counseling can be an immeasurable help and aid.[13] (1978, p. 6)

Keeping this qualification in mind, then, what can we hope to accomplish through counseling-learning?

We can hope to establish a creative dialogue between the teacher and the students even across the rift created by different language backgrounds and even in a lecture class devoted to a complex subject. Given an atmosphere of trust, the students will take active responsibility for their own learning, and they will actively engage with the teacher and with each other, fostering a learning community to which both students and teacher feel that they belong. Kenneth Bruffee says that the purpose of collaborative learning is to "redefine the roles of student and teacher, and to restructure the human relationship between people who want to learn and those whose calling is to help them learn" (1985, p. v). Bruffee's objective is identical with Curran's, for Curran's work aims at restructuring the student–teacher relationship and substituting for traditional teacher-centered pedagogy one which puts the student at the center of education. The work of both of these educators finds a common basis in a vision of human community asserted against the depersonalizing forces of contemporary industrial society and the violence of rabid nationalisms. They share a common belief in the possibility of mutual understanding among people everywhere through humane education: the initiating of students from all walks of life into the ongoing conversation of humankind.

NOTES

1. In addition to Myers, see Gere (1987) and Hawkins (1976).
2. See Rogers (1951, 1961).
3. A variety of ways of digesting the tape are described by Stevick (1980, pp. 125–133). The two works by Stevick (1976, 1980) provide very perceptive commentaries on Curran's work.

4. See the bibliographies in Curran (1968, 1972).
5. The term *nondirective* has been misunderstood and caused confusion about the role of direction in Rogerian counseling. For a balanced treatment of the question, see Rardin (1977).
6. See Pounds (1987).
7. During the 5 years in which I have followed collaborative work in English composition, I have seen no reference to Curran's work.
8. For criticism of Rorty's work, see Lentricchia (1983).
9. For a useful overview of Japanese education, see Dorfman (1987). Japan may not be as far away as it seems. Geologists tell us that it rests on the same Pacific plate as California, and that, given the present rate at which the Pacific plate is disappearing due to subduction, 50 million years from now Japan and California should collide.
10. Much of what follows summarizes parts of Chapter 9, "Cultural Learning Mechanisms," in La Forge (1983).
11. What follows summarizes parts of Pounds (1984).
12. Curran practiced this kind of pedagogy in the non-FL classroom, where students and teacher alike share native fluency in a common language. His term for it is *cognitive counseling*. See Curran (1983), index, pp. 159ff.).
13. The reader who wants further instruction in Curran's "art of understanding" should read Part 2 of *Counseling and Psychotherapy: The Pursuit of Values* (1968).

REFERENCES

Bruffee, K. (1973). Collaborative learning: Some practical models. *College English, 34,* 632–641.

Bruffee, K. (1984). Collaborative learning and the "conversation of mankind." *College English, 46,* 635–652.

Bruffee, K. (1985). *A short course in writing: Practical rhetoric for teaching composition through collaborative learning*. (3rd ed.). Boston, MA: Little, Brown.

Bruffee, K. (1986a). Kenneth A. Bruffee responds. *College English, 48,* 77–78.

Bruffee, K. (1986b). Social construction, language, and the authority of knowledge: A bibliographical essay. *College English, 48,* 773–796.

Bruffee, K. (1987). Kenneth Bruffee responds. *College English, 49,* 711–716.

Curran, C. A. (1968). *Counseling and psychotherapy: The pursuit of values*. Apple River, IL: Apple River Press, 1976.

Curran, C. A. (1972). *Counseling-learning: A whole-person model for education*. Apple River, IL: Apple River Press.

Curran, C. A. (1976). *Counseling-learning in second languages*. Apple River, IL: Apple River Press.

Curran, C. A. (1978). *Understanding: A necessary ingredient in human belonging*. Apple River, IL: Apple River Press.

Dorfman, C. H. (Ed.). (1987). *Japanese education today*. Washington, DC: U.S. Department of Education.

Gere, A. R. (1987). *Writing groups: History, theory, and implications*. Carbondale, IL: Southern Illinois University Press.

Hawkins, T. (1976). *Group inquiry techniques for teaching writing*. (ERIC Clearinghouse on Reading and Communication Skills.) Urbana, IL: National Council of Teachers of English.

Harold, B. (1972). Beyond student-centered teaching: The dialectical materialist form of a literature course. *College English, 34,* 200–223.

Holzman, M. (1984). Teaching is remembering. *College English, 46,* 229–238.

Jacoby, R. (1975). *Social amnesia: A critique of conformist psychology from Alder to Laing*. Boston, MA: Beacon Press.

La Forge, P. G. (1975). *Research profiles with community language learning*. Apple River, IL: Counseling-Learning Institutes.

La Forge, P. G. (1977). Use of social silence in the interpersonal dynamics of community language learning. *TESOL Quarterly, 11,* 373–382.

La Forge, P. G. (1983). *Counseling and culture in second language acquisition*. Oxford: Pergamon Press.

Lentricchia, F. (1983). *Criticism and social change*. Chicago, IL: University of Chicago Press.

Myers, G. (1986). Reality, consensus, and reform in the rhetoric of composition teaching. *College English, 48,* 154–174.

Pounds, W. (1984). Teaching literature with cognitive counseling. *Cross Currents, 11,* 1–14.

Pounds, W. (1987). The context of no context: A Burkean critique of Rogerian rhetoric. *Rhetoric Society Quarterly, 17,* 45–59.

Rardin, J. (1977). Comments on H. Douglas Brown's 'Some limitations of C-L/CLL models of second language learning.' *TESOL Quarterly, 11,* 463–466.

Rogers, C. R. (1951). *Client-centered therapy: Its current practice, implications, and theory*. Boston, MA: Houghton Mifflin, 1965.

Rogers, C. R. (1961). *On becoming a person*. Boston, MA: Houghton Mifflin.

Stevick, E. W. (1976). *Memory, meaning, and method: Some psychological perspectives on language learning*. Rowley, MA: Newbury House.

Stevick, E. W. (1980). *Teaching languages: A way and ways*. Rowley, MA: Newbury House.

CHAPTER 12
Attitudes and Expectations in a Shared Responsibility Classroom

Chris Madigan

Rather than the writing strategy of Rogerian rhetoric, I am more interested in Rogerian pedagogy—what Rogers calls *humanistic education* and I call the *shared responsibility classroom*. By that I mean a classroom structured so that, within the limits imposed by the institution and the teacher, students help decide and implement class content, activities, schedule, course and student evaluations. I write to synthesize experiences in two spectacular, one disastrous, and six half-hearted and therefore inconclusive shared responsibility classes. Though what follows sounds like assertion, much is really speculation and correction of my mistakes.

My discussion focuses on three questions for those who might wish to try a shared responsibility class: What can you expect to happen in a shared responsibility classroom? Why is it likely to happen? What can you do in response? I faced these questions while teaching undergraduate writing courses and graduate-level summer institutes in teaching writing, and I will discuss features peculiar to such classes. But I believe what I learned with these classes applies to shared responsibility classes in other disciplines.

INITIAL RESISTANCE

The student reaction you can be 99% certain to encounter in some form is resistance. Tell a class that you're letting them help determine what the class will do, and after polite silence and even some polite cooperation, some will complain that they took the class to learn from you, that if they knew what to do they wouldn't need you, and that you're not doing your job. Rogers notes this resistance in his own classes (1969, p. 73; 1980, p. 303), other teachers' classes (1969, pp. 14–15; 1983, p. 190), small encounter groups (1970, pp. 8, 15–17), and large encounter groups (1980, pp. 75, 319). Rogers' biographer notes resistance among Rogers' University of Chicago Counseling Center staff (Kirschenbaum, 1979, p. 172), and Elbow notes initial resistance in his classes (1986, p. 77).

In a summer writing institute for teachers, for which I was a staff member, resistance occurred after 3 days of staff-directed activities. On the fourth, we gave participants a draft of an assignment and asked for reactions to the assignment itself and for suggestions for how to structure the remaining 3 weeks to complete it. When we asked if participants wanted to change the assignment, no one answered. "So the assignment can stand as is?" Silence suggested yes. But a half-hour later, a high school teacher, shaking with suppressed anger, interjected into an unrelated discussion, "I am so upset. I just cannot accept this assignment. How could you . . . ?" Her self-disclosure released a torrent of similar frustrations by classmates and sparked a fault-finding diatribe against institute staff lasting over an hour. Backs to the wall, staff could only listen carefully, which was the best reaction.

Later, we realized participants had felt abandoned. Despite our saying we were there to help, the contrast to traditional pedagogy in which teachers decide everything made participants feel entirely on their own. Even the staff's collaborative "We will all decide what to do" was interpreted by the class as "You students will decide what to do." How recently individuals may have experienced good teacher-directed classes or poor shared responsibility classes may determine how quickly students react, but the majority will resist.

Why? Elbow (1986, p. 77) speculates that freely choosing school activity violates self-images most students cultivate over a lifetime. I agree for secondary and lower college levels, but I think even advanced students are used to being directed. Most prefer to accept what they know rather than embrace what they don't, especially when the new role adds considerable responsibility.

Shared responsibility pedagogy assumes students can plan and monitor their own learning. For example, I ask them to identify explicitly a meaningful professional or personal problem and to negotiate with classmates and me (all of us compromising when necessary) a course structure that enables everyone to solve his or her problem. The structure enlists peers to help solve those problems through sharing information, feedback, and encouragement. These assumptions contradict those of traditional classrooms, where everyone assumes that the teacher knows what the students should study, then designs a curriculum to insure learning, and monitors and evaluates student progress unilaterally. In these classrooms, peers learn alongside each other but not *with* each other in significant ways. Despite the obviously different assumptions, learning occurs in both kinds of classroom. Resistance, then, is often a class's way of voting for the familiar, traditional structure.

Will a teacher intent on a shared responsibility class allow dependence rather than independence? How should a leader respond? I try not to panic, however panicky I feel. I listen and show them I recognize their discomfort and the *depth* of their discomfort by periodically paraphrasing or summarizing their laments. I don't ask "Why do you feel that way?" and don't offer any explanation for their feelings; they only resent the psychoanalyzing. If a question surfaces several times, I may respond to it, but in general I just accept the questions and anxieties. A useful response, then, is to accept and encourage but not analyze (at least to them). Just be with students in their discomfort (Rogers, 1970, p. 48). Have faith that all of you can get past this, and, perhaps more importantly, let them know you have that faith. You can't have a new baby without pain, so accept it.

Next, be prepared with a requirement or two. These may be rules you can't teach without, e.g., an ironclad attendance policy. Or they may be no requirements at all—a set of guidelines that anxious students can perceive as a structure but, looked at more closely, really don't limit them. Rogers admits being "rather rigidly 'student-centered' " before he learned to place responsibility with the entire group (himself included) and give freely of himself (Kirschenbaum, 1979, p. 242). To alleviate student anxiety over seeming lack of structure, Rogers gave no-requirement requirements (1983, p. 27). Elbow imposes similarly minimal requirements (1986, p. 71) but cautions teachers to be unambiguous if they have real requirements, whether their own or a program's (p. 76).

If you are willing to lead some students and won't see them as second-class citizens for wanting that leadership, you might prepare an old-style syllabus for them, confer often enough to give them a sense of direction, allow them to switch from one "track" to another depending on their need for guidance, or institute short-term contracts. But then you should probably expect some resistance to those directions too. Elbow tells of students rebelling against his unambiguous guidelines (1986, p. 86), and in my Teaching Composition class that seldom got beyond resistance, new graduate teaching assistants constantly resented the eight-paper, 5,000-word requirement I levied on them despite their imposing the same requirement on their freshmen writers.

On the surface, initial resistance is a problem. It challenges a teacher's assumptions when the very students who are supposed to benefit don't want to engage the pedagogy. From another perspective, however, resistance is the first sign that participants have taken the offer of shared responsibility seriously. In how many teacher-centered classrooms do students attack the teacher the first week?

TESTING THE TEACHER

Testing the teacher follows resistance and takes several forms, e.g., verbal "what if's" about grading, submitting no work or sloppy work, talking to a nearby friend instead of participating in a group discussion, walking about the classroom at inappropriate times, wearing stereo headphones and writhing to the beat instead of listening or writing, comparing you and previous teachers in unflattering ways. If you pass, the frequency of the tests will lessen, though probably not disappear entirely.

Cooperation as well as conflict may test you. How long should this paper be? What do you want in it? Do you want research? If you answer, participants may play "yes-but" games. If you don't give options in your replies, you've given an assignment when (perhaps) you announced you wouldn't. They accuse you or merely smile knowingly and think that this is a traditional class disguised as a shared-responsibility class. It is a con, a bamboozle (Elbow, 1986, pp. 87–98).

TESTING PEERS

As you pass a few tests, students willing to share the responsibility may publicly espouse the notion, and then peer tests occur. "Maybe the teacher's serious, but are my classmates? Suppose I tell Gung-ho Joe I think his paper stinks? Or point out that Amy's last comment contradicted something she said ten minutes ago?" Can students take being honest? (Rogers, 1970, pp. 14–37).

In the class for new teaching assistants that seldom got beyond resistance, peers didn't pass their tests. For example, one new teaching assistant reported requiring her students to write papers at least one page long. Another said, "Pardon me, but I don't see how that fits the spirit of your 'Question Authority' button." Rather than merely accepting the comment, the first responded to it by re-asserting the requirement rather than discussing the apparent contradiction.

Another exchange between different participants started with one questioning another. The response didn't satisfy, so the questioner repeated the query more insistently, to which the respondent answered with an unflattering comment about the first's teaching methods. When tones of voice became acerbic, I stopped the exchange.

I believe peer tests occur to test the water. Shared responsibility implies collaboration, and both teacher and fellow students must prove themselves worthy of trust.

Britton believes a class leader must (a) establish trusting relationships with students, (b) help peers trust each other, and (c) conduct whole-class activities in ways that don't jeopardize the previous two relationships (1970, p. 188). But how? To some extent, how a leader relates to participants signals how the leader wants participants to relate to each other. As a consequence, during the crucial initial sessions, when Rogers hears no one respond to a classmate's comment, he responds himself in ways that show he's listening (1970, p. 47; 1980, p. 187). If modeling isn't enough, the leader can intervene as another member of the group rather than as teacher. If he or she has established a relationship with the person being corrected, the comment might work. Thus, Rogers talks about confronting troublesome participants with their specific behaviors (1970, pp. 54–55), e.g., "Eric, your tone of voice makes me think you're picking on Joe, so I'm getting real put-out with you." If participants are keeping journals and interpret peers' actions uncharitably, the leader can offer a more charitable interpretation, e.g., "Eric's response may suggest he dislikes you, but I wonder if he just wasn't upset over your description of his grading system. You didn't seem to think much of it." Or "Eric told me he was up all night with a sick kid. Maybe he was too tired to take the kidding today."

Theoretically, a participant who doesn't trust the teacher and so doesn't care what the teacher thinks could do considerable damage, but, if the group coalesces into community, it will protect itself in what Rogers calls "the wisdom of the organism" (1970, p. 44). In two summer writing institutes for teachers, the communities allowed critics to voice their continuing objection to the class, even on the last day, but they didn't act on critics' suggestions. For example, during one group activity, a critic didn't follow the initial instructions, then suggested the entire class change subsequent directions to do what she was doing. The group ignored her.

In groups that don't become communities for lack of trust (e.g., my class of new teaching assistants), students keep comments to themselves and play it safe with peers. During this course, a student dubbed some of his peers "sharks." A year later, a graduate student speculated that it might have been more successful but for one or two of his classmates.

If and when you and classmates pass your tests, the class will begin sharing responsibility for its actions. Independent action signals that's happening, e.g., a student suggesting the class change a teacher's suggested plan and others agreeing. For example, in a freshman English class, we'd circulated papers for classmates to read. When I suggested we move to another activity, they preferred not to, so we didn't. Or a couple of students may choose to do something other than what the class does.

As the group's wisdom becomes operational, the class will solve problems, slowly at first and later more efficiently. For example, the summer teachers' institutes (which met 4 hours daily) devoted the first 30 minutes and last 15 minutes to "homeroom." In morning homeroom, volunteers announced the day's schedule, which the class revised according to their needs for feedback or free time that day. In afternoon homeroom, the class devised next day's schedule, and individuals asked for help that peers often collected overnight and shared in the next morning's homeroom. After the first week, they no longer needed all 30 minutes to schedule the day, so volunteers demonstrated teaching tips in show-and-tell. In contrast, the teaching assistant class (partly because they met less intensively) never reached a logistical equilibrium. They began discussing day-to-day classroom problems for entire class periods, switched to 10 minutes a day, then to Fridays, then to individual conferences outside class. But this seemed more a random walk through alternatives than consensus because objections occurred to every alternative.

HERD ACTIVITY

Though the class may jell, occasionally everyone may do what one person suggests without the group validating that activity and despite some conflicting personal preferences. This might suggest a unity of intention, but if it happens consistently, it may also betray willingness to be led rather than to risk acting independently. In a summer institute, a staff member announced she'd lead an optional exercise after homeroom. When homeroom ended, all but one staff member followed her into the next room and did the exercise, even a person who did her own, different activity there. The latter obviously had her own agenda for that time period, yet she physically accompanied the group rather than doing her own activity somewhere else.

Why? Perhaps the independent thinker wanted to feel more of the group. Perhaps a staff member rather than a classmate's leading the exercise made it "less optional." Perhaps participants didn't know what they wanted. Perhaps they felt paralyzed by the many wants they did recognize and it was easier to let someone else or the group choose for them.

What can be done? Ease up. Reduce the fatigue. Give free time. Don't plan. The staff recognized herd activity and confronted the class with it. One said, "I'm concerned that the class is moving together when I've heard many of you say you wish you had time for this or that. So I'd suggest the next hour and a half be free time. What do you think?" The class decided to float. One small group discussed readings, another discussed possible projects, individuals conferred with staff, and some wrote by themselves. Afterwards, several mentioned how good it felt to choose their own activity. They felt more relaxed. Yet they'd been working. I infer that relaxation, re-creation, came from choosing their own activity rather than fitting themselves to someone else's, just as a voluntary sports workout can rejuvenate someone who went into the workout dog-tired. Re-creation comes more from the attitude in which the person acts. Staff had unintentionally fallen back into directive roles. After confronting herd activity, we refused to direct activities, and participants found ways to direct themselves.

GROUP WISDOM

The previous example illustrates a shared responsibility class's typical reaction to what Rogers' biographer calls a "leadership vacuum" (Kirschenbaum, 1979, p. 329). The group wisdom fills it. That is, what teachers don't do, students will; what teachers don't know, students will find out *if* the individual or the group needs that action or knowledge.

For example, in a teachers' writing institute that used computers, participants asked the staff questions about the word processor. If staff didn't know, participants asked each other. If peers didn't know, users found their own answers by reading the manual or experimenting. The staff wondered if refusing to answer might get participants to answer their own questions. One experienced computer teacher codified that insight into a poster—"Ask three. Then ask me"—that saved her lots of time without sacrificing student expertise.

Another summer institute committed itself to hosting an open house for principals and colleagues. When the class delayed planning it, a self-appointed committee containing no staff members decided activities, assigned jobs, set an agenda, and generally planned what the rest of the group were happy to implement. The same method of planning occurred in the next year's institute, again without any staff involvement. Leaders arose from the ranks.

Individuals as well as groups will act to fill a vacuum. In one institute, a participant was frustrated to tears that the class hadn't planned a feedback session and no staff member had asked "How's your writing coming?" She had a draft to share, so she collared some peers and asked them for comments, which they gave. Several of them had papers to share too, so when she acted on her own need, she triggered others to act on theirs.

Traditional teaching subordinates student needs to teacher needs and teacher estimation of student needs. So at first, students in shared responsibility classrooms may not know what they want, may hesitate asking for it once they do, and may need to learn strategies for operating/co-operating within a shared responsibility context. Probably the more mature the individuals, the quicker the group will develop a group wisdom. Once developed, however, defining and discussing a problem may trigger its solution through methods invisible to any one person, though "the body knows."

COLLABORATION

Given the choices shared-responsibility classrooms present, students often choose to work together, though inexperienced students don't know how. Collaborative learning can occur fairly naturally *if* the first collaborative experiences are successful.

For example, in my freshman English class, students bracketed phrases in their peers' quickwrites that they wanted to hear more about. These bracketed phrases led to more ideas for two-thirds of the class than the quickwrite's original topic. The audience helped the writers focus, and their interest stimulated ideas. Later, the Praise and Question parts of *Praise-Question-Polish* (PQP) feedback (Lyons, 1981) gave writers their "strokes" and suggested in a nonthreatening way even more information to put in their drafts. After students shared final drafts, each recalled his or her favorite passage and who wrote it. Collaboration yielded praise and interested classmates, who asked to continue reading papers and do for homework what I'd originally planned for classtime.

Consistently, summer institute participants say their favorite activities involve working together. Initial good experiences enable risk taking. During one open house, institute participants shared their writing in a writer's circle containing 60 people, 40 of whom were strangers. In contrast, because the class of teaching assistants didn't trust one another, they hesitated to share orally but did enjoy silent reading and written PQP feedback, which involved less risk. I suspect reading silently was less immediate, and the Praise-Question-Polish structure dictates praise that free-form oral response doesn't guarantee.

In collaborative classes, trust is foremost, and the teacher can stack the deck so collaborations produce trust first and "truth" later. Some things are more important than being right, and being right with each other is one, at least initially.

LISTENING AND THE POWER OF BEING HEARD

Some of my experience with collaboration obviously contradicts Elbow's finding that students don't want to test their ideas against others' reactions (1986, pp. 90–91). I, too, face "How can you tell me it's wrong when it's my opinion?" But that surfaces more in teacher–student than peer disagreements, so I suspect it's a defense against teacher-as-teacher.

My students' most determined rejection occurs when I demonstrate revision for conciseness. "How can you do that?" they ask. I originally interpreted the question as "Why make those changes?" and answered, "To make it shorter." That didn't satisfy. Even I recognized that shortness per se isn't a virtue, and they didn't care that shorter correspondence saves correspondents money. "To make it clearer" or "I like it better" was even worse, probably because it appealed to my own authority as teacher, however well- or ill-deserved.

I finally realized they questioned my right to change that paper's personality. So I sidestepped the issue by replying, "Which version do you prefer?" Most, not all, picked the concise version but continued arguing. My saying, "Which voice do you find more persuasive?" didn't stop the arguments either, though most chose the concise version again. Winning agreement to the revision seemed beside the point. Something about revising at all disturbed them.

What then was the point? I now suspect many seemingly logical "discussions" are students' emotional reactions against teachers-as-authorities. "It's not that I don't agree with you," they seem to say. "It's that I don't like you telling me."

Teachers are authority figures. Compared to students, they enjoy higher status. High status people can ignore lower status people, and teachers traditionally have shown little interest in what students have to say, more in how they've said it, and usually "how" in the limited sense of correctness. Stylistic revision suggests I'm ignoring not only the what and how but also the original writer's personality since "style is the man" (or woman). Tuning higher status people out and arguing over issues based on status are ways students reassert their identities, their wholeness (see Brooke, 1987). Students may not care whether others agree as long as they listen. Students, like the rest of us, want to be heard.

Though I may be making much over stylistic disagreements, I conclude that a shared responsibility class's greatest contribution is listening to students. Its success depends on the power of being heard. Once heard, students can hear. By hearing students, teachers earn their students' attention. Students repay being listened to by listening.

For example, in one summer institute, a very outspoken critic of the shared responsibility pedagogy complained less often once I took her criticisms seriously in my responses to her journal. She even thanked me in front of the entire class. I inferred she wasn't used to being heard, an impression later confirmed when I learned she had been a very important government official, frequently consulted by the press but, having moved across the country, she was now between jobs and a student again. Not all students have been government officials, but none of us feels listened to enough.

EMOTIONS

Rogers says empathic listening in therapy helps clients get reacquainted with themselves and eventually change whatever parts of themselves they're dissatisfied with. In a classroom, good listening helps students realize what they don't know and want to learn. Often, those things are emotionally powerful.

If a student's biggest need is figuring out how to stop fighting with his spouse and he's given permission to explore personally meaningful topics in class, he'll probably try to use the class to solve that problem, and he may confide in peers his difficulties dealing with his mate. So some participants will be frustrated, angry, anxious. Others will be joyful, enthusiastic, exhilarated. Others will be somewhere in between, including indifferent. Institute participants have reacted to the suicide of a friend's child, missing a longtime correspondent, a father's alcoholism, a grandparent's death. They've also recollected joy over washing a car with a fiancé, admiration for an immigrant father, the fruitfulness of an artist's solitude, basking in an older sister's attention, and deep pleasure in reading to a 2-year-old. When they read in writer's circle, they often cry.

Rogers (1980, p. 263) says schools embrace minds, tolerate bodies, but dismiss emotions. But heard people object to being half-heard, and people in shared responsibility classes reject being merely talking heads. I suspect the opportunity to solve personal problems is more common in humanities classrooms than others, but I can imagine a student embroiled with a spouse worrying that aching tooth in many kinds of shared responsibility classes as well. In a psychology class, he or she might investigate sexual compatibility; in a sociology class, survey reasons for divorce; in a statistics class, manipulate divorce rates; in chemistry, study the biochemistry of depression; in literature, read books portraying marriages.

How can a teacher respond? Most importantly, you must decide if you feel comfortable with strong feelings in your class. If you're uncomfortable with strong feelings or insist you are not your students' counselor, you can limit the areas of shared responsibility, e.g., insist on okaying their topics. Elbow says free spaces "can be very small and still work, so long as they are not clouded by ambiguity. A teacher can give meaningful freedom even if he works within a very tightly constrained system" (1986, p. 77).

If you recognize that emotionally facilitative roles other than therapist are open to you but feel you need skills to cope with emotions, you might take a course in "active listening." Telephone crisis intervention and "help lines" train phone workers in active listening, and communications departments teach such skills in "interpersonal communications seminars." (Call the local crisis line and ask for a referral.) But a teacher must *not* invite emotions and then rebuff them. That will likely reduce the class to an icy politeness.

Once you're ready, what can you do in class? The institutional context and personalities will dictate particulars, but a few principles bear repeating. First, help establish a climate of trust, so students needn't feel embarrassed at wanting to read about or discuss topics with emotional potential, e.g., divorce, drug abuse, physical and mental illness. Second, develop sufficiently wide-ranging interests and contacts, so you can suggest people to talk to and books to read in those subject areas. The local crisis intervention phone line, the university counseling office, and the United Way office can often refer students to community agencies and knowledgeable individuals.

Third, maintain a file of projects/papers written by previous students so that current students can see some possibilities. Used to responding only cognitively in school, even students given permission to be whole may not realize how they might proceed. Fourth, don't assume responsibility for the happiness or productivity of your students. Ultimately, they are responsible for both. But others can care for them. Let the group care for its members (Rogers, 1970, pp. 21–23, 32–33; 1980, p. 127). Fifth, admit freely when you're anxious about responding to products (papers, presentations, etc.) that are emotionally powerful. Choose not to respond if you wish. If you do respond, make it perfectly clear when you're responding as a person to a person, when you're responding as a reader to a writer's content, and (if appropriate) when you're responding as a language teacher to diction, grammar, etc. (More about evaluation later.)

Sixth, don't worry much about peer insensitivity. In my experience, students seldom risk disclosure to peers who don't deserve their trust. My students have written about bouts with bulimia, abusive alcoholic parents and spouses, parents' terminal illnesses, rape, and religious doubt. Their classmates have consistently been interested and compassionate rather than indifferent and rude (I believe) because the writer's voice is genuine and worth respect. Readers appreciate the writers as writers and as people, and the writers grow as writers and as people under that approval. In some ways, I believe that if we take care of the people, the people will take care of the discipline. Perhaps by indirection we find direction out. Finally, don't expect that all students will engage their work seriously all the time. Some will not accept your invitation to serious-mindedness; others will engage sometimes, seem indifferent other times. Nor will all topics be emotionally serious. I've also had students write how to build houses, store sailboats, enjoy Florida vacations, and cause a scene in a fancy restaurant.

Though emotions will surface when students deal with significant topics, not all emotions will be extreme, and not all will be negative. But how participants interpret their negative emotions will signal whether the class is "working" or not. In unsuccessful classes, participants perceive their anxiety as originating outside themselves (usually in the teacher) and inhibiting them. In successful classes, participants perceive most negative feelings as originating inside themselves and, if not enervating them, at least not paralyzing them. Rogers says encounter groups evoke considerable anxiety, even pain, as the price of intellectual and affective growth (1980, pp. 192–194). I suspect the same of classrooms.

PAIN

Participants in shared responsibility classes are subject to a host of painful anxieties. One anxiety is the inevitable consequence of choice. Freshman English students who chose to write about one of three essays in their readings complained of not knowing the other two essays as well as students who wrote about them and lamented the others' advantage if one of those essays appeared in a topic on the midterm. Institute participants complained they'd postponed their final presentations until it was too late to schedule them any way but concurrently, so attending one meant missing others. But all recognized these as consequences of choices they had made.

Another anxiety is fear of failure, e.g., writing a bad paper or giving a poor speech. Choosing the project themselves makes fear of failure more intense because participants can't blame the teacher's assignment for projects they pick themselves (though some try). Institute participants who'd taught for years were scared of giving stand-up demonstrations to their peers. New teaching assistants feared my opinion of their papers because some had gained admittance to writing programs through writing samples. I postponed collecting my tenure documents, lest I hurry what might be a negative decision.

GROWTH IN PAIN

The fear is familiar, the solutions iffy. One is to admit anxiety. I joke about diarrhea I suffer the first week of classes every semester, even after 18 years. I confess butterflies before making institute presentations I've never given before. Those confessions seem to relax the people I work with.

Another solution is to reinterpret the fear itself, see its presence as enhancing (or at least instructive) rather than inhibiting. When I told the teaching assistants that their anxiety in our class indicated how seriously they were preparing themselves to teach, a couple relaxed.

Another solution is to try reconceptualizing what you're afraid of, to consider that poor performances are failures only if you learn nothing from them. Only now, as I write this chapter, do I recognize that the disastrous teaching assistant class, when contrasted with successful institutes preceding and following it, helped me identify trust as the key to a shared responsibility class. What I once saw only as one of my worst semesters teaching I now see as one of the most growthful.

I find shared responsibility classrooms unusually painful places to be. As a teacher I've felt pain when students accused me of not doing my job, when teaching assistants complained to my supervisors, when course evaluations were low. In shared responsibility classes that worked, I felt pain when I couldn't reach outsiders and didn't know my role. (When you're not assigning readings and grading papers, what's to do?)

But I've felt the most pain in realizing I am not the person I thought I was. Specifically, I now realize I didn't respect students as much as I thought I did. Since Rogers' *Freedom to Learn* appeared in 1969, I'd periodically and unsuccessfully tried to implement its ideas. As part of a teaching team, I tried again in the first summer institute, but with misgivings. I feared and expected that participants might do nothing. When participants read more, wrote more, and presented better in-services than I had imagined, and when I found myself learning instead of merely teaching, I realized my previous pseudomilitary, spell-everything-out teaching style might not so much have guaranteed decent work as inhibited excellent work. I felt 60% of my teaching Self evaporate from one anomalous class. I no longer believed in some of my publications.

Students feel pain too—when they confront their own problems, reveal their Selves, don't get what they want from peers, or are confronted about their troublesome behavior. It was painful for a teaching assistant, addressing his doubts about literary scholarship in a series of expressive writing tasks, to conclude that he wasn't sure why he was in graduate school. On the last day of one summer institute, the youngest, least experienced teacher cried as she thanked her classmates for listening to and using her ideas instead of dismissing her as young and flighty, a role she admitted sometimes playing. It wasn't easy for me to say or an experienced teacher to hear that I resented her monopolizing group time by talking too much. And it has been extremely trying for all of us to evaluate ourselves according to goal statements written at midterm.

These examples illustrate how personal and professional concerns interpenetrate each other. In a few cases, this interpenetration begins changes that extend far beyond the class itself. One summer institute member resisted preparing a stand-up presentation and instead prepared stand-alone materials she could use in her classroom and give to peers. The materials worked well with institute classmates, so she started a study group in her school. Her peers' respect encouraged her to change the generally submissive role she took with her team teacher, husband, and parents, which changed her professional and personal lives radically. She credits rather than blames the institute for helping her real-ize parts of herself she now welcomes. And she's become one of the institute's most active in-service presenters. Similarly, though the participant I thought talked too much stopped talking to me for awhile, she enrolled for a class taught by another staff member, saying she "needed more of this" and has effectively shared responsibility with her own middle-school students.

A semester after the course ended, a teaching assistant who'd particularly resisted self-evaluation thanked me when she learned that her mother (a long-time public school teacher whom the daughter respects) did annual self-evaluations and found them useful. Two years after our course together, another teaching assistant apologized for her earlier criticisms, confessed she now understood what we'd argued over earlier, and wished the current course in Teaching Composition were more like the course she'd previously resisted. The teaching assistant who wondered why he was in graduate school completed his M.A. program very creditably. So despite the pain, the confrontations that a trusting atmosphere made possible have nurtured rather than debilitated people.

I'm finding pain and fear unavoidable in a shared responsibility class because when you tackle strong concerns, strong emotions are attached. When you're honest in dealing with one another, differences surface that lead to more discomfort. When you attempt to change your Self, you suffer through a new birth.

What can a teacher do? First, know when to back off. Rogers came to the uneasy conclusion that a therapist must be fairly secure in his or her own Self to avoid becoming lost in the inner turmoils of disturbed clients (1980, p. 143). Anthropologists engaged in participant observation worry lest they "go native" by identifying too strongly with their informants and thereby lose their frame of reference. Trainees in CONTACT-Albuquerque, a crisis intervention phone line, self-select and are screened by experienced phone workers lest they resonate with callers' problems too strongly to help them. If you're interested in shared responsibility classes but uncomfortable with some situations, you might announce topics you can't deal effectively with, might choose to share responsibility with only one class, or might suspend the effort entirely during semesters requiring energy elsewhere, e.g., publishing, a tenure decision, personal problems.

If you choose to share responsibility in a class, then you must prepare to "stand with" students confronting themselves and you. I do that by limiting the areas of shared responsibility when I teach several classes a semester, by actively listening in conference (and keeping tissue in my office), by responding to journal entries synthesizing students' personal and professional lives with what's happening in our class, and by trusting the class's collective wisdom and its ability to care for its members (even when I, perhaps because the conflict is with me, cannot). I don't always succeed.

OUTSIDERS

My failures are the "outsiders," and outsiders have appeared in every shared-responsibility classroom I've worked in and several I've heard about. Outsiders refuse to collaborate, but the ways in which they refuse vary.

One way is constantly finding fault with the class structure. The fault-finders argue that the staff should shoulder responsibility as experts, not share it with amateurs. Having erected an appropriately academic (and often flattering) objection, these outsiders avoid engaging the pedagogy altogether.

Other outsiders set themselves apart, see the group wisdom as inapplicable to themselves. They cite differences in experience or training or motivation to justify rejecting group standards for their own, often very high ones—for example, choosing to complete two papers instead of the class's one. To objections about premature closure or unnecessarily high self-expectations, these outsiders re-assert "high standards" and "personal goals." I suspect they need to see themselves as superior.

Still other outsiders pursue their own agendas ruthlessly and don't allow others to help. They stay busy, so they're hard to recognize, but they're often alone. If staff object that something doesn't feel right (and feelings may be the only indicator), these outsiders claim they're being subjected to coercion, which violates the intent of the class.

Outsiders present the greatest challenge to a shared responsibility pedagogy because they incarnate the question, "In a participatory pedagogy, can someone choose not to participate?" Not to allow outsiders seems to violate the assumption of free choice.

If outsiders find one another and circle their wagons, they can be formidable opponents. A group of outsiders in one of my classes collaborated on student evaluations in what another student called a "lynching party." A group in a colleague's class collected enough signatures on a petition objecting to his approach that he asked another colleague to replace him. "They fired me," he said.

Why do outsiders act this way? The outsiders I've encountered seem in turmoil already, and the demands of a shared responsibility class put stresses on their Selves that they refuse to bear, perhaps with good reason. For example, a major change in a Self's social or professional identity— e.g., marriage or divorce, birth or death in family, relocation, new job, new role — can cause barely-manageable stress. Faced with added responsibilities of articulating what, of all the possibilities, that Self-in-turmoil wants right now and how that Self will get them in a roomful of strangers, it is much easier to say "To hell with this!" and find some way of escaping physically or mentally or both.

Corey (1985, p. 67) identifies people who tend to disrupt groups or prevent their forming, but since teachers can't select their students, they can only deal with them once they appear. So what can a leader do for outsiders? Rogers (1980, p. 160) says genuineness is most important in ordinary interactions like those between teacher and student, but for people who are hurting, confused, alienated, doubting their self-worth, or uncertain about their self-identities, he recommends empathy. Having tried genuineness with outsiders and found they withdraw from me, I'm ready to try empathy. Empathy is the power of being heard, and I'm struck at how outsiders don't hear how they sound to others. Perhaps if I could really listen to them, they could listen to themselves.

Jeanne Whitehouse, another institute staff member, stresses helping students set their own boundaries as soon as they get anxious over all the freedom they confront. This involves "standing with" students even more intimately than giving them a pseudorequirement because the teacher must first face some students' notions that an internally imposed boundary, because it carries no external sanction, is no boundary at all. Secondly, the teacher standing with such a student may find herself opposing the very structure she determined to be for the student's own good. To perceive an opponent's point of view is difficult enough. To feel it and actually help that opponent further his or her good rather than the good you want for that student is an acid test of empathy. Teachers who can do that are rare. Those who can exercise such empathy may ease their student's stress enough to earn the student's reconsideration for the teacher's point of view—"the power of being heard" leading to "the power to hear"—but in many cases, that will not happen.

Whether teachers can practice that degree of empathy or not, they should not browbeat themselves for "failing" outsiders. Though some people won't let you help them, others can't accept help and achieve their goals. Struggling to define themselves, some outsiders resemble children trying to break from their families, who can't risk getting help from parents. You don't know what you've done for outsiders. Inexplicably, three of four outsiders I've recently encountered later praised the classes they didn't fully participate in.

EVALUATION DIFFICULTIES

Evaluation, including grading, is the most difficult job I face because I answer to several groups. To students during the semester, I feel responsible for honestly responding to (not necessarily grading) their process and their products in ways that will help them improve both. To students at end of term, I feel responsible for an equally honest response, including disclosure of how I, as a representative of my university and my academic discipline, have graded their performance. To my institution and society, I feel responsible for grading that product performance, not improvement or good intentions. Elbow (1986) aptly identifies the contraries involved in these responsibilities.

Shared responsibility classrooms involve even more contraries because students share goal making and evaluation, and they are often the only legitimate evaluators of their performance. For example, if a writer intends to overcome writing anxiety or boost self-confidence, he or she is the legitimate evaluator of her own achievement.

So how do I grade students in a shared responsibility classroom? My system changes slightly each semester, but one current procedure requires students to write a goals statement by midterm and revise it a few weeks before end of term. Students and I then write evaluations (including grades) of their performance and share and answer questions about those in final conferences, settling on their final grade before they leave. So far I've accepted their self-evaluations as their final grades. In one or two cases, I've persuaded them to let me raise their grades.

I've usually been satisfied with all but outsiders' self-evaluations and grades, which exceeded mine. But having discharged my primary responsibility (i.e., to them) by an honest written evaluation, I felt challenging their self-assigned grade would hurt more than benefit either of us. I didn't consider the difference between their As and my Bs (even from teachers' and employers' viewpoints) significant enough to fight about, and fewer outsiders con self-evaluative grading than grade-grubbers con traditional grading systems.

As I write, I recognize the potential confusion a student may experience from my mixing signals, e.g., my writing a less-than-laudatory narrative before accepting an A grade. Next time, I may use Rogers' technique of having students I disagree with call me a day after conference with their final grade (1969, p. 91). Both of us feel defensive when our grades disagree, and that need to justify ourselves sometimes warps the rest of our conference. Perhaps a little time would give us both enough distance to consider the other's evaluation.

There are other ways to determine final grades. Elbow gives As to anyone meeting minimal requirements (1986, p. 20). At one time, Rogers asked all students if they would accept Bs (Kirschenbaum, 1979, p. 174). Rogers also recommends contracts (1983, pp. 149–154). In one summer institute, we accepted participants self-evaluations and offered teacher evaluations only if asked. In another, we accepted self-evaluations, but three staff members wrote separate evaluations. In the University of New Mexico's freshman English program, which mandates outside readers' evaluations of final exams, I allow students to choose their best papers, which I grade and average with the readers' final exam grades for the semester grade. Whatever the particulars, the grading method should be determined early, and students should get a significant (but not necessarily complete) role in evaluating themselves.

SHARED RESPONSIBILITY CLASSES IN WRITING

Staff in shared responsibility writing classes can expect several things peculiar to writing classes. First, given a choice of topics, participants will choose nonacademic topics more than they would in a traditional writing class. Few writers are thinking/feeling literary criticism or impersonal, analytic topics. Even experienced English and language arts teachers in the summer institute write about family relationships and personal challenges and triumphs in their open topic pieces.

Second, given a choice of discourse modes, participants choose poetry and narrative at least as often as nonfiction prose. Britton (1970) defines *poetic discourse* as discourse whose forms are particularly suited to what needs expressing, and these forms are very suited to the emotional messages that shared responsibility classes permit writers to explore.

Third, participants write to discover rather than to declare. The final products surprise the writers, and sometimes the tone is more here's-where-I-am-now than here's-the-way-it is. Papers seldom sound definitive, much less dogmatic.

These consequences of choice can trouble service-oriented writing programs intent on academic discourse. If listened to, students will listen. They'll often agree with and accept program-imposed goals as their own. But then program goals and methods compete with student goals and methods, and it's easier for large programs to dictate rather than share responsibilities. So the teacher must mediate between the program and the students. Rogers says there's no similarity between a traditional teacher and a facilitator of learning (1983, p. 135). The same applies to the apparatus of a traditional course and a shared responsibility course.

Unless staff are adept at coordinating student goals and program goals, for example, through teaching expressive and poetic discourse as routes to more transactional discourse so students focus on their goals while staff focus on program goals, this pedagogy may more likely survive in upper-level electives than service-oriented programs like freshman English. This is especially true in programs employing the same final exam for all sections, where teachers tend to teach to the test.

I am *not* saying shared responsibility classrooms are incompatible with mastery. Quite the contrary. I believe a shared responsibility pedagogy to be *most likely* to produce genuine competence for the *greatest percent* of students, but given students' lack of experience with shared responsibility classrooms, I suspect mastery would take more than a semester. But many universities (not to mention legislatures) won't wait that long. And most writing staffs do not believe in shared responsibility pedagogy in the first place, so they're not likely to implement it genuinely. Rogers says transformation is different from reform, that you can't put wings on a caterpillar and expect it to fly like a butterfly, and that colleges and their faculty are among the least likely groups to facilitate whole-person learning rather than merely profess it (1980, p. 252). Better support individuals who can make shared responsibility classes work in a few low-profile upper level classes than halfheartedly attempt the pedagogy throughout a lower level program and fail, thereby souring students on the approach.

POLITICS

That last concern is political because shared responsibility classes have political consequences. You can't cause students this must frustration, even temporarily, and keep colleagues from hearing about it. My experience is that outsiders will savage staff with extremely low course evaluations, and even students who eventually take to sharing responsibility may recall their initial frustrations come evaluation time.

Low evaluations will attract attention of department administrators, who may not have the time to examine more than evaluation averages and fear that bad publicity may reach their deans, students' parents, and legislators. Averages low in the department's range of student evaluations will at least require the teacher to justify a pedagogy while simultaneously clarifying it for himself or herself. Low evaluations give less-scrupulous administrators a convenient excuse to discipline a teacher they oppose for reasons those administrators couldn't publicly defend. At worst, low evaluations can sabotage tenure decisions. I therefore suggest waiting till you're tenured before trying a shared responsibility pedagogy. Rogers tells of humanistic educators, even school district superintendents, being fired, schools closed, colleges dissolved (1983, pp. 227–252).

But some teachers can't wait. Whether foolhardy or courageous, they take the risk. So what can they do?

First, know yourself. Ask yourself tough questions. What freedoms can the system I teach in realistically allow and not allow? What requirements of the program must be met, regardless of the pedagogy? What freedom can *I* allow and not allow? What requirements must students meet for me to succeed in my classroom? Can they reject a shared responsibility pedagogy? Can I afford and am I willing to accept the consequences if this turns out badly?

A way to know yourself is to practice what you teach. Put yourself into shared responsibility enterprises to feel what it will be like for participants. Team teach, share responsibility in committees, and serve in task-oriented groups outside the university where you have no particular prestige or expertise. After many years of leading encounter groups, Rogers says the best preparation for staff is to encounter each other (1980, pp. 186–187).

Second, cover yourself. Which colleagues, especially supervisors, should you keep informed about what you're doing? What experiences and ideas of theirs can you build into the pedagogy? Who can support you in and outside the classroom, psychologically as well as politically? Until I sought allies, I thought few teachers shared responsibility in their classrooms. Now I know better.

Questions of logistics and techniques arise too, but teachers routinely solve such problems, and Rogers says techniques aren't as important as attitudes. If we expect that students given freedom will do nothing, we will adopt attitudes that they can't be trusted. Students will detect those attitudes and will tend to fulfill the expectations (Rosenthal, 1976). But if we expect that students given freedom will work hard, we will assume they can be trusted, and they'll tend to fulfill those expectations. In relating what I've found for my classes, I hope I've helped you develop realistic expectations for your own.

Most results of a shared responsibility class are welcome. Some are not. Shared responsibility classrooms present a context within which teachers and students can listen to one another. Teachers can benefit by knowing more about students, which can lead to more appropriate instruction. By being heard, students are more likely to listen to their listeners, their teachers, and therefore learn more. So from a viewpoint of subject mastery, the results are promising (Rogers, 1983, p. 203), and I've experienced and therefore believe in that improvement. But I've also experienced the benefits as much, much more.

REFERENCES

Britton, J. (1970). *Language and learning.* London: Allen Lane.

Brooke, R. (1987). Underlife and writing instruction. *College Composition and Communication, 38,* 141–153.

Corey, G. (1985). *Theory and practice of group counseling* (2nd ed.). Monterey, CA: Brooks/Cole.

Elbow, P. (1986). *Embracing contraries: Explorations in learning and teaching.* New York: Oxford University Press.

Ferguson, M. (1980). *The Aquarian conspiracy: Person and social transformation in the 1980's.* Los Angeles, CA: J. P. Tarcher.

Kirschenbaum, H. (1979). *On becoming Carl Rogers.* New York: Delacorte.

Lyons, B. (1981). The PQP method of responding to writing. *English Journal, 70,* 42–43.

Rogers, C. R. (1969). *Freedom to learn.* Columbus, OH: Merrill.

Rogers, C. R. (1970). *Carl Rogers on encounter groups.* New York: Harper & Row.

Rogers, C. R. (1980). *A way of being.* Boston, MA: Houghton Mifflin.

Rogers, C. R. (1983). *Freedom to learn for the 80's.* Columbus, OH: Merrill.

Rosenthal, R. (1976). *Experimenter effects in behavorial research.* (enlarged ed.). New York: Irvington.

CHAPTER 13
Carl Rogers and the Teaching of Rhetoric and Composition

Paul Bator

Early presentation explaining how the work of Carl Rogers might be applied to the teaching of rhetoric and composition sought to distinguish Rogers' ideas from more traditional or classical models of persuasion (Young, Becker, & Pike 1970; Hairston, 1976; Bator 1980). Part of our effort was not to raise the flag of discovery so much as to draw attention to what we believed was a novel psychological perspective that might be cast usefully upon well-founded rhetorical grounds. While staking claims around an application of Rogers' principles to composition theory and practice, we never actually abandoned the rhetorical roadmap originally charted by Aristotle. All along, Rogerian proponents have sought to delineate and demonstrate those rhetorical situations in which a Rogerian-based rhetoric might apply. While not claiming that Rogers' psychological approach provided an epistemological basis for a rhetoric apart from an Aristotelian rhetoric, we were, nonetheless, positing certain epistemic implications insofar as such might affect the shape and meaning of rhetorical discourse. Theorists applying Rogers' work to rhetoric and composition sought to distinguish rhetorical situations wherein the application of Rogerian principles might be particularly effective. My own writing earlier noted that a Rogerian approach could be useful particularly in nonadvocacy situations where the writer is "exploring a problem, defining a concept, or conveying information" (Bator, 1980). Richard Young has observed that Rogerian argument may really be concerned with "the situation prior to the situation that Aristotle is concerned with" (this volume, Chapter 4).

Rogers' work and insights had and continue to have import for a variety of rhetorical situations, implications for the way rhetorical transactions are studied, taught, and conducted. Now that Rogers' communication approach has become more a more familiar—albeit debatable—part of composition parlance (Corder, 1985; Ede, 1984; Lunsford, 1979; Teich, 1987) it needs to be cast in a larger rhetorical relief that includes Perelman's *new rhetoric,* Toulmin's approach to argument, the *good reasons* movement as articulated by Wayne Booth, and other rhetorical approaches that have been characterized as a *rhetoric of inquiry* (Nelson & Megill, 1986). None of these approaches sets out to refute an Aristotelian or Ciceronian rhetorical tradition. Rather, in a post-Freudian age, they seek to offer students of rhetoric a perspective which accentuates the dialogical upon the dialectical, the empathic upon the agonistic, the provisional upon the dogmatic. Fundamentalist positions, whether anti-Rogerian or Rogerian in nature, for example, move our discussion little. The daily classroom problems facing us as teachers and theoreticians are harder and more subtle than a single foundationalist position can account for. Models of discourse such as those based upon Rogerian psychological principles recommend neither a strictly classical, romantic, nor analytic view; instead, they recommend a pluralistic persuasion theory that is inclusive rather than exclusive. The more integrated a Rogerian-based rhetoric becomes with forms of the new rhetoric, or a *rhetoric of inquiry,* the more widely applicable it becomes also.

The present chapter offers a practical way of assessing the impact of a Rogerian-based rhetoric by examining the reactions of student writers to Carl Rogers' principles of communication. Student reactions can reveal useful information for rhetoric and composition instructors planning to incorporate a "Rogerian-based rhetoric" as part of a design to teach persuasive writing. The following discussion of my experiences trying to teach composition students how they might apply principles from Carl Rogers' work to their own writing is based, in part, upon written responses to informal survey questions that I distributed to my freshperson composition students. While I don't claim to have been wholly successful in my attempts to encourage students to adapt Rogerian communication principles to their writing, I do believe that I've been able to gauge student writers' reactions and am able to comment informatively here upon their efforts to understand and apply select Rogerian principles to their papers. As might be expected, many student writers find a "Rogerian-based rhetoric" (hereafter, RR) to be impractical, unrealistic, or too mixed in intention. Others find RR more comfortable and similar to a style of writing they have already been using. Yet for all writers, I've found, applying Rogerian principles of communication to their persuasive papers causes them to reexamine their own stance on the problem situation at hand, to re-evaluate the writer/audience relationship, and to view writing as part of an ongoing process of discourse.

Student writers' responses to Rogerian-based rhetoric can also inform the way we as teachers establish our pedagogical presentation of this rhetorical perspective. Within the context of my composition classes I have found it reasonable to approach and teach Rogerian principles as an underlying framework for a collaborative, problem-solving approach toward persuasion and not to insist upon a uniquely or exclusively "Rogerian" rhetorical strategy. Thus, my students are borrowing from their prior argumentative writing experiences and our discussion of classical approaches toward argumentation as well as their new-found interest in principles of Rogerian, collaborative, problem-posing, and problem-solving persuasion. Since the introduction and adaptation of Rogerian principles to rhetoric by Young et al. (1970) and Hairston (1976, 1982), those of us who have been applying Rogerian principles in our classes have qualified, refined, and re-articulated our methods. Thus, many teachers I've worked and talked with have found it theoretically sound and pedagogically effective to teach Rogers' ideas as part of a larger rhetorical framework that encompasses a rhetoric of inquiry and good reasons. For convenience here, however, the abbreviation RR, indicating a Rogerian-based rhetoric, will be used as a shorthand to characterize students' reactions. Among the several areas to be discussed are: initial student reactions to Rogerian principles, student writers' attempts to incorporate the several phases of RR, student views of the advantages and disadvantages of RR, and student comments upon the ethicality of Rogerian-based method of persuasive writing.

INITIAL STUDENT REACTIONS

Initially, many students tend to be neutral, sceptical, or negative about the goals of Rogerian principles of communication. Most seem to be uncertain about whether or not they'll actually be able to apply RR to their own writing. As one student said, "It seemed that it would be extremely difficult to compose a paper in such a neutral manner." Another stated, "It seemed as if this strategy was trying to please everyone at the same time—too idealistic." Often for good reason, some student writers are reluctant to think in terms of any given strategy: "I didn't want to use any strategy at all—it's not that I didn't want to use the Rogerian particularly"; "I was never required to write in a style of writing different from my own."

Student writers need an actual chance to apply a Rogerian-based rhetoric before they can be expected to understand it. Theoretically, it appears abstract to many. Students noted, "Before using the Rogerian, actually writing using it, I didn't know how it would work. But after writing out the paper, I could see how all the elements came together to show a clear explanation/solution to the problem"; "I am used to arguing by the Rogerian strategy verbally; I have noticed that solutions to problems are most easily reached in an atmosphere of understanding"; "At first I thought of it as any other assignment. Incorporating it made me realize its purpose." Another observed, "It was hard to switch from the traditional argumentative strategy to the 'nice,' compromising Rogerian strategy. I've been used to debating in high school and the instant transition was hard, but this approach can be more useful and would have been even in my debating."

Then there are those students whose initial reaction was more receptive: "I seem to write in terms of a nonthreatening argument naturally. It seems to be the fairest way." Others said, "I liked the way this strategy approaches the problem open-mindedly and looked at both sides objectively"; "I was very interested in this strategy mainly because it approached a problem in a positive way, without threats or criticism"; "When going over the strategy in class I realized that it is a very logical approach to persuasive writing. It also seems to be based on some firm psychological ground"; "It verbalized something I already practiced and believed in." Another noted, "Since I always try to be objective, it was a legitimization of sorts." Others picked-up on the dynamic, or dialogical nature of the Rogerian strategy: "I saw immediately that it was an effective strategy of reconciliation between parties. The strategy reminded me of the way I thought all debates should be structured. I also liked the strategy's sense of realism. It acknowledged that no single paper or debate can permanently change anyone's mind. It recognized that resolutions come about in small steps over the long-term. An essay should serve only to contribute to a resolution, not to mandate it."

DIFFICULT PHASE TO APPLY

Of the several phases of the Rogerian strategy described by Young, Hairston, and others, students are of mixed view as to which phase is the more difficult to apply to their essays. Typically, however, the

Statement of the Audience's Position and the *Compromise* phases pose difficulty.

One student commented, "The phase of trying to view the other side's perspective on the problem was especially hard. I had to leave my stance on the subject for a time and write on how the other side felt about the subject. It was a trying task." Another said, "The most difficulty arose in trying to state, objectively, the other side of an issue. It was difficult for me to remain neutral on an issue especially if I had predetermined views about it. Giving this phase equal time in the paper for a proper balance was not always easy." Similarly, another writer commented, "Objectivity in the presentation of the opposing view's points was tough to maintain, especially on a topic which I already had a clear opinion on."

One word of guidance to students having difficulty comprehending and describing the audience's perspective is to write with "two pens"—one in each hand, so to speak—and to use separate sheets of paper or notebooks or computer files to differentiate and "store" the audience's position almost physically apart from the writer's. Providing a list of questions, or a heuristic, for analyzing the audience's views can be effective for some students. Once students understand that RR does not invariably demand a "unitary" audience position, and that there are levels or layers of the audience which represent positions held with varying degrees of intensity, they are better able to "relax" enough to make inferences and write about the audience's views. Having students role-play audience members for each other and write a response as if from the primary audience is another way of providing students with insight into the audience's perspective. Encouraging students to interview representative primary audience members and/or to conduct an informal survey of audience members are but two other techniques for assessing audience perspectives.

It is critical that we remind students that, while the Rogerian strategy encourages them to consider and state differing audience perspectives, it does not conversely require that they give up their own opinions, feelings, or stance on the problem situation at hand. Indeed, any rhetorical strategy which would do so would be counterproductive. Student writers need to be guided to express their own thoughts, feelings, and opinions as a legitimate response to the problem or issue at hand. What a Rogerian-based rhetoric recommends, however, is that writers not be forwarded the responsibility of assuming that it is their opinion solely that bears the burden of the argument or necessarily weighs most heavily in terms of the several audience perspectives involved.

Those student writers who were able to incorporate the audience phase more readily found further advantages. "Presenting both sides of the argument was difficult, but once that had been accomplished it was easier to come up with a 'compromise' between the two views." "Stating the point of view of those who might differ from my own view of the problem seemed easier. During the course of my research, I was able to find a sufficient amount of information which expressed the opposing views." These observations stress the significance of long-range planning or thinking and the importance of conducting adequate research on the problem, research which deliberately seeks out all quarters or perspectives—usually meaning locating journals with which the writer is unfamiliar. And then one student relied upon past experience in a turn-about way: "Presenting the opposing view toward the beginning was not too difficult. One may simply list the arguments he or she would disprove right away in other more traditional writing strategies."

The *compromise* phase is often seemingly more problematic for certain students who observe, "Trying to apply the audience's views to the writer's (that is, incorporating the two) was difficult. It was a compromising position to be in, and I did not want to lose my focus through compromising too much." "I could picture myself in their shoes, I could speak objectively but that compromise was crazy. It's hard to give up your position." Usually, students such as these came from writing backgrounds that had stressed the necessity of the writer's position prevailing, as expressed by this writer: "Trying to find common ground/compromises was the hardest. My old English teacher was also our debate coach, and in debate a compromise often means the opposing side is correct in some way. If you admit this you lose!"

I've found it necessary and helpful to talk about the word *compromise* and its connotations. Not surprisingly, perhaps, many students view the term less than positively. One student observed: "When I first started to 'get a grip,' that compromise stuff didn't sound so hot. But when it became clear, you understand the rationale behind it." Another said, "I don't like to compromise in arguments usually, so at first I felt that this belief of realizing the view of your audience and possibly compromising sounded as if one was getting low." Another student observed generally, "Initially, I considered a persuasive paper as one which argued a point. The Rogerian strategy seemed like a spineless form of persuasion." "I don't fully understand this part, but I refuse to compromise when arguing a point. I feel I can say at the end—'This is the best way to do it—don't you agree?' And of course emphasize why they should agree."

Interestingly, some student writers begin to adapt the concept of compromise in useful ways and apply those adaptations to their papers, one student commenting: "Compromising is something that I learned as a child since I've always had to deal with a twin. When we combined our ideas, our outcome always came out better. I believe in compromising." With many writers, introducing the relatively synonymous term *consensus* provides a more neutral, or acceptable, way of characterizing any negotiation between writer and audience. While an isolated-from-the-text example, the following passage from a student essay on "Indian Burial Rights" demonstrates how the writer was sensitive to the compromise phase:

> Indians are willing to cooperate if given the opportunity. Roger Lewin writes in *Science,* "American Indians for the most part are cooperating with archeological and anthropological researchers . . . entering into a collaborative scholarly appreciation of [their heritage]" (citation). Despite Mr. Lewin's rosy picture of the current relationship between many Indians and researchers, substantial numbers of tribes have never been given the opportunity to cooperate because archaeologists have been their opponents from the very outset. Too many cases of "Who owns the bones?" have went to court unnecessarily when cooperation would have been the ideal alternative. The fears of archaeologists and Indians often breed miscommunication and conflicts that seem to have no definite resolution except in the courts. . . . The reality for archaeologists is that they are starting to lose decisive court battles. If they really want to keep open opportunities for further Indian excavations, they should seek out-of-court settlements and propose plans for more collaboration between Indians and archaeologists, especially with regard to excavation site decisions.

The need for attentive use of language also caused problems for some students, even for those who found stating the audience's position relatively manageable: "The easiest phase was explaining the position of both sides in the debate. It is easy to be objective enough to at least recognize the opposing side's viewpoints; one need only keep his or her eyes and ears open. However, even this "easy" task had its sticking points. Avoiding the use of indirectly subjective language was difficult. It was hard to recognize what words or phrases might be interpreted by the opposing side as loaded words or preconceived notions. Other students noted: "I found it very difficult because you have to write with rhetorical sensitivity so that no one is offended"; "Keeping myself from stating opinions in too strong a manner was difficult. I was used to a basic persuasive paper, in which you state outright what you believe and why. It was sometimes hard to make statements 'nonthreatening.' " "The most difficult for me was to give my arguments without upsetting my audience. Although it wasn't really that hard to do, it was the most difficult because I had to pay more attention to word choice and other details like that."

Some students experience a true sense of cognitive dissonance insofar as they feel constrained by language demands while writing a paper incorporating RR: "A strong argument becomes somewhat flimsy because the language must be downplayed, and the full effect may be lost"; "The Rogerian strategy does not let you manipulate the audience as much through selective presentation of information and colored wording." Response to the concern about language leads to discussion of tone, voice, diction, and connotation. Helping students to consider the bases for distinctions between objective and subjective observations, between inferences and opinions, between facts and hypotheses, proves necessary in this context. Having students work in peer groups, marking with highlighters offensive or threatening words in each other's papers can also be a useful activity leading toward group or individual revision. Here, for example, is a *(highlighted)* passage from a paper on the problem of smoking in the workplace which had business employers designated as part of its primary audience:

> Smoking employees should also be allowed to smoke at home. Employers can *really not justify barging into the private lives of employees in such a manner*. If people were allowed to smoke at home, it might be more reasonable to ban smoking completely in the office since it is a great hazard. Employers should also not refuse to hire smokers just because they smoke. The act *really is discrimination and very unfair*. If the companies really would like their employees not to smoke, they should offer incentive programs if people quit smoking, for example a bonus or free help to quit smoking might be good ways to get people to quit.

Working with writers to help them strike a clear, forceful, persuasive, yet nonthreatening tone requires patience and deliberativeness on all parts; for many writers this is the first time they've considered closely the impact their choice of words might have on people whom they are attempting to persuade.

SUITABLE TOPICS FOR THE ROGERIAN STRATEGY

In response to the question: "What types of arguments do you believe are particularly suitable for the Rogerian strategy," student writers responded in terms of arguments that dealt with morals, ethics, or emotions. Writers observed that RR seemed most suited for: "Questions that are more flexible than just resulting in a 'yes' or 'no' response"; "Arguments that cause strong emotional reactions for people both for and against the topic"; "Social issues involving values, morals, sensitive matters. Issues in which both sides have some common ground"; "Highly personal & controversial issues in which the views of people are very emotional" (e.g., abortion, surrogate parenting). Perhaps being overly cautious about their abilities to persuade others through a single piece of writing, some students adopt the Rogerian method as a way of cooling down arguments about issues which have been heated but frustratingly nonproductive for them in the past. One writer, for example, found: "Those that involve emotional issues are very well suited for the Rogerian strategy. Emotional arguments tend to develop into irrational fights. The Rogerian strategy slows down the pace of the argument to avoid heated debates." Another noted, "The Rogerian strategy is suited when there are two distinct views of a problem. These two views, however, cannot be so opposed that compromise is impossible. Cooperation between the two sides must be possible."

Emphasis upon the multiple rhetorical intentions of the writer also makes those students who were frustrated previously in writing argument papers when they were unable to "win" the argument find the Rogerian strategy less frustrating in terms of their being able to strive for a measured degree of success in their persuasive papers. One student, for example, drew this conclusion: "I think arguments aimed for compromise solutions are most suitable, even if the writer is clearly a supporter of one side of the debate. Any sign of reconciliation eases tension between the opposing sides. If a Rogerian paper succeeds in bringing the two sides closer to even the slightest degree, it has fulfilled its purpose. One can always use more traditional argumentation to 'shock' the opponent, but Rogerian strategy is a reprieve from this."

Thus, through my teaching, I have come to modify my earlier belief that a Rogerian-based persuasive strategy might be applied most effectively to select rhetorical situations. Working with my student writers has led me to realize the diversity of topics to which they are often comfortably and successfully able to apply Rogerian principles of communication. Viewed as a tool to bring parties to a bargaining table, the Rogerian approach can be seen equally as operative during negotiations resolving differences, establishing policy, or promoting a course of action.

STRONG POINTS OF ROGERIAN RHETORIC

In response to the question, "What do you believe are the strong points of Rogerian rhetoric," students offer a variety of responses. Many writers find that the writer/audience relationship is significantly different than the one they have been used to in the past—one which posits a competitive or agonistic relationship. Rogers' *principle of threat* is grasped readily by all students, even if applying the principle to their writing is more difficult to accomplish. One student commented, "The only way someone will listen to you is if they aren't threatened by you. This 'gentleness' gets them listening. Then, showing them that you know and understand and respect them will get them to listen even more—they may try to know, understand and respect your views as well." Another said, "It doesn't offend the other side if you use it right."

It is useful to promote the ongoing nature of persuasive writing which the Rogerian strategy implies. Students find: "It gives the audience a clear idea of the issue concerned and an objective view of the two sides of it. If used effectively, the reader will tend to at least read through the whole essay and be more open to the writer's viewpoint"; "It presents an argument that is non-threatening, yet in its subtle way, manages to get the audience to at least think about the opposing argument without turning the people away in the process"; "The strong point of RR is that both sides of a problem are explored. When a person knows that his argument has been considered, he will not block out the discussion." Viewing a paper as part of the process of persuasion relieves the total burden of responsibility from any single piece of discourse. I encourage my students to view their essays as a way to promote continued dialogue on the problem at hand. In some classes, for example, I've had students draft cover letters and mail copies of their essays to representative members of their primary audience as a way of soliciting feedback and engendering discussion.

For the first time, many students become aware of the fact that audiences can literally stop reading their essays if the audience is so moved. Previously, I've found, most students took it for granted that they had a captive audience which would continue reading inevitably. Certainly, those students who looked upon the composition teacher as their sole audience assumed that—even if "offended"—the teacher would read through to the end because he or she had to give the paper a grade. Increasingly aware of the dimensions (primary and secondary) of the audience, students applying the Rogerian approach become quickly more attuned not only to gaining their audience's initial attention, but toward the rhetorical importance of maintaining the audience's open mind throughout the discourse. As one writer observed, "I think, psychologically, RR works to change someone's position or at least make them take a look at the other side without being completely turned off." Another agreed, "Since it's nonthreatening, the audience listens to the whole argument instead of getting turned off by offensive assertions early on." One writer expressed RR as "keeping people with opinions opposite yours from turning you out before you can get your ideas expressed." Here, for example, is a sample passage from a student paper on off-shore oil-drilling which demonstrates how the writer was able to take account of the audience's view:

> The main concern of the environmentalists and residents is that the oil platforms constitute a risk to the marine life found off the coast and should not be allowed in the area. The Santa Barbara Channel and Farallon Islands, outside the San Francisco Bay, are home to a number of species of birds along with sea otters and the elephant seals which are making a comeback from possible extinction. Citizen groups, constituting residents and environmentalists, have lobbied to create various reserves and sanctuaries in these coastal regions and due to their efforts, 12 million acres of land have been taken off a list of possible lease sites (citation). Additionally, Doug Smith, a writer for the Los Angeles Times, reports the residents of the coastal communities contend the platforms blight heavily-used scenic areas (citation).

In practice, students also come to see that the novel characterization of the writer/audience relationship serves not only to maintain the dialogue but also can serve to support the writer's own position: "It doesn't anger the audience; by considering the audience's ideas, it makes the audience more likely to consider the writer's." Another writer found that RR allows for "objectivity in the presentation of your own subjective opinion." One summarized: "The solution is more likely to work in real life."

Many writers come away from the experience of incorporating Rogerian principles of persuasion with a new perspective upon their own "writerly selves"—a perspective they may not have considered or articulated before: "The Rogerian strategy stimulates independent thinking and very often self reflection. This strategy shows the reader that you, the author, understand and appreciate both sides of the issue"; "Definitely the strong points are the compromise and the attempt to view the other side. It gave me a whole new perspective and I became not as stubborn in my position"; "In general, it allows the person presenting the argument to step to the 'middle' and present both sides objectively, weighing the individual arguments. It doesn't 'point the finger.' You can effectively use terminology such as 'I' and

'We' and 'Us' *not* 'you'." Another writer concluded that RR "gives a person the ability to learn to listen and understand another's point of view."

WEAK POINTS OF ROGERIAN RHETORIC

Class discussion also needs to be focused upon the weak points of the Rogerian strategy, for many student writers remain uncomfortable with RR throughout their practice of it. Talking about the weak points, moreover, can generate spirited exchanges between those who find RR an effective persuasive strategy and those who feel as these writers expressed: "The writer can appear 'wimpy'—especially in issues that require a firm stance"; "The strategy can be too wishy-washy at times because no strong, outright, opinions are presented." As a related observation here, I have not observed consistent gender distinctions with regard to those students who find Rogerian rhetoric "weak-kneed" and those who select it as a preferable, and often powerful, form of persuasive writing. The "camps" appear relatively mixed in terms of male and female students' responses, leading to the conjecture that past socialization into and experience with the (persuasive) writing process has more bearing upon argumentative styles than gender alone.

Discussion about weak points reveals, in part, how well students have been instructed in more traditional methods of argumentation—particularly those methods which place a premium upon authority, facts, and proof. As several writers found: "It may not convince people who require hard facts or strong proof to be persuaded"; "Sometimes it may be too unauthoritative"; "It is weaker in the sense that it is less supported by indisputable facts." The extent to which these writers misunderstood the nature and applicability of empirical data and proof in RR, indicates the need for instructors of RR to demonstrate how such persuasive elements are integral to RR and can be incorporated in a nonthreatening yet convincing style.

One of the more interesting drawback features of RR, according to some students, is that it "can lead to compromising a bit too much." "Sometimes one side is clearly weaker than the other, thus making it difficult to defend or understand." Or, as other writers found: "Sometimes the argument for the other side seems stronger than the one you're arguing for"; "With the Rogerian Strategy you can sometimes put too much emphasis in the wrong direction. You might end up proving the other side's points"; "If you are trying to persuade some one and not reach a compromise about a point, then this style fails." "One way in which RR may be viewed as a weak argument is in the compromise. The author may have to alter his opinion in order to come to this compromise." While there is clear danger implied in the preceding comments, the danger of student writers feeling unable or unsure of speaking their mind to their audience, there is a concomitant challenge of the risk value inherent in applying Rogerian principles of communication. The risk value is one of having your own image or view of the problem at hand altered or changed significantly in the course of the give-and-take of persuasion.

FUTURE WRITING ASSIGNMENTS

One of the less-predicted sets of reasons for some writers' preference for RR involved the structure of the argument. Some students felt that RR gave them a clearer pattern or picture of their paper in advance, with which they felt comfortable. Class discussion can stress that there is no set or ordered hierarchy of elements or phases in the Rogerian strategy and the several variations upon the typical essay structure available. We also discuss the point that Young et al. (1970) make in regard to a persuasive paper whose structure can be anticipated in advance by the audience as having a more difficult time maintaining the audience's interest and attention in the argument. Nevertheless, due in part no doubt to our spending class time exploring the several phases of RR, many students discover that it gives them a handle upon their papers: "I think RR is a good way to organize a paper; I like the style better than other argumentative styles"; "Definitely—it gives a paper some direction and organization"; "Yes—because of how logical it is in solving an argument"; "I enjoyed a more structured technique in which to guide my writing."

In terms of whether or not they would consider using RR in one of their future papers outside of the composition class, student writers were cautious in their responses: "I would try to incorporate it if I were writing to a 'mixed' audience"; "I'd use RR only for those issues where the justification for the arguments of each side involve a moral, ethical, religious, or personal issue"; "My final paper—Rogerian—worked well. Maybe it will on another also—never thought I'd say that!" The audience came into clear view for many writers who found that they would use RR in future papers: "The Rogerian Strategy coincides more with my style, in that I usually try to write subtly when directing an argument toward a very opposing audience"; "I plan to use RR again because of the 'mellow' persuasiveness it provides. By not putting the reader on the defensive right away, I feel I can present my method of a possible solution that may agree with my audience's, or at least implement part of their solution. It doesn't shove an issue, one-sidedly, down the reader's throat."

ETHICS OF ROGERIAN RHETORIC

Students had a difficult time responding to a question about the *ethicality* of the Rogerian argument, many unsure how to picture a relationship between writing and ethics in the first place. But those who did grasp the query and responded found that the Rogerian Strategy was "at least as" ethical as other persuasive writing strategies they had used: "I think RR is ethical since it is not prejudiced toward one aspect only of an issue. Rather, this style of writing covers the entire spectrum of possible viewpoints without insulting or judging"; "RR is a little more ethical since you are at least acknowledging the audience and trying to reach a common ground in the end"; "Other times I have argued without giving respect to the other side. Well, I never realized they wouldn't read it most likely if they were 'threatened.' "

The writers' heightened sense of audience was, as is apparent in several of the responses which follow, related to their awareness of the ethical situation: "It is more ethical in that it seems that less deception is involved or could be involved in this type of argument"; "Because it doesn't snowball the audience with one side, RR is especially ethical for uninformed audiences"; "I think it's good, but it's almost more manipulative because of the non-thretening language"; "RR is ethical because it shows both sides and doesn't make low blows"; "It seems to take into account the opposing viewpoints rather than hacking away at them"; "Usually, I've only written one-sided arguments"; "It doesn't 'point the finger.' It allows the person presenting the argument to be much more objective"; "RR recognizes other points of view as well as your own—very fair and sportsmanlike!"

In applying RR, students faced the practical demands of an in-class writing situation, finding frequently that it places special constraints upon the writer. One student summarized: "I don't really like to argue in the traditional sense—it's like two people talking (or writing) at each other, but not taking anything else into consideration. This is not to say I don't have strong convictions—I do. The Rogerian strategy helps me convey my ideas without putting anyone on the defensive." Another, similarly, said, "I think that the most ethical argumentation brings both sides of an issue closer to an acceptable resolution or, equivalently, eases tensions between the two. RR is built on the premise of realism in terms of what a single paper or debate could best accomplish and in terms of reconciliation."

Discussions with student writers about the ethics of a Rogerian-based rhetoric have led me to see that consideration of the concept of ethics entails an exploration of traditional issues and questions central to the study of the ethics of rhetoric. Ordinarily there is little time in our composition classes—or composition texts—to explore the ethical ramifications of a rhetorical strategy. Trying to apply Carl Rogers's principles to persuasive discourse in our writing classes has the benefit of redirecting attention toward the ethics of rhetoric. Thus, as time might allow, considerations such as the following emerge for class discussion.

A Rogerian-based rhetoric, ultimately, will not answer a question about which course of action or which given rhetorical discourse is *more* ethical than another. Rather, it refocuses or reframes the query toward an assessment of the inherent validity of premises, morality of positions held, respect for differing audience views entailed, and provision of public justification for positions demonstrated. What Rogerian-based rhetoric does is suggest an underlying framework for an ethics of rhetoric. The guidelines which recommend that writers applying a Rogerian strategy provide—up front as it were—an explicit, written statement of the problem, the perspectives of the audience on the problem, and the possible contexts within which the problem might be discussed, reorient both writer and audience toward the problem situation under discussion and—intentionally—away from implied or perceived threats to communication. Such a process can provide the basis for a more open evaluation of the grounds upon which a problem rests, the nature of the evidence being called forth, the extent to which beliefs and accepted facts, proven data and testimony, are being brought to bear upon the problem situation.

A Rogerian-based rhetoric is not prescriptive in its ethical stance. Its stress upon multiple perspectives, for example, allows an outsider, or third-party to come in and offer an ethical assessment of the rhetorical situation in a way that he or she was less able to before—in part because previously the third-party was not privy to sufficient information. When applied to a given rhetorical interchange, a Rogerian-based rhetoric allows parties to it to make reasoned judgments about the ethics of the argument that take into account the nature of the problem under discussion, the relevance of the research data, the several audience perspectives involved, the discourse tone and style, and the contextual reasonableness of proposed courses of action. A Rogerian-based rhetoric recognizes the danger of appeals to truth collapsing into appeals to belief and thus strives toward providing public justification for those beliefs.

CONCLUSION

A Rogerian-based approach to argumentation provides no panacea for either teachers or student writers in rhetoric and composition courses. As the foregoing student reactions have indicated, there are advantages and disadvantages to be realized from trying to adapt Carl Rogers' principles of communication to a persuasive or argumentative paper (Baumlin, 1987; Zappen, 1980). Nevertheless, the positive reactions of many student writers are encouraging and recommend further application and experimentation. Future application would be well advised to place Rogerian principles in a larger context of a problem-solving persuasion approach that encourages a rhetorical stance characterized by inquiry, dialogue, and good reasons. Future application should also try to remain open-minded about the multiplicity of rhetorical situations within which a Rogerian-based approach might operate and be effective. Experimentation will need also, importantly, to establish means and measures for assessing the reader's or audience's reactions to written discourse that is applying Rogers' principles of communication.

Only indirectly suggested by the foregoing student reactions is a potentially significant by-product of incorporating the Rogerian approach in rhetoric and composition classes. Framed within a dialogic *rhetoric of inquiry,* applying Rogers' principles can help foster a pluralism of values in the classroom. Discussion can be turned fruitfully toward examining absolutist and relativist responses to problems in a way which encourages students to act and write within pragmatic and realistic social situations and contexts. Students and teachers can come to see value, at times, even when a problem is not resolved successfully—the value inherent in entering in to dialogue as a way of extending the vitality and significance of an issue. In difficult cases, a rhetoric of inquiry frequently calls forth an exercise of practical rationality, a sense of fairness and justice which demands that the writer place him- or herself in a social setting. The groundwork for a collaborative approach toward writing may thus emerge naturally and productively.

REFERENCES

Bator, P. (1980). Aristotelian and Rogerian rhetoric. *College Composition and Communication, 31,* 427–432.

Bator, P. G. (1988). The 'good reasons movement': A 'confounding' of dialectic and rhetoric? *Philosophy and Rhetoric, 21,* 38–47.

Baumlin, J. S. (1987). Persuasion, Rogerian rhetoric, and imaginative play. *Rhetoric Society Quarterly, 7,* 33–44.

Corder, J. W. (1985). Argument as emergence, rhetoric as love. *Rhetoric Review, 4,* 16–32.

Ede, L. (1984). Is Rogerian rhetoric really Rogerian? *Rhetoric Review, 3,* 40–48.

Hairston, M. (1976). Carl Rogers' alternative to traditional rhetoric. *College Composition and Communication, 27,* 373–377.

Hairston, M. (1982). Using Carl Rogers' communication theories in the composition classroom. *Rhetoric Review, 1,* 50–55.

Lunsford, A. A. (1979). Aristotelian vs. Rogerian argument: A reassessment. *College Composition and Communication, 30,* 146–151.

Nelson, J. S., & Megill, A. (1986). Rhetoric of inquiry: Projects and prospects. *The Quarterly Journal of Speech, 72,* 20–37.

Teich, N. (1987). Rogerian problem-solving and the rhetoric of argumentation. *Journal of Advanced Composition, 7,* 52–61.

Young, R. E., Becker, A. L., & Pike, K. L. (1970). *Rhetoric: Discovery and change.* New York: Harcourt, Brace.

Zappen, J. P. (1980). Carl R. Rogers and political rhetoric. *PRE/TEXT, 1,* 95–113.

PART 3
Empathy: The Heart of Collaborative Communication

INTRODUCTION

Perhaps the most familiar way of referring to empathy is that you try to put yourself into another person's shoes (e.g., Basch, 1983; Katz, 1963; Fliess, 1942). While this analogy has become a commonplace, one of its most memorable appearances is in Harper Lee's novel, *To Kill A Mockingbird* (1960). At the end of the novel, Scout, the child narrator, says: "Atticus was right. One time he said you never really know a man until you stand in his shoes and walk around in them" (p. 282). Early in the novel, Atticus had said: "if you can learn a simple trick, Scout, you'll get along a lot better with all kinds of folks. You never really understand a person until you consider things from his point of view . . . until you climb into his skin and walk around in it" (p. 34).

The images of entering another's shoes or skin are sufficiently visual, even tactile, to evoke notions of empathy. The responses of projection, identification, and kinesthetics are all commonly associated with empathy. But it is as difficult to arrive at acceptable definitions of empathy, as it is to find the origins of these frequently used images. The Native American folklorist Barre Toelkin pointed out to me the parallel of "putting yourself in another's shoes" with the Navaho proverb: "Don't judge me until you walk a mile in my moccasins." He emphasized the aptness of moccasins, rather than shoes, since the contours of the owner's feet would impress a personal shape.[1]

Empathy is a key topic in relation to Carl Rogers, because it is at the foundation of his theory and practice. Moreover, it is inherent in applications of his principles to communication, rhetoric, and composition—such as *Rogerian argument, Rogerian problem solving,* and *active listening.* When we expand our field of vision for a broader survey of the concept of empathy, however, many complex and tangled strands compete for our attention. But, given the space available, I have limited the discussion in the four chapters of this part by excluding certain issues in psychology, philosophy, and literature. For instance, I will not examine experimental studies which measure the expression of empathy in controlled conditions, nor do I have space to explore in detail the implications of empathy in ethics and cultural criticism, or various current theories of audience response as they relate to empathy. Rather, I will focus on empathy in theory and practice immediately relevant to communication, especially the fields of rhetoric and writing.

To begin, in Chapter 14 I will briefly summarize backgrounds of the contemporary concept of empathy: derivations of the term; its origins and locations in the fields of aesthetics, ethics, and premodern psychology; and its emergence in 20th-century psychoanalysis and psychotherapy. In the next chapter (15), I will trace Rogers' developing views on empathy, as one of the three interrelated principles fundamental to his thought and practice. In the following chapter (16), I will examine in detail ideas of psychoanalyst Heinz Kohut, whose work since the 1950s has revitalized the concept of empathy in his field, and whose expanding ideas about the centrality and applications of empathy could serve as a model for developing our own views and our teaching about empathy. In the final chapter (17), I will relate empathy, as a key to human intersubjectivity and understanding through language, to our teaching in the fields of rhetoric and composition, reading and writing, literature, and cultural studies generally.

Specialists have agreed that empathy can be taught or improved as a skill, through role playing, imagination and visualizing, and critical thinking activities, as well as by specialized professional training. Empathy, then, has increasing relevance to the new emphases on collaborative writing, on the social contexts of discourse communities, and on critical thinking skills. Throughout my investigation of empathy to follow, I will stress certain implications that point toward my concluding chapter, in which I discuss the pedagogical values of considering the empathic process as a rhetoric of collaboration. Viewing empathy this way—as a creative, imaginative, dialogic, collaborative process—my aim is to show those of us trained in rhetoric, composition, and literary studies how empathy can be better acknowledged and used in our own work and in teaching our students to understand language and to engage in constructive discourse.

NOTE

1. Another version has been attributed to "the old Sioux Indian prayer: 'Oh Great Spirit, grant me the wisdom to walk in another's moccasins before I criticize or pass judgment' " (Waitley, 1983, p. 131). The prevalence of such folk expressions is evident from Fliess's quotes of German and French: "sich in jemanden hinein-versetzen" and "se mettre dans la peau de quelqu'un" (1942, p. 213).

REFERENCES

Basch, M. F. (1983). Empathic understanding: A review of the concept and some theoretical considerations. *Journal of the American Psychoanalytic Association, 31,* 101–126.

Fliess, R. (1942). The metapsychology of the analyst. *Psychoanalytic Quarterly, 11,* 211–227.

Katz, R. L. (1963). *Empathy: Its nature and uses.* New York: Free Press.

Lee, H. (1960). *To kill a mockingbird.* Philadelphia: Lippincott.

Waitley, D. (1983). *Seeds of greatness.* Old Tappan, NJ: Revell.

CHAPTER 14
Backgrounds: Origins, Locations, and Multiple Definitions of Empathy

Nathaniel Teich

The term *empathy,* a 20th-century neologism in English, has acquired enough contradictory meanings that some critics have proposed abandoning it, while others have attempted to clarify it as necessary for psychoanalytic theory and clinical practice, as well as other human studies. Problems in defining empathy range from the biological, through the psychological, to the social and ethical. Do humans have an innate capacity for empathy, which is evident from infancy? How is empathy related developmentally to human growth? Is empathy intuitive, and is what it produces like intuitive knowing? Does it involve only affect (feelings and emotions), or also cognitive dimensions? Is it a process of identification, in which one loses one's identity or self in merging with the other? Is it a positive attribute, like altruism, love, sympathy? Or is it value-neutral? Basch (1983) asked: "Is empathy an end result, a tool, a skill, a kind of communication, a listening stance, a type of introspection, a capacity . . . a disposition . . . or a feeling?" (p. 102).

Several commentators have traced the origins of the word *empathy* to the word *Einfuhlung,* used by the German psychologist and aesthetician Theodor Lipps in the late 19th and early 20th centuries. But the subsequent locations and uses of these two words (empathy and *Einfuhlung)* have been variously debated (e.g., Reed, 1984; Olinick, 1984; Noy, 1984). Regardless of who was responsible for the early uses of the two words, it is clear that their initial context was aesthetic perception, referring to effects on an observer perceiving physical objects. Thus, empathy initially did not have to do with understanding other people (Noy, 1984, p. 171). Freud probably limited his use of the term *Einfuhlung,* according to Agosta (1984), to avoid association with Lipps's metaphysical psychology. Lipps's concept of *Einfuhlung* corresponded to what is now called *projection* (Agosta, 1984, p. 44) or *projective identification* (Olinick, 1984, p. 151).

Although the English word *empathy* was created to translate *Einfuhlung,* few commentators have investigated the etymology of the two terms, as did Basch (1983). He analyzed the German term *Einfuhlung* to disclose that it connotes more than just affective experiencing. This broader connotation was intended in the English coinage of *empathy,* derived from the Greek (as "feeling within"), which was designed to parallel *sympathy* ("feeling along with"). These precise meanings were not always reflected in ordinary or specialized usage. As a result, according to Basch, the word

> "empathy" has led to a confusion of "feeling with" with the much broader concept of *Einfuhlung* or "feeling into," i.e., "finding" or "searching" one's way into the experience of another without specifying or limiting the means by which this occurs. (pp. 110–111)

For Basch and others of the analytic school of psychotherapy, empathy is appropriate in theory and practice only if it involves "a reasoned . . . interpretation" of the affective experience of another (the patient) and subsequent "validation or disconfirmation . . . through further reflection, observation, or experiment." These psychoanalysts "deplore" those schools of therapy whose less rationalized definitions and applications of empathy "implied resignation of intellect and considered judgment in favor of a prerational affective experience with the patient" (p. 111). While this indictment appears aimed at those like the humanistic school of therapy, including Rogers, it is certainly not accurate regarding Rogers' fully developed ideas, as I shall discuss below.

Yet, in the psychoanalytic schools, as well as other schools of therapy, definitions and applications of empathy vary widely. For example, another etymological study (Olinick, 1984) compared empathy and sympathy to correct the blurred distinctions in both popular usage and psychoanalysis. In summarizing "the nuances of the various types of sympathy" in German, which were not as precisely distinguished in English, Olinick stated that it would be more appropriate to refer to "the sympathies," among which empathy would be "a special case" (cf. Marshall's [1988] more literary analysis of the cultural origins of sympathy in the 18th century, this volume, Chapter 17). In contrast to sympathy, as "frequently an affect-laden attitude" which can involve relationships of "dominance and submission and/or dependence," he described empathy as "conflict-free and autonomous" (pp. 145, 163). As a result of his discriminations, Olinick denied that empathy was mystical or incompatible with scientific psychoanalytic principles. But he regarded empathy more as an "attitudinal state," in the service of maintaining communicative understanding, than as a mode of analysis and understanding (pp. 101, 163).

In contrast to this narrower construction of empathy, Lichtenberg (1984) construed empathy as a "vantage point" from which the analyst "orients his listening stance to be from within the perspective, the state of mind of the analysand." To Lichtenberg, this means more than simply being in touch with the patient's feelings and emotional state (pp. 115–116). Similarly, Schwaber (1984) called this broader empathy "a mode of analytic listening"; it is what Rogers and his colleagues called *active listening*. In addition, we should note here the frequent use of positional/spatial metaphors to locate empathy *(perspective, vantage point)*. Symbolizing empathy in figures of space and place suggests the arrangements of subjects and objects that the empathic process signifies.

At this point, it is important for us to keep in mind the contested definitions of empathy as a process, as evidenced in the psychoanalytical discussions. There may be a greater demand for precision in defining empathy for its specialized use in psychoanalysis than in other disciplines. Yet I believe that, for rhetoricians and critics of literature and the other arts, as well as for psychotherapists, the key issues involving empathy are the same: primarily, "empathy as a general process and a mode of analytic listening," empathy as balanced between "rational understanding" and "emotionality and sympathetic affective attunement," and "empathy as a special mode of affective communication" (Bornstein, 1984, p. 111).

While the psychotherapeutic perspective on empathy seems most useful for my focus on rhetoric and writing, I will turn briefly here to other perspectives on empathy. They open up much broader psychological and philosophical views, from intuition and mysticism to ethics and aesthetics. Historically, as already mentioned, the first instances of *Einfuhlung* and *empathy* occurred in psychological explanations of aesthetic experience. Lipps used *Einfuhlung* to describe an observer's loss of self-awareness in experiencing a natural object or an art object (painting, sculpture). Lipps postulated an *inner imitation,* including muscular responses, leading to the observer's loss of identity and merging with the object (Olinick, 1984; Katz, 1963).

In earlier philosophies and psychologies, what could be called empathy has been identified as intuition, a sixth sense, which has been regarded as an ethical sense of sympathy, sensitivity, and benevolence. In early 18th-century England, Shaftesbury was the spokesman for the new philosophy of sensibility, postulating a special moral sense in human nature. This notion continued throughout the century. Adam Smith (1976), in his 1759 *The Theory of Moral Sentiments,* based his ideas on Hume's and identified sympathy as an imaginative process of thinking about and emotionally responding to the suffering of others.

Similarly, Kames (1836), in his 1762 *Elements of Criticism,* considered sympathy the cement of society and attributed it to the benevolence of human nature which found "gratification . . . to relieve a fellow-creature from distress" (pp. 98, 213). In recent scholarship, Katz (1963) traced the ethical and spiritual roots of empathy back to Hebrew scriptures. Stewart (1956) traced origins to Plato and St. Thomas Aquinas, in a study centered on personal knowing and empathy as "a postulate of all ethics."

However, it is revealing to note that these ethical and religious culminations of empathy in the studies by Stewart and Katz are grounded in their analyses of "scientific" psychology and psychotherapy. They concluded that empathy must be regarded as signifying universal personal action "of the highest importance to ethics, to psychology, to art—perhaps even to science" (Stewart, 1956, pp. 154–155). This view has a counterpart in the nontheistic humanism of Rogers and Kohut, as we shall see in the next two chapters examining their developing theories and applications of empathy.

Before turning to Rogers, let me present four pre-Rogerian positions on empathy: the first by Freud and the others by three of Rogers contemporaries in the 1940s. While these statements make clear that the term was present, if not central, in psychology and ethics before Rogers and Kohut, the statements also prepare us to see the importance of Rogers' contributions—especially introducing a means of putting empathy into practice. Rogers not only defined the empathic process as central to the therapeutic situation, but also provided for operational terms and strategies. His principle of *reflecting* the client's feelings, that is, *saying back* what the therapist empathically feels, not only provided therapists with a specific action to indicate their empathic experience with clients, but also helped maintain open channels of communication so that the empathic process could continue.

Freud wrote little about empathy. His most quoted remark was paraphrased by Basch as stressing the "indispensable" aspect of empathy. Basch noted problems with the standard translation (1921) of Freud: "A path leads from identification by way of imitation to empathy, that is, to the comprehension of the mechanism by means of which we are enabled to take up any attitude at all toward another mental life" (1983, p. 103). Freud's focus on identification has directed many commentators to emphasize this part of the sequence in "the psychogenesis of empathy" (Basch, 1983, pp. 104–106; Stewart, 1956, pp. 37–41). But the empathic process remained ill-defined and little explored until Rogers and Kohut.

Theodor Reik (1948), in *Listening with the Third Ear,* vigorously rejected "the theory of empathy . . . as inadequate"; yet, in his traditional psychological perspective of ego and unconscious, he stated: "to comprehend the unconscious of another person, we must, at least for a moment, change ourselves into and become that person" (pp. 360–361). What Reik proposed instead of empathy resembled it in all but the name (and some commentators have simply equated Reik's theories with empathy).[1]

To Reik the universal process of "unconscious sharing of emotion" occurred by means of "introjection" and "projection."

> The special form in which the ego is transformed by taking another person into itself for a moment can only be called an introjection. . . . And then the process of introjection is followed by projection, whereby the transformed ego is thrown outward and perceived as a psychological object. . . . This . . . incorporation of the psychological Thou into the ego and its ejection . . . constitute the primary psychological condition for the comprehension of other people's unconscious processes. (p. 362)

However, the psychoanalyst's ego is not permanently transformed because he employs "temporary introjection." Although Reik's theorizing is limited by the concepts of ego and unconscious, his explanations are notable for considering the process of analysis. He was additionally concerned with the problem of accurately perceiving the other, without imposing one's ego or only seeing one's self in the other. He proposed "the careful observation of the subject, free from presuppositions" (p. 464), which we find more fully developed in Rogerian acceptance and unconditional positive regard.

Earlier, in 1940, Harry S. Sullivan insisted "that the psychiatrist . . . take the role of his patient" but "must not abdicate in a complete identification with the patient . . . must continue to function in his own role and in the role of observer . . . to place himself in the psychological shoes of the patient and perceive the situation from that perspective" (Natale, 1972, pp. 35–36). Sullivan continued to talk about empathy through the 1950s, although granting that it remained undefined as an "interpersonal process" (Shapiro, 1984, pp. 112–113; Grotstein, 1984, p. 201).

Martin Buber, the Hebrew philosopher writing on both worldly and religious dialogue, objected to the aesthetic identification theory of empathy, because he was committed to the idea of retaining one's identity when experiencing along with others. He prefered such terms as "inclusion" and "seeing the other" rather than empathy. As Katz noted, Buber's 1948 description of empathy reminds us of Lipps.

> Empathy means . . . to glide with one's own feeling into the dynamic structure of an object [in nature] . . ., or even of an animal or a man, and as it were to trace it from within, understanding the formation and motoriality of the object with the perceptions of one's own muscles; it means to "transpose" oneself over there and in there. (Katz, 1963, pp. 39, 87)

Rogers evidently had not studied Buber until the early 1950s. But Rogers responded positively to his ideas and in 1957 engaged in a public dialogue with him (Kirschenbaum, 1979, pp. 231–232, 393; Evans, 1975, pp. 70–71). Whether or not Rogers was influenced by these or other prior statements about empathy (and he gave no indication that he was), his contributions were new and essential for popularizing and applying the empathic process in counseling and other interpersonal situations.

NOTE

1. Katz (1963, pp. 41–54) schematized Reik's theories into four phases, which go beyond and, in some places, distort his views. Natale (1972, p. 35) appears to have taken these phases from Katz and attributed them to Reik. Here is a good example of why theorist-practitioners, like Rogers, complain about the reduction of their ideas into mechanical steps.

REFERENCES

Agosta, L. (1984). Empathy and intersubjectivity. In J. Lichtenberg, M. Bornstein, & D. Silver (Eds.), *Empathy I* (pp. 43–61). Hillsdale, NJ: Erlbaum.

Basch, M. F. (1983). Empathic understanding: A review of the concept and some theoretical considerations. *Journal of the American Psychoanlaytic Association, 31,* 101–126.

Bornstein, M. (1984). Introductory remarks. In J. Lichtenberg, M. Bornstein, & D. Silver (Eds.), *Empathy II* (pp. 107–112). Hillsdale, NJ: Erlbaum.

Evans, R. I. (1975). *Carl Rogers: The man and his ideas.* New York: Dutton.

Grotstein, J. S. (1984). Some perspectives on empathy from others and toward oneself. In J. Lichtenberg, M. Bornstein, & D. Silver (Eds.), *Empathy I* (pp. 201–215). Hillsdale, NJ: Erlbaum.

Kames, Lord. (1836). *Elements of criticism.* New York: Conner & Cooke. (Original work published 1762)

Katz, R. L. (1963). *Empathy: Its nature and uses*. New York: Free Press.
Kirschenbaum, H. (1979). *On becoming Carl Rogers*. New York: Delta/Dell.
Lichtenberg, J. D. (1984). The empathic mode of perception and alternative vantage points for psychoanalytic work. In J. Lichtenberg, M. Bornstein, & D. Silver (Eds.), *Empathy II* (pp. 113–115). Hillsdale, NJ: Erlbaum.
Marshall, D. (1988). *The surprising effects of sympathy*. Chicago, IL: University of Chicago Press.
Natale, S. (1972). *An experiment in empathy*. Berkshire, U.K.: National Foundation for Educational Research in England and Wales.
Noy, P. (1984). The three components of empathy: Normal and pathological development. In J. Lichtenberg, M. Bornstein, & D. Silver (Eds.), *Empathy I* (pp. 167–199). Hillsdale, NJ: Erlbaum.
Olinick, S. L. (1984). A critique of empathy and sympathy. In J. Lichtenberg, M. Bornstein, & D. Silver (Eds.), *Empathy I* (pp. 137–166). Hillsdale, NJ: Erlbaum.
Reed, G. S. (1984). The antithetical meaning of the term 'empathy' in psychoanalytic discourse. In J. Lichtenberg, M. Bornstein, & D. Silver (Eds.), *Empathy I* (pp. 7–24). Hillsdale, NJ: Erlbaum.
Reik, T. (1948). *Listening with the third ear: The inner experience of a psychoanalyst*. New York: Farrar, Straus.
Schwaber, E. (1984). Discussion. In J. Lichtenberg, M. Bornstein, & D. Silver (Eds.), *Empathy I* (pp. 25–30). Hillsdale, NJ: Erlbaum.
Shapiro, T. (1984). Empathy: A critical reevaluation. In J. Lichtenberg, M. Bornstein, & D. Silver (Eds.), *Empathy I* (pp. 103–128). Hillsdale, NJ: Erlbaum.
Smith, A. (1976). *The theory of moral sentiments*. Oxford: Clarendon. (Original work published in 1759)
Stewart, D. A. (1956). *Preface to empathy*. New York: Philosophical Library.

CHAPTER 15
Rogerian Empathy

Nathaniel Teich

Empathy—as a concept and in its practical application—is one of the cornerstones of Carl Rogers' work and life. The development of Rogers' ideas about empathy is nearly inseparable from the evolution of his client-centered therapy and the articulation of the three facilitative attitudes that he insisted therapists must hold to provide the psychological conditions for growth and wellness. Moreover, Rogers (1980) posited that these "three attitudinal elements making for growth" applied to "any situation in which the development of the person is a goal." He gave as examples, "the relationship between therapist and client, parent and child, leader and group, teacher and student, or administrator and staff" (p. 115).

Let me summarize these three attitudinal elements briefly. The first is *congruence* or genuineness. The therapist, as model communicator, does not play a role, but "is himself or herself in the relationship, putting up no professional front or personal facade." The therapist appears "transparent," in that "the client can see right through what the therapist *is* in the relationship. . . . As for the therapist, what he or she is experiencing is available for awareness, can be lived in the relationship, and can be communicated, if appropriate" (p. 115). (Rogers recognized that not everything may be appropriate for presentation to the client; see also, this volume, Chapter 3, R.3.)

The second attitudinal element includes caring, prizing, acceptance—what Rogers labeled *unconditional positive regard*. "When the therapist is experiencing a positive, acceptant attitude toward whatever the client is at that moment, therapeutic movement or change is more likely to occur" (p. 116). Thus, the therapist's stance is nonjudgmental.

The third attitudinal element is empathic understanding.

> This means that the therapist senses accurately the feelings and personal meanings that the client is experiencing and communicates this understanding to the client. When functioning best, the therapist is so much inside the private world of the other that he or she can clarify not only the meanings of which the client is aware but even those just below the level of awareness. This kind of sensitive, active listening is exceedingly rare in our lives. . . . Yet listening, of this very special kind, is one of the most potent forces for chance that I know. (p. 116)

Let me turn next to Rogers' origination and development of these attitudinal principles. Rogers, reportedly, was an experimenter and observer/listener first, and only later did he theorize based on his "direct experiences in therapy and human interaction" (Kirschenbaum, 1979, pp. 158, 195). In keeping with a tradition of pragmatism and empiricism, Rogers formed his theories from his praxis, which gave them a positivistic cast. In the following discussion of Rogerian empathy, I will summarize, condense, and in some cases interpret Rogers' views from several sources.

Rogers began to define empathy and describe applications of empathic understanding in the late 1940s, after moving from Ohio State to establish the University of Chicago's Counseling Center. Rogers' innovative *nondirective* approach to therapy was controversial and difficult to teach effectively to counselors-in-training. According to Rogers, the counselor's role was not to advise or interpret matters for the client, but to *reflect* the client's feelings about the matter being discussed; and not to reflect simply the content of the matter, but the emotions connected to it. Later, to correct the misconceptions and distortions of this approach, Rogers insisted that nondirective therapy was not a method or technique that might be applied superficially, by merely reflecting or *saying back* the client's feelings. Rather, he insisted that the counselor must genuinely hold a *set of attitudes* which are coherently related to the principles of the nondirective approach (Kirschenbaum, 1979, pp. 158–159).

As Rogers progressively articulated the three attitudes (of congruence, acceptance, and empathy), the therapist's attitudes and stance became inherently connected with the client's attitudes to himself or herself. If therapists approach clients by accepting them unconditionally and understanding them empathically, then the clients are better able to accept and understand themselves in the process of their growth to resolve their problems. As Rogers refined the concept of client-centered therapy, he used the term *empathy* to describe the kind of understanding required: "the therapist's sensitive ability and willingness to understand the client's thoughts, feelings, and struggles from the client's point of view. This ability to see completely through the client's eyes, to adopt his frame of reference, . . . is the basis for the use of the term 'client-centered' " (Kirschenbaum, 1979, p. 164).

This broader concept of "adopting the client's frame of reference" implied much more than reflecting the client's feelings. In a 1958 article, Rogers asked:

> Can I let myself enter fully into the world of his feelings and personal meanings and see these as he does? Can I step into his private world so completely that I lose all desire to evaluate or judge it? Can I enter it so sensitively that I can move about in it freely, without trampling on meanings which are precious to him? Can I sense it so accurately that I can catch not only the meanings of his experience which are obvious to him, but those meanings which are only implicit, which he sees only dimly or as confusion? Can I extend this understanding without limit? (Rogers, 1961, p. 53)

Although the term *empathy* had been used in psychotherapy since the early part of the century, Rogers extended and popularized its meanings; the terms *empathic listening* and *active listening* originated with Rogers and his Chicago colleagues (Kirschenbaum, 1979, pp. 165, 178, 195; see also, this volume, Chapter 3, R.13).

In his article on empathy, published in 1975 and reprinted in *A Way of Being* (1980), Rogers summed up his early antipathy to the reductionism often applied to the empathic approach. He noted the "appalling consequences" of schematizing the "reflecting" (or "say back") principle into a "technique."

> I was so shocked by these complete distortions of our approach that for a number of years I said almost nothing about empathic listening, and when I did it was to stress an empathic attitude, with little comment as to how this might be implemented in the relationship. I preferred to discuss the qualities of positive regard and therapist congruence, which, together with empathy, I hypothesized as promoting the therapeutic process. (Rogers, 1980, pp. 138–139)

Rogers' abhorrence and repudiation of techniques and strategies stemmed from their reductionism and abstraction from genuine empathy and congruence. Empathy, as a therapist's helping stance, is a mode of experiencing another person in more than just cognitive, egocentered, and formulaic terms.

Moreover, Rogerian empathy is not *identification* with the other, as he stressed in a 1959 definition:

> empathy, or being empathic, is to perceive the internal frame of reference of another with accuracy and with the emotional components and meanings which pertain thereto as if one were the person, but without ever losing the "as if" condition. . . . If this "as if" quality is lost, then the state is one of identification. (Rogers, 1980, pp. 140–141)

Rogers' definitions of empathy, differentiating it from identification, distinguish themselves from Kenneth Burke's (1969) ideas of identification in the rhetorical process of persuasion.

It is important to note that Rogers' definition of empathy here maintains a self-conscious and analytical distinction between simple identification and the awareness of the "as if" condition of a relationship. Yet, as Rogers stated in 1975: "To be with another in this way means that . . . you lay aside your own views and values in order to enter another's world without prejudice. In some sense it means that you lay aside your self;" of necessity, the practitioner must be a "secure" and stable self (Rogers, 1980, p. 143).

In his 1975 article, Rogers presented current definitions and implications of research on empathy, stressing the effect of the empathic process on the recipients. To Rogers, being empathic "means entering the private perceptual world of the other and becoming thoroughly at home in it. . . . It includes communicating your sensings of the person's world . . . [and] frequently checking with the person as to the accuracy of your sensings." What the therapist is attempting to sense are the feelings and emotions which lie behind or within the client's experiencing at a particular moment. The "empathic therapist points sensitively to the 'felt meaning' which the client is experiencing . . ." by reflecting a provisional understanding of these feelings back to the client. "By pointing to the possible meanings," the therapist allows the client "to experience the meanings more fully" and to understand and clarify the feelings (Rogers, 1980, pp. 141–142; see also, this volume, Chapter 3, R.9).

In the last section of this article, Rogers summarized the positive effects of "an empathic climate," which he extended from the clinical setting to wider contexts of parents, teachers, and other social interactions. "An empathic way of being can be learned from empathic persons," he observed; "the more sensitively understanding is the therapist or teacher, the more likely are constructive learning and change to take place" (Rogers, 1980, pp. 150–151). Rogers presented two consequences of empathy for the recipient: that it "dissolves alienation" and "that the recipient feels valued, cared for, accepted as the person that he or she is." It provides "needed confirmation," he noted in Buber's terms, for the recipient's sense of identity. But mixed in with the consequences for the recipient, Rogers discussed the "accepting and nonjudgmental quality" of empathy provided by the therapist or initiator; "true empathy is always free of any evaluative or diagnostic quality." If the recipient is not judged, "the possibility of self-acceptance is gradually increased" (Rogers, 1980, pp. 151–155).

In his conclusion, Rogers stressed that the empathy of the initiator eventually leads to the recipient's own empathic activity and healthy growth:

> when persons find themselves sensitively and accurately understood, they develop a set of growth-promoting or therapeutic attitudes toward themselves. . . . The self is now more congruent with the experiencing. Thus, the persons have become, in their attitudes toward themselves, more caring and acceptant, more empathic and understanding, more real and congruent. But these three elements are the very ones that both experience and research indicate are the attitudes of an effective therapist. So we are perhaps not overstating the total picture if we say that an empathic understanding of another enables a person to become a more effective growth enhancer, a more effective therapist, for himself or herself. (Rogers, 1980, p. 159)

In concluding with "the three attitudinal elements making for growth," Rogers implied that "an empathic stance," which "provides illumination and healing," is dependent on the other two attitudes: congruence and caring, nonjudgmental acceptance. All three are interrelated, but Rogers noted that congruence is primary.

> In the ordinary interactions of life—between marital and sex partners, between teacher and student, employer and employee, or between colleagues or friends—congruence is probably the most important element. Congruence, or genuineness, involves letting the other person know "where you are" emotionally. . . . Thus, congruence is a basis for living together in a climate of realness. (Rogers, 1980, pp. 160–161)

These three interrelated attitudes also serve as the necessary conditions to facilitate *genuine communication,* although Rogers did not directly introduce them in his 1951 article on communication. Instead, what he presented for the purpose of communication generally was a nonclinical version of his reflection or say-back principle, which I called his *restatement rule.*[1]

> Each person can speak up for himself only *after* he has first restated the ideas and feelings of the previous speaker accurately, and to that speaker's satisfaction. It . . . would be necessary for you to really achieve the other speaker's frame of reference—to understand his thoughts and feelings so well that you could summarize them for him. (Rogers, 1961, p. 332)

Rogers formulated this rule from his conception of empathic understanding; yet the other two attitudes are clearly interconnected. Congruence is implicit in the goals of genuine communication and mutually satisfactory solutions to common problems. We can see nonjudgmental acceptance in operation by a negative example which Rogers provided in his later chapter on empathy. To prove that "it is impossible to be accurately perceptive of another's inner world if you have formed an evaluative opinion of that person," Rogers proposed a test of the restatement rule:

> choose someone you know with whom you deeply disagree and who is, in your judgment, definitely wrong or mistaken. Now try to state that individual's views, beliefs, and feelings so accurately that he or she will agree that you have sensitively and correctly described his or her stance. I predict that nine times out of ten you will fail, because your judgment of the person's views creeps into your description of them. (1980, p. 154)

Because Rogerian empathy is linked with attitudes of the initiator toward himself or herself (congruence) and toward the other (acceptance), we might say, in rhetorical terms, that empathy is linked to *ethos*—the personal character and presentational qualities of the initiator. Although we might explain aspects of Rogerian empathy rhetorically, Rogers himself was concerned less with the logos of rhetoric and more with the attitudinal climate for interpersonal communication. Rogers' models throughout his theory and practice were clinical not rhetorical. And the clinical situation to Rogers was a helping relationship.

As Rogers described helping clients, there is a reiterated idea of empowering them to cope with and solve their future problems as well as their immediate difficulties. According to Rogers' humanistic assumptions:

> the individual has within himself vast resources for self-understanding, for altering his self-concept, his attitudes, and his self-directed behavior—and that these resources can be tapped if only a definable climate of facilitative psychological attitudes can be provided [i.e., congruence, acceptance, empathy]. (1980, p. 49)

Moreover, Rogers took the goal of mobilizing the individual's inner resources beyond the bounds of the therapeutic situation to "locate power in the person, not the expert" (1980, p. 140; Zappen, Chapter 10, this volume). This stress on the individual allowed Rogers to present similarities not differences between therapeutic and nontherapeutic situations of empathy. There could be similar goals for empathic understanding in all manner of relationships: from close, interpersonal living to professional interactions with therapists, parents, teachers, religious leaders, supervisors, politicians, etc. As Rogers claimed in his 1951 paper on communication, empathic, active listening and restatement could be applied to a wide range of situations beyond the therapeutic context.

> Just as clients in psychotherapy find that empathy provides a climate for learning more of themselves, so students in the classroom find themselves in a climate for learning subject matter when they are in the presence of an understanding teacher. (Rogers, 1980, pp. 155–156)

For Rogers' applications of empathy, the structural relationship of a situation would not matter; it could be strictly dyadic or multiple (groups of clients, students, believers). What would matter, however, would be the assumptions and intentions of those involved. Rogerian empathy would work best if all parties (for example, a couple in a family or those in multiple business negotiations) were willing to pursue such strategies as cooperative action, mutual respect, reciprocity, possibility of compromise, and mutually satisfactory solutions to resolve conflicts (Teich, 1987).

Beyond these favorable conditions, Rogers proposed that his principles were applicable to hostile, highly charged conflict situations, such as violent social conflict (here Rogers cited his work with Catholics and Protestants in Northern Ireland; this volume, Chapters 2 and 3, R.4), family tensions, labor disputes, and political negotiations (cf. Young, Chapter 6, this volume). Rogers contended that trained facilitators can employ empathy to reduce tensions between factions and make them feel understood; as a result, their defensiveness would diminish and their rationality would emerge to resolve the differences. Yet, as some critics of Rogers claim, the greater the stress on individuality and individuals' inner resources, especially in nonclinical contexts, the less that social, political, and historical determinants of the situation may be taken into account and recognized as integral to the structure of a problem (cf. Pounds, 1987).

When we observe the broad range of claims made for Rogerian empathy, we may well ask for more direct and concrete discussion of its usefulness in rhetoric, argumentation, and writing. In the last chapter (17) of this part, I will explore more fully the implications and applications of empathy for these fields. But first, to supply additional grounding for that discussion, I will examine important recent psychoanalytic perspectives on empathy.

Unlike, for example, psychoanalyst Heinz Kohut's positions on empathy (which I will examine next), Rogers' humanistic assumptions invested more potential in the personal resources of individuals for their own healthful change and growth in response to a therapist's empathy. Moreover, Rogerian empathy, as it is often taken from its clinical context and transformed into a humanistic ideal, does not always entail the final step of analytic interpretation of the empathic experience, which is characteristic of traditional psychoanalytic theory and practice.

NOTE

1. See Teich, 1987; also this volume, Chapter 3, R.9–R.15, for Rogers' comments on this principle of restatement.

REFERENCES

Burke, K. (1969). *A rhetoric of motives*. Berkeley, CA: University of California Press.

Kirschenbaum, H. (1979). *On becoming Carl Rogers*. New York: Delta/Dell.

Pounds, W. (1987). The context of no context: A Burkean critique of Rogerian rhetoric. *Rhetoric Society Quarterly, 17*, 45–59.

Rogers, C. R. (1961). *On becoming a person*. Boston, MA: Houghton Mifflin.

Rogers, C. R. (1980). *A way of being*. Boston, MA: Houghton Mifflin.

Teich, N. (1987). Rogerian problem-solving and the rhetoric of argumentation. *Journal of Advanced Composition, 7*, 52–61.

CHAPTER 16
Heinz Kohut: Empathy in and Beyond Psychoanalysis

Nathaniel Teich

In conjunction with Rogers' views on empathy and with the aim of identifying the role of empathy in communication and writing, it is instructive to examine psychoanalyst Heinz Kohut's influential theorizing about empathy. Rather than attempting to sort out innumerable definitions of empathy offered by psychotherapists (in a futile effort to establish universals), I will focus on Kohut's work to reveal his broadening conception of empathy. He extended it from initially restricted applications in psychoanalysis to wider personal, social, historical, and literary contexts.

Heinz Kohut (1913–1981) may not be popularly known, but has been influential in his field well beyond the University of Chicago and other Chicago area institutions where he worked as a psychoanalytic theorist, practitioner, and teacher. According to many commentators, Kohut expanded classical psychoanalytic theory and practice by formulating a new "psychology of the self." Kohut went beyond Freudian drive psychology and the subsequent ego psychology in his exploration and treatment of narcissistic personality disorders. As the fundamental methodological approach for his work and, he insisted, for that of all psychoanalysts, Kohut formulated what he termed "our empathic-introspective observational stance" (1977, p. 309). In fact he posited that "the field of psychoanalytic depth psychology *is* the dimension of reality that is perceived via introspection and empathy" (1977, p. 244).

That Rogers was familiar with Kohut's work, and that Kohut knew about Rogers, can both be substantiated; however, what cannot be established is the matter of influences. Rogers mentioned Kohut positively in our interview, especially regarding the issue of the negative uses of empathy (this volume, Chapter 3, R.3). Rogers' formative work appeared earlier than Kohut's 1959 article, "Introspection, Empathy, and Psychoanalysis" (Kohut, 1978). But Rogers' own 1975 article on empathy, which became a chapter in *A Way of Being* (1980), contained no reference to Kohut in its many citations.

As for Kohut, he deliberately avoided references and connections to similarities with contemporary thinkers. After noting in the Preface to *The Restoration of the Self* that critics had identified similarities in his work with many others, from Sartre to Winnicott, Adler, Lacan, and Rogers' client-centered therapy, Kohut acknowledged "overlap," but resisted the "integration" of other views (1977, pp. xix–xx). By making the claim of struggling to work out his individual ideas for himself, Kohut had no attributions to Rogers or others and ultimately denied any debts. In several places, however, Kohut grounded his view on "the irreplaceable role of empathy in psychology" by quoting the sentence by Freud on empathy (e.g., 1977, pp. 143, 306n; see also, this volume, Chapter 14). Yet, innovatively, Kohut's controversial elevation of empathy as the essential analytic mode for psychology opened a debate which continues today. For instance, his new, "scientific" definition of empathy as *vicarious introspection* has proven epistemologically troublesome, as we shall see.

In Kohut's major 1959 paper on the subject, "Introspection, Empathy, and Psychoanalysis," he first advanced an "operational" definition of the field of psychology as that which is accessible by means of the empathic-introspective stance of the observer. Like Rogers, Kohut conceived this stance "in the widest sense of the total attitude of the observer toward the phenomena under investigation" (1978, p. 206). Although Kohut did not deny other tools and components for psychoanalytic observation (as some of his critics claimed), he proposed "introspection and empathy as an essential constituent." They constitute "the usual analytic situation" for both parties:

> it is the introspective self-observation of the analysand to which the analyst is a witness. It is true that the psychological insights of the analyst are frequently ahead of the analysand's comprehension of himself. [cf. Rogers, this volume, Chapter 3, R.3] These psychological insights are, however, the result of the trained introspective skill which the analyst used in the extension of introspection (vicarious introspection) that is called empathy. (1978, p. 209)

Kohut repeatedly argued for a scientific conception of empathy and developed an analogy with the empirical methods of the physical sciences, which he would use again in future writings. Just as theories about phenomena in the external world are constructed from observations by our senses (augmented by instruments like telescopes, microscopes, and now computers), so Kohut stated:

> Our thoughts, wishes, feelings, and fantasies . . . have no existence in physical space, and yet they are real, and we can observe them as they occur in time: through introspection in ourselves, and through empathy (i.e., vicarious introspection) in others. (1978, pp. 205–206)

The functional, phenomenological nature of his definitions, at this time in his work, resulted in a focus exclusively on the individual, to the exclusion of broader social and political contexts.

> Only a phenomenon that we can attempt to observe by introspection or by empathy with another's introspection may be called psychological. A phenomenon is "somatic," "behavioristic," or "social" if our methods of observation do not predominantly include introspection and empathy. (1978, pp. 208–209)

In a lengthy passage, Kohut distinguished between his definition of scientific empathy as an "observational method" and "the use of empathy outside of scientific psychology." "In everyday life," he noted, we arrive more easily at a "psychological understanding" of people from "our own cultural background" than people "from a different background." We empathize "most easily" with people whose "movements, verbal behavior, desires, and sensitivities are similar to our own."

> Yet even when we observe people from a different culture whose experience is unlike our own, we usually trust that we will be able to understand them psychologically through the discovery of some common experiences with which we can empathize. Similarly with animals: when a dog greets his master after a separation, we know that there is a common denominator between our experiences and what the dog experiences at the end of a separation from a beloved "you," and we can begin to think in psychological terms even if we should be inclined to stress that the differences between human and animal experience must be great. (1978, pp. 210–211)

Kohut's positivistic orientation emerged in his subsequent examples. "Hardly anyone," he asserted, "would talk about a plant psychology."

> True, some enthusiastic observer of flowers may conceivably see in the turning of plants toward the sun and toward warmth something with which he can empathize, an inner striving, yearning, or wish—but this

> will be more in the sense of allegory or poetry because we cannot concede to plants (as we do, for example, to some animals) the capacity of rudimentary self-awareness. There are, however, still further gradations. We observe water running down a hill, seeking the shortest route, avoiding obstacles, and even describe these facts in anthropomorphic terms (running, seeking, avoiding); yet we do not speak of a psychology of inanimate bodies—much less of a psychology of plants. (1978, pp. 210–211)

Given Kohut's technical conception of scientific empathy here, any empathic response directed to imaginative, aesthetic, or natural constructs would have to be consigned to the nonscientific realm of poetic figuration (a distinction reminiscent of the duality of verifiable statements vs. pseudostatements posited by the logical positivists of the early 20th century).

In his writings prior to 1973, Kohut reiterated and refined this definition of scientific empathy, which focused on empathy from the analyst's point of view. He also formulated a developmental interpretation of *primary empathy,* which occurred in the relationship between mother and infant and influenced the growth of narcissistic object relations. Since among Kohut's major contributions are his theories, discussions, and treatments of narcissistic personality disorders, it is important to recognize connections between his views of narcissism and empathy. In a 1961 letter, he replied: "When we speak of narcissism we do not mean that there is no other person involved, but that the other person is not experienced as separate, with individual motivation and individual freedom" (1978, pp. 852–853). Such narcissism, Kohut noted later, is marked by inadequate empathy.

In his 1966 paper, "Forms and Transformations of Narcissism," Kohut began to shift his focus from only discussing the analyst's scientific empathy to hypothesizing about the growth of empathy in human development and its function in people's relationships in society.

> Just as the child's *primary empathy* with the mother is the precursor of the adult's ability to be empathetic, so his *primary identity* with her must be considered the precursor of an expansion of the self, late in life, when the finiteness of individual existence is acknowledged. (1978, pp. 455–456)

In Freudian and existential terms, Kohut pondered the human "capacity to acknowledge the finiteness of his existence," to accept "transcience" and "the impermanence of objects, be they beloved people or cherished values" (1978, p. 454). In conclusion, he stated that the most "genuine and valid results of therapy" were "the reshaping of the narcissistic structures and their integration into the personality—the strengthening of ideals, and the achievement, even to a modest degree, of such wholesome transformations of narcissism as humor, creativity, empathy, and wisdom" (1978, p. 460).

Kohut's first book, *The Analysis of the Self* (1971), contained little on empathy, because he concentrated on new theories of self-psychology and treatment of narcissistic personality disorders. Then in a 1973 paper, Kohut offered a more speculative view of "the ideal of achieving an ever broadening and deepening scientific empathy"—"a new kind of humanitarianism in the form of a scientific empathy"—"the empathic expansion of the self with the aid of scientifically trained cognition" (1978, pp. 678, 683). "Empathy is," Kohut stated, "not just a poor relation of those other forms of cognition that we hold in high esteem. . . . Empathic modes of perceiving ourselves and our surroundings exist from the beginning of our lives side by side with other, nonempathetic, modes of perception" (1978, p. 678). Again Kohut linked developmental and existential views to portray "the expansion of the self, its increasing capacity to embrace a greater number and a greater variety of others through a consciously renewed and cultivated deepened empathy" (1978, p. 682).

> From the beginning of life, it is empathy, the psychological extension of an understanding human environment, that protects the infant. . . . And it is human empathy, as we mirror and confirm the other and as the other confirms and mirrors us, that butresses an enclave of human meaning—of hate, love, triumph, and defeat—within a universe of senseless spaces. . . .

Finally, as we face death, empathy provides, in Kohut's existential terms, "a sense of continuing life, of the survival of essential human sameness, and thus protection against the fallacy of pairing finiteness and death with meaninglessness and despair" (1978, p. 682).

In another 1973 paper, "The Psychoanalyst in the Community of Scholars," Kohut proposed the centrality of empathy to all the sciences to prevent the isolation of scientific knowledge from the rest of human life. The psychoanalyst, according to Kohut, "has the broadest access to the relevant data" concerning empathy.

> He knows that, despite its essentially narcissistic nature, empathy is a fundamental mode of human relatedness; that it is not only a powerful basic psychological bond between individuals, but that indeed it constitutes the very matrix of man's psychological survival. (1978, p. 704)

In a succinct paragraph which evinces how far he had come from considering empathy only from the analyst's perspective, Kohut summarized his view "of the important role empathy plays in all human life."

> (1) Empathy, the recognition of the self in the other, is an indispensable tool of observation, without which vast areas of human life, including man's behavior in the social field, remain unintelligible. (2) Empathy, the expansion of the self to include the other, constitutes a powerful psychological bond between individuals which—more perhaps even than love, the expression and sublimation of the sexual drive—counteracts man's destructiveness against his fellows. And (3), empathy, the accepting, confirming, and understanding human echo evoked by the self, is a psychological nutriment without which human life as we know and cherish it could not be sustained. (1978, pp. 704–705)

This Rogerian-sounding summary highlights the multiple modes and functions that Kohut assigned to empathy. His refinements and innovations regarding the role of empathy extended into literature, social relations, and communication.

In the remainder of his paper, Kohut discussed examples of great artists, popular figures, and anonymous clients to illustrate "the interaction between the empathic process as a mode of cognition, on the one hand, and the wholesome social effects of empathy, on the other hand, in order to illuminate the potential role empathy can play for science" (1978, p. 707). Kohut's idealized goal was to encourage "the infusion of our specialized activities with a new kind of humanitarianism," from the collaboration of the sciences in applying "their knowledge to life-sustaining goals," which would "give the fundamental emotional sustenance to man that he needs for his psychological survival" (1978, pp. 714–715).

Yet Kohut acknowledged the limitations of the empathic process when applied beyond the therapeutic or dyadic relational situation to larger social contexts. In concluding his paper, he proposed collaborative action by the community of scholars to investigate both "the limitations" and "the possible extension of the effectiveness of empathy in the social field." Although he was committed to his "maxim of the life-sustaining, civilizing, curative power of empathy," he admitted that

> as soon as we turn from the assessment of the role it plays in the relationships of two individuals—be it mother and child, or psychotherapist and patient—and begin to examine its potentialities in the social arena, the psychoanalyst's knowledge alone will not carry much weight.

> Clearly, it would be suicidal to apply the two-step procedure of empathic understanding and scientific explanation directly to some of the sources of evil in our world. (1978, pp. 717–718)

From Kohut's (1985) recently published writings and interviews, it is evident that, from the early 1970s, he was studying both evil and heroic behaviors, pursuing psychohistorical interpretations (especially of Hitler and Nazi Germany) and discussions of artists and the characters they created. Despite his earlier disavowals, he developed connections from individual to social psychology. But if his work was more theoretical and speculative than Rogers' group and workshop experiences, it was also more tempered and less optimistic in its promises for beneficial change. Kohut lamented in his conclusion to his 1973 paper:

> It is one thing to grasp the human suffering hidden behind a patient's cruelty to animals[;] it is another thing to be tolerant and understanding toward the antihumanitarian activities of a dangerous fascist politician and the appeal he exerts upon the multitudes. Even if we acquire increasing understanding of the psychology . . ., our tolerant communication will not set up the move toward health in the political arena that we are able to achieve in the therapeutic situation. (1978, p. 717)

Yet Kohut returned to "scientific" justifications for empathy in his second book, *The Restoration of the Self* (1977). Although he introduced some new theoretical concepts for self psychology, he stressed "more explicitly my reliance on the empathic-introspective stance" (1977, p. xiii). Throughout he repeated his basic tenets, including: (a) "the definition of the psychological field as the aspect of reality that is accessible via introspection and empathy" and (b) "a methodology of the observer's long-term empathic immersion in the psychological field" (1977, pp. xxi–xxii).

In Kohut's scientism, empathy is called an *instrument,* analogous to the tools and software of natural scientists and technicians.

> The enormous number of variables contained in the psychological field dooms a purely cognitive approach to failure. The refined empathy of the trained human observer, however, constitutes a potentially adequate instrument for the performance of the first step—understanding—of the two-step procedure—understanding-explaining—that characterizes depth psychology. (1977, p. 142)

Empathy, as "refined" and "trained," however, is not "purely cognitive." According to Kohut, it can produce knowledge that is pre- or nonverbal; yet it contributes to rational understanding.

> The ability of the analyst to conceive of psychic conditions that cannot be described in terms of verbalizable meaning allows him to consider an important band in the spectrum of possibilities as he scrutinizes the analysand's anxiety. (1977, p. 105)

As Kohut's metaphors develop, "refined" empathy, and empathic "immersion" imply greater "scientific" precision than we might be prepared to grant. Moreover, his metaphors from the physical sciences not only attribute greater authority, but also connect the nonverbal, psychological reality to the objective, physical universe. Bands on a spectrum (as quoted above) suggest wave-lengths that are not evident to the senses unaided by technical instruments. However, Kohut posited empathy as a natural instrument analogous to the other human senses, which scientists supplement with their technology. Thus, Kohut's empathy became both a natural sense and an enhancing instrument, for which any difficulties could be resolved by additional scientific advancements.

> Valid scientific research in psychoanalysis is nevertheless possible because (1) the empathic understanding of the experiences of other human beings is as basic an endowment of man as his vision, hearing, touch, taste, and smell; and (2) psychoanalysis can deal with the obstacles that stand in the way of empathic comprehension just as other sciences have learned to deal with the obstacles that stood in the way of . . . the observational tools. (1977, p. 144)

To support his notion of empathy as a basic endowment like our senses, Kohut also used other developmental analogies with the physical world, for example, comparing the child's need for empathy to the need for oxygen.

To anticipate objections by his critics, Kohut denied any connection of his scientific conception of empathy with popular uses of the term: "such fuzzily related meanings as kindness, compassion, and sympathy, on the one hand, and intuition, sixth-sense perception, and inspiration, on the other." So as not to be taken as nonscientific, he denied abandoning "the cold facts of reality" for sentimentalism, "a quasi-religious or mystical approach," or for therapies offering to "cure through love and . . . suggestion" (1977, p. 304). Yet his previous descriptions of empathy certainly evoked notions of intuition and a sixth sense—an unusual mixture of scientism and what resembles romantic organicism.

A few pages earlier, Kohut claimed that the conception of empathy in the development of psychoanalysis provided "a new direction. . .to human thought." It was not simply a new explanatory paradigm (in the Kuhnian sense), but rather a "revolutionizing new technique. . .and theory. . .—and, being both, it is more than both."

> It is an advance on that basic level of man's relationship to reality where we cannot yet differentiate data from theory, where external discovery and internal shift in attitude are still one and the same, where the primary unit between observer and observed is still unobstructed and unobscured by secondary abstracting reflection. On this basic level of experience, the most primitive and the most developed mental functions appear to be at work simultaneously, with the result not only that there is no clear separation between observer and observed, but also that thought and action are still one. (1977, pp. 299–300)

Kohut's claim for empathy as a whole that is greater than the sum of its parts, and as an undifferentiated union that reconciles opposites and contraries, reminds me of the holistic, organic theorizing developed by Herder, Goethe, and the Schlegels in Germany and adopted by Coleridge in England during the late 1700s and early 1800s. According to Wellek (1955), this view in aesthetics had a tendency to dissolve into mysticism. Perhaps to compensate for or resist this tendency, Kohut also defended his conceptions of empathy as scientific. Yet, after his excursion into romantic organicism, we should not be surprised a few pages later to find Kohut quoting Coleridge. Here Kohut described the empathic process as "temporarily but for sufficiently long stretches of time adopting the attitude that Coleridge (1817) referred to as the 'willing suspension of disbelief' " (1977, p. 309). Coleridge made this now-famous remark in an aesthetic context, discussing what constitutes "poetic faith" *(Biographia Literaria,* chap. 14, in Perkins, 1967). For my purposes of examining empathy and rhetoric, this reference will get more attention in the next chapter.

At this point, we should note how deeply implicated Kohut's scientism is with aesthetics and language. He stated: "I am trying to observe and explain inner experience—including the experience of objects, of the self, and of their various relationships" (1977, p. xxii). But his epistemological position regarding introspection and empathy is not sufficiently clear. Certainly, the evidence of the client's introspection is (along with nonverbal cues and cues of spoken delivery) the client's words, just as the therapist's explanation is also words—whether more or less consciously and metaphorically structured discourse. Poststructuralist psychological theorists like Lacan, Foucault, and Kristeva recognized the determinate influences of language in constructing meaning and the impossibility of an objectivity transcending the discourse situation.[1] But Kohut, and perhaps Rogers (see this volume, Part 1, Introduction; Chapter 3, R.19), assumed a prelinguistic reality prior to articulate language and accessible by means of empathy.

In his last book, *How Does Analysis Cure?* (1984b), Kohut skirted the epistemological/linguistic problems of his basic concepts and, ultimately, the status of psychoanalytic explanations.

> If . . . the concepts of a self and of a selfobject refer to inner experiences . . ., that they are not part of physical reality but of psychological reality, observable only via introspection and empathy, how then can we speak of relationships between them as if we were dealing with actors on the stage of external reality? (1984b, p. 50)

In the pragmatics of a clinician, his justification was that it is "expedient . . . in the service of scientific communication" to, in effect, reify and personify concepts, rather than qualify them as abstract constructs in every usage.

The *self* to Kohut, however, was not a metaphysical entity, but rather a construct—a structure—that is built by the individual in relation to external conditions. What psychoanalysts call *structure building,* according to Kohut, is successful to the extent that "a healthy self . . . is not prone to become fragmented, weakened, or disharmonious during maturity, at least not severely and/or for long periods" (1984b, p. 70). In reexamining and summarizing many of his major ideas, Kohut continued to link definitions of empathy to the developmental processes starting in infancy "that build up the healthy self" (p. 70).

Kohut offered an ordinary-language definition of empathy in an extended passage which proclaimed the centrality of empathy not only for depth psychologists but also for all human life.

> The best definition of empathy—the analogue to my terse scientific definition of empathy as "vicarious introspection" . . .—is that it is the capacity to think and feel oneself into the inner life of another person. It is our lifelong ability to experience what another person experiences, though usually, and appropriately, to an attenuated degree. (1984b, p. 82)

This attentuation is necessary because "the baby's empathic perception of his surroundings seems to be tantamount to total suffusion with the emotional state of the other," and these "archaic needs . . . for merger" and the later "wish for closeness via perfect empathy" must be transmuted into attenuated empathy for adults to build healthy personality structures (1984b, pp. 6, 82–83). As in previous works, Kohut discussed the formative role of the mother's empathic responses to the infant. Where it is inadequate and traumatizing, from her anxiety, panic, or neglect, the result "may foster in the child an impoverished psychic organization," producing "a person . . . unable to be empathic," unable, "in essence, to be fully human" (1984b, p. 83).

Kohut insisted that "training and learning make the difference" in employing empathy, although some people are "severely restricted" in their empathic abilities while others are "unusually great" (1984b, p. 83). Thus, there are no special qualifications for an individual to engage in the empathic process, since it is our more or less fully human response; psychotherapists simply apply the process scientifically for the two-step purpose of understanding and explaining the patient's situation. Here Kohut sounded much like Rogers:

> In the understanding phase, the analyst verbalizes . . . that he has grasped what the patient feels . . . thus demonstrating to him that he has been "understood," that is, that another person has been able to experience, at least in approximation, what he himself experienced, whether, for example, the experience in question is one of inner emptiness and depression or of pride and enhanced self-esteem. (1984b, pp. 176–177)

There is a further innovation which Kohut introduced in his conception of empathy, as he discussed "the curative effects of analysis." In an isolated remark, he contended that the analyst's empathy can be informed and even surpassed by the patient's own self-empathy. The analytic process remains the collaborative (affective and cognitive) construction of narrative discourse about the self; however, the patient may discover

> that his own understanding of his mental states and attitudes is at times better than that of the analyst, that the analyst['s] . . . empathy is fallible, and that the patient's empathy with himself, including, par excellence, his empathy with his childhood experiences, is often superior. (1984b, p. 72)

At this point, Kohut felt the need of an explanatory note, given his definition of empathy as vicarious introspection:

> my use of the phrase "the patient's empathy with himself" might seem to be strangely inconsistent at first glance. Still, if one considers our ability to step away from ourselves and look at ourselves as objectively as possible, i.e., as if we were another person, the differentiation between "introspection" (the directly perceived experience of one's inner life) and "empathy with oneself" (the indirectly perceived experience of one's inner life) will make sense. (1984b, p. 220 n9)

The stance of objectivity and distancing oneself even from one's previous experiences constitutes Kohut's definition of mature empathy as attenuated. It is consonant with Rogers' position that the empathic process does not produce identification with the other. Although Kohut's further distinction between "introspection" and "empathy with oneself" threatens, on one hand, to dissolve the usefulness of the terms, it provides, on the other hand, a further blending of empathy with the imaginative, self-reflexive creative process of both famous and ordinary writers who narrate their recollected experiences.

In the next chapter, I will explore implications of Kohut's distinction between "introspection" and "self-empathy." If introspection is restricted to current states (the present timeframe, which could be reflected in immediate conversation and recorded in automatic and spontaneous writing), then self-empathy would include the imaginative process of most writers who attempt to understand and express any memory or self-conscious recollection of past states. This process was perhaps best described in the incompletely-known passage by that first great modern poet of self-consciousness, William Wordsworth, in his 1802 Preface to *Lyrical Ballads*.

> I have said that Poetry is the spontaneous overflow of powerful feelings; it takes its origin from emotion recollected in tranquillity: the emotion is contemplated till, by a species of reaction, the tranquillity gradually disappears, and an emotion, kindred to that[2] which was before the subject of contemplation, is gradually produced, and does itself actually exist in the mind. In this mood successful composition generally begins, and in a mood similar to this it is carried on. (Perkins, 1967, p. 328)

The valuation of empathy and its products was one of the most significant issues discussed, albeit briefly, by both Rogers and Kohut. They noted that not just the results of the empathic process, but also the process itself can be valued as positive or negative, good or ill. In 1973 Kohut stated that "empathy . . . can serve inimical ends, is often used for destructive and asocial purposes." As examples he listed "war propaganda" and unscrupulous salesmen (1978, p. 706). Rogers, in our interview, referred to the harmful effects of therapists' communicating their understandings and the matter of brainwashing techniques (this volume, Chapter 3, R.3). Kohut summarized these issues in his 1984 restatement of empathy as:

> a value-neutral tool of observation which (a) can lead to correct or incorrect results, (b) can be used in the service of either compassionate, inimical, or dispassionate-neutral purposes, and (c) can be employed either rapidly and outside awareness or slowly and deliberately, with

> focused conscious attention. We define it as "vicarious introspection" or, more simply, as one person's (attempt to) experience the inner life of another while simultaneously retaining the stance of an objective observer. (1984b, p. 175)

Kohut had explored the issue of valuation in the context of empathy as an investigative tool in studying psychohistory, political figures, and other cultural topics in essays from the early 1970s, unpublished until the posthumous collection, *Self Psychology and the Humanities* (1985). He insisted that the scientific, objective use of empathy made it not only possible but also necessary to study historical and fictional subjects, from evil figures, like Hitler, to the heroic and tragic in literature and life, like Hamlet and individuals in the Nazi resistance.

> If the depth psychologist is to make a contribution to the understanding of man's role in history and his control over his destiny, then he must try to extend his empathic observation not only to the victims but also to the persecutors, not only to the martyrs but also to their torturers. . . . Furthermore, he must not focus only on the historically distant past . . . [because] our emotional involvement declines . . . [as] does our empathic attunement. (1985, p. 65)

In a 1981 interview, Kohut commented on the issue of "the researcher's empathy with the [historical] past."

> So long as another culture is totally foreign to us, it is like psychosis. It's so easy to say the Nazis were beasts and that Germany then regressed to untamed callousness and animal-like passions. The trouble is that Nazi Germany is understandable. There is an empathic bridge, however difficult to maintain.
>
> [Q.] If psychosis is defined by the inability to establish and maintain empathy, is there a group analogue to that?
>
> [K.] That's what I'm talking about. Can we build an empathic bridge to those who committed these horrors? As soon as we can they are no longer a psychotic culture. I don't know whether we can. I think up to now we can't; it's too close. . . . In principle, it should be possible. (1985, pp. 250–251)

Kohut's last paper, "Introspection, Empathy, and the Semicircle of Mental Health," written in 1982, has a Rogerian cast in its personalized reflection and first-person narration. Kohut looked back at the reception and controversies surrounding his first paper, the 1959 "Introspection, Empathy, and Psychoanalysis," and reiterated and defended his scientific conceptions of empathy. They were presented, he said, from the "high road" of epistemological theorizing, as opposed to the pragmatic, low road of "data collection and experience-near theory." Thus, from the high road, "in an epistemological context . . ., empathy is a value-neutral mode of observation . . . attuned to the inner life of man." From the low road, Kohut balanced his views by describing empathy "in an empirical context as a mental *activity*, whether employed in everyday life or in scientific pursuits."

Operationally, in the empirical context, Kohut distinguished between "two levels" of empathy: (a) "as an information-gathering activity" and (b) "as a powerful emotional bond between people" (1984a, p. 84). Regarding empathy at the first level, Kohut repeated his prior views that it "can be right or wrong, in the service of compassion or hostility, pursued slowly . . . or [what appears to be] 'intuitively,' that is, at great speed." At this level, empathy is "never by itself supportive and therapeutic," but "a necessary precondition" for the success of these functions.

Although Kohut would have preferred to stop at this point, he felt compelled to travel further down the conceptual road to a point that, he said, "appears to contradict everything that I have said so far." He was compelled by his adherence to "scientific rigor" to acknowledge the (quintessential Rogerian) point that "the mere presence of empathy" has beneficial and therapeutic effects "both in the clinical setting and in human life, in general." This claim, he noted "unfortunately," is supportable as "a scientific hypothesis and not an outgrowth of vague sentimentality or mysticism," and not grounded in "wishes" or a "more or less hidden morality" (p. 85).

Despite his reluctance to deviate from the traditional scientism of the psychoanalytic path, Kohut's final position on empathy in theoretical and operational terms is compatible with Rogers. Also compatible with Rogerian humanism is Kohut's optimistic, humanistic orientation for self psychology, placing the concept of the self at the center of psychoanalytic theory and practice, and emphasizing developmental transformations leading to normal, cohesive personality structures.

For much of Kohut's final paper, he presented a personal story of his dissatisfactions with traditional Freudian perspectives, which led Kohut to formulate his new views of self psychology and empathy. He sought to supplement and redirect the established theory and practice. As an example, he reviewed his dissatisfaction with the Freudian mythologizing of the Oedipus complex, with its characterization of man as "guilty." As a substitute, Kohut offered his own mythos of the sane, clever, ultimately normative response of Odysseus to the intergenerational issue, which embodied an existential characterization of the human struggle.

Finally, Kohut sought to change the psychoanalytical outlook from being "hampered by such misleading medical analogies as the removal of disease" to a positive emphasis on "the reestablishment of psychological health" (p. 99). Rogers, in his language, made just such a dramatic move from medical to humanistic signification by referring to "clients" rather than "patients." As Rogers said in our interview (this volume, Chapter 3, R.11), it is important to understand the feelings with which people hold their views. We see Kohut, in his last paper, as a fuller figure in the landscape—with personal feeling, intellectual honesty, and social responsibility.

After examining closely Kohut's writings on empathy, we are better positioned to see how controversy grew, spawning a range of responses that turned empathy into a highly conflicted term in psychotherapy. At various times, Kohut referred to empathy as: an observational method (1959), tool (1973), and instrument (1977); a mode of perception, cognition, and human relatedness (1973); a stance (1977) and a vantage point (1982). Kohut spanned the extremes, starting from detached scientism and reaching unabashed, existential humanism (by 1973). In my detailed presentation of Kohut's views in this chapter, I allowed him a fuller voice than most of his critics have within the limits of their papers. With this fair hearing, we are prepared for the next chapter, to take up the conflictedness of the term *empathy* and to determine how we can turn the apparent contradictions to our benefit in the field of communication.

NOTES

1. For example, psychiatrist W. W. Meissner, SJ (1988) states "that psychoanalysis is a hermeneutic and linguistic discipline, that the exclusive focus of psychoanalysis is on the patient's use of words, and that the flow of analytic material is subject to linguistic examination according to the laws of linguistic analysis. The major modality of therapeutic intervention is interpretation, so that the dimensions of the interpretative process assume core significance" (p. 59). Cf. Lacan (1977) and McGee (1987); Foucault (1987) and Spellmeyer (1989); Kristeva (1986).
2. Wordsworth's 1800 version originally stated "an emotion, similar to that," but in the 1802 and later editions he changed it to "an emotion, kindred to that." His change implied the effort to distinguish between the original and the recreated imaginative experience; the latter is not identical, but indeed a mental creation, an offspring related to the original.

REFERENCES

Foucault, M. (1987). *The care of the self: The history of sexuality* (Vol. 3). New York: Pantheon.

Kohut, H. (1971). *The analysis of the self.* New York: International Universities Press.

Kohut, H. (1977). *The restoration of the self.* New York: International Universities Press.

Kohut, H. (1978). *The search for the self: Selected writings of Heinz Kohut, 1950–1978* (2 vols). New York: International Universities Press.

Kohut, H. (1984a). Introspection, empathy, and the semicircle of mental health. In J. Lichtenberg, M. Bornstein, & D. Silver (Eds.), *Empathy I* (pp. 81–100). Hillsdale, NJ: Erlbaum.

Kohut, H. (1984b). *How does analysis cure?* Chicago, IL: University of Chicago Press.

Kohut, H. (1985). *Self psychology and the humanities: Reflections on a new psychoanalytic approach* (C. P. Strozier, Ed.). New York: Norton.

Kristeva, J. (1986). *The Kristeva reader.* New York: Columbia University Press.

Lacan, J. (1977). *Ecrits: A selection.* New York: Norton.

McGee, P. (1987). Truth and resistance: Teaching as a form of analysis. *College English, 49,* 667–678.

Meissner, W. W. (1988). A place for Freud. *Boston College Magazine, 47,* 59.

Perkins, D. (1967). *English romantic writers.* New York: Harcourt, Brace, & World.

Spellmeyer, K. (1989). Foucault and the freshman writer: Considering the self in discourse. *College English, 51,* 715–729.

Rogers, C. R. (1980). *A way of being.* Boston, MA: Houghton Mifflin.

Wellek, R. (1955). *A history of modern criticism: 1750–1950. Vol. 2. The romantic age.* New Haven, CT: Yale University Press.

CHAPTER 17
Teaching for and about Empathy as Collaborative Rhetoric

Nathaniel Teich

By examining empathy in the works of Rogers and Kohut, I have traced the extension of empathy in theory and practice from the therapeutic context to communication generally. These broader contexts may range from interpersonal external dialogues to individual internal interactions with texts or events in history or present society. However, all nonclinical situations of empathy inescapably raise rhetorical problems.[1] Is the situation appropriate for empathy? Is the empathy difficult to achieve and maintain? What is the desired goal or outcome in the situation? Is the *other* (individual discourser, or collective audience) hostile or cooperative? And in personal terms, each of us must ask: can I genuinely be empathic in this situation?

In answering this last question, we and our students might agree that the empathic process is not universally applicable in all discourse situations. Yet there is a fundamental philosophical sense in which empathy serves universally "as the functional foundation of human intersubjectivity" (Agosta, 1984). I will explore this view more fully below. Let me begin by focusing on practical classroom considerations of teaching for and about empathy, so that this pedagogical aim will remain evident throughout the chapter.

While we and our students can easily provide examples from experience and common-sense reasoning to show where empathy has not worked or would not work, nevertheless, the empathic process remains valid and uniquely suited to certain situations. For example, empathy is important generally (although little mentioned) in the reading process, as readers understand and develop their responses to literary texts. In courses devoted to oral and written communication, argumentation, and rhetoric, I believe that it is important specifically to study empathy—as important, say, as studying formal logic. Studying the empathic process provides supplementary and alternative understandings about discourse. As we have seen from the discussions of Rogers and Kohut, the empathic process will operate successfully both with the give-and-take of face-to-face dialogues and with imaginative, internal dialogues in interpersonal, historical, and literary contexts.

To introduce the study of empathy to our students, we might start by pointing out examples of its double origins in aesthetic perception and clinical helping relationships (this volume, Chapter 14). Next, students could easily offer examples of situations where they felt empathy would or would not be appropriate. In my teaching, I might begin by contributing a timely example; for instance: who would want to walk in the steel-tipped boots of teenage neo-Nazis or other violence-prone bigots? Personally, I would agree with those who could not bring themselves to be empathic in this situation. But, then I could show a magazine article in which the writer did employ empathy toward such people, although ultimately judging them unfavorably. Moreover, I would point out that Kohut (1985) talked about building "an empathic bridge" to understand Nazi Germany, and Rogers brought together hostile factions in Northern Ireland. My goal in such discussions is for students to conclude that empathy is determined by individual and situational factors when it is applied in nontherapeutic contexts.

To pursue this conclusion further in another example, let us consider the legal context. There are pleadings, presented in written documents or orally in courtrooms, that obviously require forensic, not empathic, methods for criminal and tort (personal damages) cases. Yet, there are provisions for pretrial conferences, exchanging of information and evidence, and bargaining which need not be as formally adversarial as a trial. Moreover, incorporated into the legal system now are increasing opportunities to resolve disputes by mediation, not litigation, in personal relations (such as family problems, no-fault divorce, custody arrangements for children). There are also a variety of means for nonadversarial resolution of issues by arbitration and by cooperative not adversarial collective bargaining in labor relations.[2]

After viewing empathy as a function of individual and situational factors, we could discuss with students that what is common to empathy in all situations is its grounding in discourse. Empathy—whether as defined and practiced by Rogers, Kohut, and other therapists, or as employed in nonclinical communication and rhetoric—is discourse based, because felt meanings must be articulated to be shared, checked, and revised. Rogers' restatement rule provides an operational foundation for discursive empathy: providing the means for maintaining the connections and flow of communication, checking perceptions, and revising understandings. The empathic process initiates a rhetoric of collaboration, in both external and internal contexts. Empathic dialogues between the self and other (in the external world or in one's imagination) create and clarify new verbal realities. Thus, theoretically, empathy involves more epistemological issues than we might have expected.

Empathy, conceptually and operationally, appears to be a touchstone or litmus test that can indicate a range of conflicting epistemological positions. The debates about empathy involve the status of such paired constructs as: subject and object, detachment and involvement, rationality and intuition, cognitive and affective modes. While some interpreters have privileged one polarity of these pairs, others have tried (with varying success, like Kohut and Rogers) to maintain a balance or plurality of modes within the bounds of the empathic process.

PLURALISTIC MODELS OF EMPATHY

The theoretical challenge for such pluralists is both to account for and to harness operationally the dichotomous and contradictory conceptions attributed to empathy. While this pluralistic task may be logically indefensible to monists, who insist on unified resolutions of discordant elements, we can explain this pluralistic balancing to our students in Rogerian terms, and they should find it quite acceptable and workable both inside and outside school settings. Rogers' restatement rule provides the basis for understanding others' feelings and ideas without passing judgment and without immediately or necessarily giving up one's own feelings and ideas. Students, drawing on their own life experiences, can accept and practice this dual and divergent way of thinking. It is not uncommon in their experiences of fictional or actual situations. It can be explained well in terms of Bakhtin's dialogical theories (Schuster, 1985; Halasek, Chapter 8, this volume). Coleridge's phrase "willing suspension of disbelief" describes the common attitude toward such dialogical situations. This example and others from literary history (which I will discuss throughout) should provide additional illustrations.

Holding two different, even contradictory, ideas in mind simultaneously is not inconceivable. Students can be asked to supply examples in which two ideas or feelings do not cancel each other out or blend into a single, new combination. For instance, students have identified the feelings of both pride in our country, but disgust at treatment of the homeless, at corrupt politicians, or other negative conditions. Another type of example familiar in literary criticism may be instructive. Dr. Johnson (1779) described the 17th-century metaphysical poets as frequently using "a combination of dissimilar images. . . . The most heterogeneous ideas are yoked by violence together" (Wellek, 1955, pp. 98–99). Although Johnson did not judge this rhetorical practice favorably, we could present to our students examples of discordant images and discuss whether they are effective logically and emotionally. Then, we can draw students' attention to such mental acts as rational analysis, suspension of disbelief, and empathy operating in the process of our responses to what Johnson called the *"discordia concors"* (harmonious discord) of the combined and perhaps contradictory ideas.[3]

Empathy itself is a term that embodies contradictions in its multiple connotations (as we have seen in the previous chapters). One particular contradiction is that empathy signifies both active and passive, intrusive and receptive, modes. The more evocative figurations of empathy, such as *empathic immersion* (which connotes active entering in) and *empathic resonance* (which connotes passive receiving), do not resolve the problem of contradictory modes. Reik (1948) used a multisensory metaphor to describe the psychoanalyst's attitude of both involvement and detachment: "he can vibrate unconsciously in the rhythm of the other person's impulse and yet be capable of grasping it as something outside himself and comprehending it psychologically" (p. 468). But "comprehension" to Reik, as he discussed its etymology, meant "a kind of taking possession . . . of things, seizing them."

Thus, both elements of Reik's model of *introjection* (incorporating the other within us) and *projection* (externalizing the experience as an object for psychological comprehension) involved "man's craving for power" and possession.

> Psychological comprehension of another person is a special case of this sublimated seizure and incorporation. It is, in a sense, psychological cannibalism. The other person is taken into your ego and becomes, for the time being, a part of your ego. (p. 233)

We have become sensitized to the connotations of such language, and, accordingly, we should not be surprised to find stereotypical gender dichotomies inherent in discussions of empathy (see this volume, Introduction, Section 6).

Reed (1984) examined the psychoanalytic discourse on empathy and identified the major uses of the term as "antithetical." In particular, she classified characteristics of empathy as dichotomously feminine or masculine: the analyst's passive receptivity vs. active intrusion into the patient's state, maternal nurturing vs. symbolic (phallic) penetration, organic oneness vs. mechanistic instrumentality. Such polarities, however, indicate the unsatisfactoriness of dichotomous models (in this case gender stereotypes associated with empathy). Whatever the truth signified by a conception of the allegedly masculine drive for logic and explicit analysis dominating the allegedly feminine direct mystical union and felt identity of experience, a satisfactory resolution to avoid automatically privileging one mode and rejecting the other must go beyond dichotomous, either/or, conceptual models (cf. Schafer, 1984, pp. 31–33).

Reed (1984) discussed the possibilities and limitations of employing one construction of empathy which would signify "a creative synthesis . . . of its antithetical components" (p. 21). However, there is no reason to assume that closure, or an organic unity, is possible or desirable within a traditional synthesis of antithetical elements. It may be an unwarranted assumption that the component elements—such as the modes of masculinity and femininity, rationality and intuition—are dichotomous and mutually exclusive. Rather than assuming that empathy represents antithetical elements, let us consider them as contraries or opposites which can be complementary and mutually supportive. Accordingly, these elements will not cancel each other, as an equal and opposite binary relation, nor will they be dissolved and blended homogeneously into a new organic whole. Rather, each element will retain its differences while contributing to a new dialogical discourse relationship in a specific rhetorical situation.

When instructing students to use the empathic process (and when attempting it ourselves), we should reinforce the rhetorical assumption that its application and outcome depend on contextual and situational conditions. A discussion of people's different roles, and the attitudes appropriate to these roles, will draw useful distinctions for the applicability of empathy: for example, differences between psychoanalysts and patients, teachers and students; and differences among family members, friends, and co-workers. We expect the certified therapist to employ empathy in a professionally objective manner, while in one's personal relationships the degree of involvement and commitment of self in the empathic process may vary with the importance of the issues. Moreover, there are always some highly charged issues that seem intractable. Everyone could list topics on which one might strongly resist being empathic: abortion, drug use, gun control, rape, sadistic torture, Hitler's personality.

In a recent writing class, after just such a discussion of topics resistant to empathy, I asked students to share with the class the issues that they were planning to treat according to Rogerian empathic understanding. In one case, a student (whom I will call Janet) seemed to be convinced by comments from the class that she could not present an empathic or balanced expository treatment of abortion issues, because of her unequivocal prochoice values. The paper she turned in, however, was such an effective dramatization of a high school girl's agonizing decision about whether to choose abortion that I could not help wondering whether the account was an actual personal experience or fictional. Janet, by substituting the model of a literary narrative with a dialogic double voice for the pro/con expository argument model, engaged the empathic process not only for herself but also for her audience. She evoked the human complexity and mixed feelings involved in the debate over abortion, which logical exposition can only tell. Her paper showed that there was not a single truth or simple reconciliation for the problem.

In our teaching and our own expressions of empathy, the most effective model for empathy will not simply produce a conventional dialectical synthesis, but rather engage a pluralistic rhetoric of collaboration. Collaboration will be evident not only from oral, face-to-face dialogues (therapist and client, student and classmates), but also from the writer's internal dialogical acts. Janet's empathic collaboration took place both with her classmates and with her imaginative apprehension and understanding of various conflicting perspectives. Each of us could supply numerous examples, like Janet, to illustrate the interrelation of the empathic process and the writing process as a collaborative pluralism.

For purposes of communication in most contexts, the diversity of empathic theory and practice can be maintained within a pluralistic perspective. Such a pluralism would not be simply eclecticism, but a more rigorous *methodological pluralism* in the manner of Wayne Booth (1979). Pluralistic methodology would authorize pragmatic, functional applications of empathy as an operational process for communication and understanding. Reik's effort to maintain multiple rather than monistic or synthetic modes offered an early, albeit metaphoric, model. "The analytic technique of cognition of unconscious processes is marked by oscillation between the conscious and unconscious labors of the intellect and imagination" (1948, p. 389). With this figure of oscillation, I turn to a more recent and comprehensive model.

EMPATHY AS HERMENEUTIC PROCESS

Empathy, as I am presenting it here—as a rhetoric of collaboration in creating and responding to discourse—is a special kind of intersubjectivity. Yet, in a larger sense, as Agosta (1984) argued, empathy must be regarded as the basis for all human intersubjectivity. Agosta's model of empathy (as I see it in my own figurative terms) bends the straight line of the continuum, which connects the two ends of the dichotomous polarities attributed to empathy, into the hermeneutic circle—symbolized by such shapes as the circular ouroboros and the yin-yang, which stand for bringing opposites together, counterbalancing them, and providing continuity in situations of contradiction (Cirlot, 1962, pp. 235, 360).

Agosta's connection of empathy with intersubjectivity, from his philosophical perspective, reoriented the view of empathy as comprised of antithetical elements. He noted that the many dichotomous conceptions of empathy "incorporate a circular or spiraling movement," between passive receptivity and active interpretation (1984, p. 44). To account for this oscillation, Agosta described the empathic process as taking the form of a hermeneutic circle—that circular process of knowing in which the parts "take their meaning from the whole of which they are a part and, in turn, lend meaning to that whole" (p. 45).

> If empathy is to escape the arbitrary caprice of conflicting intuitions, then it must be related to the act of interpretation. This mutual interrelation of empathic receptivity and interpretation constitutes a kind of "hermeneutic circle," in which both components are needed to constitute interhuman knowledge in the full sense. Empathy most authentically becomes a mode of understanding as it is transformed into and communicated as an interpretation. (p. 51)

By proposing that empathy, "as a form of human understanding," operates as a hermeneutic process, Agosta established the connection between empathic interpretation in psychoanalysis and in other discourse situations, from literature to rhetoric in real life. Accordingly, the analysts' use of empathy in the circular process of interpretation—moving back and forth between self and other, receptively participating in the experience and then reflecting for the purpose of understanding—is only a special case of the general human activity of interpretation via the hermeneutic process. As Agosta stressed, "the paradigm for hermeneutics is a written text," but hermeneutics can be applied to "symbolic action of all kinds." Moreover, "empathy is a hermeneuticaly relevant skill," because it is "the functional foundation of human intersubjectivity" (pp. 43–45).

Following his Kantian mode of argument, Agosta posited empathy "as a general interhuman . . . capacity or competence" which makes human "inner life intelligible and meaningful by constituting it as a field of study." Agosta followed Kohut, who posited empathy as constituting the field of study for psychology.

> Here the phenomena (feelings, emotions, thoughts) are dependent on that function which makes possible our access to them. . . . Empathy is the function through which intersubjectivity makes sense, insofar as without empathy we would not even be able to conceive of human beings as capable of expressing and being receptive to expressions of feelings. (Agosta, 1984, p. 49)

Empathy, then, is complementary to, and copresent with, the other constituents, like language and logic, that determine the fields and boundaries of our communicable understandings.

Therefore, when we ask students to use empathy in reading and writing about a literary text, or an issue in society, or their own lives, we are not asking them to do something unnatural; rather, we are helping them practice making their assumptions and responses conscious, first, in apprehending the irreducible otherness outside the self and, second, in understanding self and other through honest interpretation that can be shared, checked, and revised. The Rogerian and psychoanalytic conceptions of empathy differ here from Kenneth Burke's (1969) ideas of identification in the rhetoric of persuasion. For both practice and "real" situations, Rogers provided the test for the analytical aspect of empathy. His restatement rule invokes the collaborative principles of dialogue for the purposes of mutual understanding, reduction of misinterpretation, and cooperative solutions of problems. For the subjective operations of empathy, however, neither Rogers nor Kohut and contemporary psychoanalysts fully explained the general principles.

Here Agosta also contributed to understanding the operational principles of empathy by reorienting our view of Kohut's concept of empathy as *vicarious introspection*. Agosta explored the operational implications of this idea in a way that Kohut did not, and offered a basic clarification of how the empathic process takes place. From Kohut's words (and the many other notions of empathy as *feeling into* another), we might infer the distinction that when we engage in introspection we are examining our own inner states, while when we engage in vicarious introspection we are examining the inner states of another. But Agosta claimed that we do not vicariously participate in the other person's introspection; rather we directly introspect in ourselves the vicariously experienced states of the other.

This distinction is significant and bears repeating, for it further entrenches empathy in the field of rationalized interpretation and understanding required by psychoanalysts and others, like rhetoricians, concerned with rigorously analysing discourse. Thus, it opens up opportunities for pedagogy and praxis by rationalistically qualifying notions that empathy is only found in the direct, mystical, intuitive senses of knowing and sharing experiences of another.

> In defining "empathy" as "vicarious introspection," misplacement of the stress may mistakenly suggest that empathizing consists in directly introspecting another's inner life. . . . In vicarious introspection one is not introspecting the feelings, emotions, sensations, or experiences of the other at all. . . . Rather, empathy consists in introspecting one's own vicarious experience of another's experience, and thus establishing a connection between self and other through this vicarious dimension of experience. (Agosta, 1984, p. 51)

We should find that it is both easy to explain the concept of empathy as vicarious introspection to our students and easy for them to grasp it, especially when coupled with Kohut's idea of self-empathy. If the empathic process is seen in the context of self-reflection, it will be appropriately demystified, although it may well be practiced by some people with greater sensitivity and speed (which is what Kohut called *intuition)*. The implications of Kohut's note on self-empathy clearly relate the process of empathy to introspection of one's own vicarious experiences (Kohut, 1984, p. 220, n9; this volume, Chapter 16). Students will quickly realize this distinction if we ask them, first, to remember a childhood incident and, next, to determine how they felt at the time (whether or not they were conscious of and understood the feeling then). Finally, they should recognize that, in the present, they were engaging in self-empathy regarding their past state and experience. Or we might illustrate self-empathy by literary examples, such as Wordsworth's "Tintern Abbey," Turgenev's "First Love," or Anne Sexton's poems. From examples of self-empathy, it should be clear that to empathize is to feel and examine one's experiences of previous or foreign experience.

Agosta further described the empathic process of vicarious introspection as constituted by a *double representation* that corresponds to the two basic elements of empathy—receptivity and understanding—which earlier he reformulated from dichotomous polarities into the hermeneutic circle of empathic interpretation. The double representation of empathy involves, first, "a representation of another's feelings"—to which we are receptive; second, "it entails a representation of the other as such as the source of the first representation"—that is, our understanding of the other as the cause of the feeling. Intersubjective interpretation is present in this second phase because, as he said, I understand that the feeling "does not come from me alone, but originates with the other and, by implication, with my interaction with him" or her (1984, p. 55).

Finally, Agosta described three ways we engage the empathic process to enter the hermeneutic circle of empathic interpretation. "First, when I experience a vicarious feeling, the possibility opens up that empathy can be directly grounded in the intersubjective communicability of affect." Second, through what we called *analogical recollection,* Agosta stated that "I can recall an experience similar to or resembling that of the speaker." Third, through *analogical apperception,* fantasies, rather than memories of actual past experiences, can be imaginatively constructed "in which some aspect of the other's experience is paired with my own" (p. 57). Also, I would add that there is a mixed mode (evident from our own introspection) mingling the recollection of actual experiences with fantasies.

In all these cases the empathic process would operate similarly (at the general level of the process of receptivity and interpretation) with different subject matter or situations. That is, empathy could occur in oral or written contexts: whether one was engaged in oral discourse either informally or in the psychoanalytic situation, or whether one was experiencing the written discourse of literary fiction or expository argument.

From Agosta's analysis of empathy and intersubjectivity in relation to one's vicarious introspection, it follows that the empathic process in its widest applicability is analogous to the creative, meaning-making process possible in all discourse situations. Process and product are inherently connected when we discuss communication, writing, literature, the other arts, and the roles of creators and responders. Similarly, there is a commonality in the act of listeners and readers engaging empathy and producing new understandings (affectively and cognitively responding and interpreting), whether the discourse originates from actual life or fiction, from narratives or exposition.

Empathy in the field of psychoanalysis signifies both process and product, according to Schafer (1984). He noted that this interconnection posed "an expository problem" for psychoanalysts writing about empathy (and we have certainly seen many such problems in their writings), but he proposed to define empathy as appropriately "conflictual." That is, pluralistically, he sought to retain the diversity signified by the concept without harmonizing or blending the opposites. Moreover, he stated that within the conflictedness, "the process and the product are not only close to unconscious modes of thought . . . they are also references to the analyst rather than the analysand. They are self-descriptions of a sort" (p. 33). Here Schafer lends support to Agosta's interpretation of "vicarious introspection" as focused on the self. Because analysts use "figurative language," "analogs of dream work," and fantasies, what they report as empathy can tell us about the analyst as well as the analysand (p. 33). Reik (1948) also noted that the analyst learns about himself or herself in a process of "reciprocal illumination" (pp. 397, 433).[4]

Rogers' recognition that a person who engages in the empathic process may well be affected and changed as a result led him to expand the applicability of empathy beyond the clinical situation. In our teaching situations, we can show our students, by examples from rhetoric, writing, and literature, that empathy produces distinctly individual results. They vary, according to the doubleness of empathy as receptivity and understanding, from one's willingness to risk a change of feelings and opinions to one's resisting change after empathic activity and evaluation. Students should not reject trying out empathy on topics about which they feel strongly. Despite the "corollary" I proposed to Rogers' restatement rule—that one should be prepared to change one's mind before applying empathy in an argumentative situation (Teich, 1987)—I am persuaded by the new essays of rhetoricians in this volume, by the psychoanalytic commentaries, and by students' work that a collaborative process of empathy can operate significantly even if no effective changes in actual positions occur.

Students have reported and written about their perceptions and understandings of others whose feelings were ultimately unacceptable or unsharable: racists, radical environmental activists, Vietnam vets, drug users. One student, specializing in sports medicine, disagreed with athletes' use of performance-enhancing procedures like blood doping, but described vividly the athletes' drive to win and ambivalent feelings which motivated them to choose such procedures. If we emphasize the use of imagination, focused fantasy, and visualization in a creative sense, we and our students can draw upon our capacities for collaboration and dialogue with people, either in actuality or in our heads.

As noted above, some psychoanalysts have found that, in the empathic process, the analyst engaged in his or her own fantasies in response to the analysand's fantasies (cf. Olinick, 1984, pp. 158–159). If we pursue the idea that the empathic process can involve shared or equivalent fantasies, analogs of dreams, and descriptive language such that both participants share or collaborate in producing and experiencing a common affect, we are led again to consider parallels with the aesthetic experience: the creative process and the response process.

Upon further consideration, we will have additional evidence for the pragmatic usefulness of a pluralistic approach to empathy. This approach both explains and harnesses for use the ideological variability (that conflictedness) registered by the term *empathy*. In the following brief excursion into aesthetic criticism, we will see early examples of the cognitive and affective dichotomies associated with what we now call empathy. In addition, we will have further evidence of how conventional (nonpluralistic) psychoanalytic approaches to empathy are stuck in early-modern dichotomous conceptions of common-sense realism vs. imagination. They posit rationalistic and singular interpretations of empathy rather than accept the conflictedness and tensions of pluralism (which can entertain both realism and fantasy). By examining some examples of mid-18th to early 19th century psychological aesthetics of response, I will introduce a link between literary theory and empathy that supports our use of a pluralistic, collaborative model for empathy in communication and rhetoric.

PRECURSORS OF EMPATHY IN LITERARY HISTORY

The etymological origins of the term *empathy* (see this volume, Chapter 14) came from the direction of 19th-century psychological aesthetics and emphasized the *primary* psychological processes of projection and identification. The *secondary* process of empathy—the phase of understanding and interpreting—also can be traced to aesthetic locations. These are the psychologized aesthetics of audience response developed from the mid-18th to the early 19th centuries. If we turn to the literary history of that period, we can see the two aspects, which Agosta (1984) defined as the double representation of empathy, present in the writings of poets and critics.

How will these historical examples help justify the use and value of empathy for rhetoric and communication? My illustrations will show that what we refer to as empathy has been part of the established critical tradition and debates about how writers and readers, speakers and spectators, create and respond to art, if not all discourse. Although the exact term *empathy* had not yet been coined, from the mid-18th century there were critics beginning to formulate psychological explanations of moral behavior and aesthetic experience.

In such diverse works as Hume's 1751 *An Inquiry Concerning the Principles of Morals,* Adam Smith's 1759 *The Theory of Moral Sentiments,* and Rousseau's 1762 *Émile: or Concerning Education,* enlightenment ideas about "the human capacity for vicarious experiencing another person's feelings," especially suffering and distress, were regarded as "an essential basis for social life and moral action" (Hoffman, 1977, p. 713). The moral and social dimensions of enlightenment sympathy are evident in its many significations: sentiment, sentimental, sensibilité, and (especially) fellow-feeling. Smith stressed "our fellow-feeling with the sorrows of others" (Marshall, 1988, p. 3). Yet, when he stated that sympathy had come "to denote our fellow-feeling with any passion whatever," Smith acknowledged the broadening and universalizing 18th-century conception of this construct. During the 18th century, "the transition from classical aesthetics . . . to the pre-Romantic aesthetics . . . (with its emphasis on subjectivity and affect) centered on the question of the *effects* that a work of art had on its reader or beholder" (Marshall, 1988, p. 2).

For a representative example, it is appropriate to examine the common-sense realism in the aesthetics of Henry Home, Lord Kames. In his 1762 *Principles of Criticism* (1836), Kames discussed the arts, especially literature, according to standards of verisimilitude and fidelity to the prevalent notions of universal norms of human nature. Accordingly, Kames described a uniform state of aesthetic receptivity as what I would call responding without conscious reflection. Kames defined this state as a dream-like *ideal presence,* which he compared to "a walking dream . . . because, like a dream, it vanishes the moment we reflect upon our present situation." In contrast, that present situation Kames defined as *real presence,* the common-sense world of actual life (p. 52). To explain this dichotomous existence of a reality principle vs. the principle of unreflective participation in waking dreams, Kames introduced the efficient cause of delusion—spectators being deluded by the stories they viewed or read.

In discussing epic and dramatic compositions, Kames illustrated his "doctrine, that fable [story] operates on our passions, by representing its events as passing in our sight, and by deluding us into a conviction of reality" (p. 419). But at one point he qualified the passive response of delusion by noting the spectator's active, volitional behavior of "willing to" go along with the idealized presence of the waking dream.

> While the [stage] dialogue goes on, a thousand particulars concur to delude us into an impression of reality; . . . the spectator once engaged, is willing to be deceived, loses sight of himself, and without scruple enjoys the spectacle as a reality. From this absent state, he is roused by violent action: he wakes as from a pleasing dream, and gathers his senses about him, finds all to be a fiction. (p. 426)

Of course, from our 20th-century perspectives, which reject Kames's limited realism and uniformitarianism, we recognize that receptivity without reflection is not the only possible state of aesthetic response. We can envision being simultaneously conscious of the aesthetic illusion, yet willing to participate and be emotionally moved. We can also envision an additional phase—that of interpretation and conscious understanding—alternating with the others, but not cancelling them out. This multiple and overlapping set of responses is exactly what the pluralistic conception of empathy signifies.

According to Wellek (1955), Kames did not recognize "all the difficulties implicit" in his psychologized aesthetics centered around art "as communication of emotion," especially "in distinguishing between art and life" (p. 116). Wellek noted that Kames's statements on dreams and delusions probably provoked Dr. Johnson "when he argued that the spectator is always in his senses" (p. 119). A pluralistic conception of empathy, however, allows us to recognize the double representation, in which emotional effects are experienced, but need not be dichotomized as art or life, another's fantasy vs. my reality. Indeed, whether intersubjective collaboration occurs in fictional or real situations, both the art and life of others can be transformed into my lived reality and continue to influence me. As Rogers proposed, through our acts of acceptance and suspending judgment, we allow the empathic transformations to operate. But, also, given the phase of empathic interpretation and understanding, which may appear simultaneously or alternating with the receptivity of affect, we have the potential to be "in our senses" to choose how to accept and evaluate those influences.

Kames's work proved influential, with its rationalistic explanation of audience delusion and waking dreams, and it was reprinted in many editions in Britain and America for more than 100 years. In the generation following Kames and Dr. Johnson, Coleridge was next to advance the debate over audience response. In his 1817 *Biographia Literaria,* he offered that memorable phrase "willing suspension of disbelief." We should note, however, that it occurred in the context of emotional responses attributed to delusions of supernatural influence. As he described his early poetic goals for readers' responses to such poems as "The Ancient Mariner" and "Christabel," Coleridge emphasized psychological verisimilitude in portraying "the dramatic truth of such emotions, as would naturally accompany" experiences of being "under supernatural agency." Although he called this original feeling of supernatural influence a "delusion," when it came to eliciting dramatically such a feeling in his audience, Coleridge, unlike Kames, described his task in volitional and affirmative, rather than delusional, terms. He sought

> to transfer from our inward nature a human interest and a semblance of truth sufficient to procure for these shadows of imagination that willing suspension of disbelief for the moment which constitutes poetic faith. (Perkins, 1967, p. 452)

This "willing suspension of disbelief" is affirmative rather than neutral or negative, because it signifies a positive negation: a choice of *not* not believing. Faith is placed in the imaginative illusion. Similarly, Rogers' conditions for empathy can be regarded as an *empathic faith* in the willingness to affirm the irreducible otherness, the Thou that cannot be totally appropriated into the I. Later in the *Biographia,* Coleridge added to his description of poetic faith. As he presented examples to distinguish between the audience's sense of falseness in a fiction and their acceptance of successful fictitiousness as dramatic truth, he expanded the idea of poetic faith as illusion in contrast to delusion:

> That illusion, contra-distinguished from delusion, that negative faith, which simply permits the images presented to work by their own force, without either denial or affirmation of their real existence by the judgment. (Perkins, 1967, p. 481)

Coleridge implies that, as individuals consciously or unconsciously suspend judgment, they accept and participate in the fiction as illusion, without resistance. While suspending the imposition of standards of truth from the actual world, they willingly participate in the verisimilitude of fictitious truth in an imaginative world. To Coleridge, this "negative faith" is not a pejorative, because it applies to the world of imagination. Like a mirror world, it simply parallels positive faith (religious belief) in the actual world. If we accord Coleridge's poetic/negative faith its appropriate affirmative value, we can apply this faith to both the aesthetic process and the empathic process. It refers to situations bracketed off from real-life truth but eliciting genuine emotions.

There are two aspects of Coleridge's definition that are common to both the aesthetic process and the empathic process: lack of resistance to the story/discourse, and limited time span for the experience. Given these two conditions, the aesthetic experience and the empathic experience are embedded one within the other. In both response situations, the imaginative experience of shared affect, memory, or fantasy is of brief duration, perhaps interrupted often by varying degrees of participation and detachment.

This provisional and temporary aspect was recognized by many of the psychoanalytic commentators on empathy. Reik (1948) called his receptive stage *temporary introjection* (p. 362). Fliess's (1942) definition of *trial identification* as a synonym for empathy reflects his attempt to retain the traditional Freudian concept of identification. But the substitution of the equally conflicted term of *identification* did not help. Basch (1983) considered the idea of "trial identification . . . to be a contradiction in terms," given the distinction that empathy has a component of understanding and interpretation not present in identification (pp. 104–106). But Fliess's term has been variously transformed as: *trial empathy* by Kohut (1977), *partial identification* (Olinick, 1984), and *transient identification* (Spencer, 1984).

If we stress to students this temporary and provisional aspect of the empathic process, perhaps they will be less resistant to experimenting with it. In situations of argumentation and problem solving, perhaps they will be more open to risking genuine acceptance and understanding of another's position and even modifying their own. In aesthetic situations, application of Rogers' restatement rule and Elbow's (1986) believing and doubting games should help turn spectators into participants who are willing to believe temporarily in the imaginative experience created collaboratively with a performance or a text. Empathy for Hamlet's difficult situation should make us feel personally, not just intellectually, his doubts and torments.

Underlying Coleridge's doctrine that "poetic faith" is "for the moment," however, is a fundamentally rationalistic standpoint like Kames's. Wordsworth, Coleridge's friend and collaborator, also employed the Kamesian vocabulary in the 1802 Preface to *Lyrical Ballads:* "it will be the wish of the Poet to bring his feelings near to those of the persons whose feelings he describes, nay, for short spaces of time, perhaps, to let himself slip into an entire delusion, and even confound and identify his own feelings with theirs" (Perkins, 1967, p. 325).

In contrast, Keats rejected such rationalism and, ironically, judged Coleridge incapable of suspending judgment, according to the Keatsian notion of *negative capability*. Keats expressed this idea in a letter (December 1817) in the same year that Coleridge's work appeared. Keats's memorable phrase, like Coleridge's, has often been taken out of context to connote empathy. Keats went further than Coleridge, however, in illustrating varieties of the empathic process from the poet's perspective:

> at once it struck me, what quality . . . which Shakespeare possessed so enormously—I mean Negative Capability, that is when man is capable of being in uncertainties, Mysteries, doubts, without any irritable reaching after fact & reason—Coleridge, for instance, would let go by a fine isolated verisimilitude caught from the Penetralium of mystery, from being incapable of remaining content with half knowledge. (Perkins, 1967, p. 1209)

Keats did not dwell on rationalistic explanations of illusion or delusion from an audience point of view, but rather offered subjective descriptions of his mental and poetic processes, which we now define as empathy. In an earlier letter (November 1817), Keats wrote: "if a Sparrow come before my Window I take part in its existence and pick about the Gravel" (Perkins, 1967, p. 1208). Keats recognized that there was not simply one way for the poet's merger of self with the external world to occur. He presented two figurations: the controlling ego and the "negative" or annihilated self.

In a subsequent letter (October 1818), Keats described the "poetical character" by calling his own chameleon-like, as "distinguished from the [W]ordsworthian or egotistical sublime." Wordsworth's strong ego absorbed everything into himself but retained his own identity. In contrast to Wordsworth's introjection, Keats experienced otherness to the point of losing himself and annihilating his ego.

> A Poet is the most unpoetical of . . . all of God's creatures . . . because he has no Identity . . . no self. . . . [Shakespeare's poetical character] has as much delight in conceiving an Iago as an Imogen. What shocks the virtuous philosop[h]er, delights the camelion [sic] Poet. . . . When I am in a room with People if I ever am free from speculating on creations of my own brain, then not myself goes home to myself: but the identity of every one in the room begins to press upon me that, I am in a very little time an[ni]hilated. (Perkins, 1967, p. 1220)

Perkins noted that Keats was influenced in his descriptions of Shakespeare's empathy by Hazlitt's 1818 *Lectures on the English Poets,* which Keats attended. In describing Shakespeare's genius, Hazlitt attributed it to what we now take as obvious aspects of literary empathy.

> The striking peculiarity of Shakespeare's mind was its generic quality, its power of communication with all other minds. . . . He was the least of an egotist that it was possible to be. He was nothing in himself; but he was all that others were, or that they could become. . . . When he conceived of a character, whether real or imaginary, he not only entered into all its thoughts and feelings, but seemed instantly, and as if by touching a secret spring, to be surrounded with all the same objects . . . and unforeseen accidents which would occur in reality. (Perkins, 1967, pp. 621–622)

Keats's contemporary, Shelley, in his 1821 "A Defence of Poetry," wrote about not only the annihilation of self in merging with another, but also the moral effects of "poetry" (imaginative literature, generally) on society. He traced a path of audience sympathy from admiration and imitation of ideal characters to identification with them.

> The great secret of morals is love; or a going out of our own nature, and an identification of ourselves with the beautiful which exists in thought, action, or person, not our own. A man, to be greatly good, must imagine intensely and comprehensively; he must put himself in the place of another and of many others; the pains and pleasures of his species must become his own. The great instrument of moral good is the imagination; and poetry administers to the effect by acting upon the cause. (Perkins, 1967, pp. 1075–1076)

Shelley, in a romantic sense, connected empathy to positive imaginative activity leading beyond the individual to humanitarian love and social morality. In contrast to this, 20th-century psychoanalytic commentators on empathy have restricted their definitions to exclude the more subjective and sentimental, romantic associations, like that of love. As opposed to Shelley's idealism, Kohut's notions of love were more materialistic. He parenthetically described love as "the expression and sublimation of the sexual drive" (Kohut, 1978, p. 705), in contrast to what he saw as the more expansive notion of empathy. In a letter he argued that there was no place for love in the "therapeutic milieu," which must be "psychologically neutral."

> I reject love, as I understand this term, not only because it is not essential, but because it is to my understanding a faulty, unempathic response. . . . I see no advantage and many disadvantages in calling love the analyst's ability to be in touch with the patient's needs and to tell him about them in a noncensorious, accepting way. (1978, pp. 928–929)

Yet one aspect in the romantic-idealist description of love involved that very figuration of empathy as being *in harmony* with another. As we have noted previously, Reik talked about *vibrations*, and Kohut and later commentators used the term *resonance* to describe the empathic process. In one of Shelley's many metaphoric descriptions of love, he exclaimed that "another's nerves should vibrate to our own . . . like the chords of two exquisite lyres, strung to the accompaniment of one delightful voice" (Perkins, 1967, pp. 1070–1071). Kohut denied love as a component of scientific empathy so that the psychoanalysts' rational, cognitive understanding and interpretation would not be contaminated by humanist or sentimental elements. In his later work, however, Kohut was able to express broader notions of empathy in a humanistic context (Chapter 16, this volume).

In a concluding literary example, we can see that Brecht's views on empathy also broadened from his initial dismissal of it, whether as a technique of the actor and dramatist, or a goal for audience involvement. In the 1920s and 1930s, Brecht equated empathy with simple identification of spectators with stage characters. Because he construed this empathy as emotional and lacking critical understanding, he rejected it in favor of his *alienation effect*.

> The spectator was no longer in any way allowed to submit to an experience uncritically (and without practical consequences) by means of simple empathy with the characters in a play. The production took the subject matter and the incidents shown and put them through a process of alienation: [*Entfremdung*] the alienation that is necessary to all understanding. (Brecht, 1964, p. 71)

But later, Brecht distinguished between expressions of empathy from the spectators' point of view and that of the actors'.

> It is well known that contact between audience and stage is normally made on the basis of empathy. . . . The technique which produces an Alienation-effect is the exact opposite of that which aims at empathy. . . . Yet in [actors'] efforts to reproduce particular characters and show their behavior [they] need not renounce the means of empathy entirely. . . . They do feel their way into their characters' skins with a view to acquiring their characteristics. (Brecht, 1964, pp. 136–137)

Brecht denied that he had "objections to feeling in art," since he did not avoid portraying characters' emotions on stage. What he did object to was that a simple empathic identification led to a lack of critical understanding, which prevented ideological awareness and practical action.

By the 1950s, Brecht was writing about a more complex conception of empathy from the spectators' point of view. The feelings created by the play should not be "impulsive" and "blind" but "conscious," "acquired . . . through the understanding" (p. 247). Elsewhere he stated that "our actual emotion will come from recognizing and feeling the incident's double aspect" (p. 271). This double aspect of empathy—collaboratively engaging in an experience and then understanding and explaining that experience—is evident in the many 20th-century conceptions of the empathic process that I have discussed previously.

* * *

The examples I have presented of aesthetic discussion about the effects of empathy in the context of literary texts and dramatic performances illuminate the activities of teaching about and experiencing empathy in other contexts of oral and written discourse. Moreover, as we have seen with Rogers, Kohut, and other psychoanalytic theorists, there should be no contradiction today in construing empathy from multiple perspectives: aesthetic, scientific, and the humanistic caring and facilitating of personal and social growth.

In our personal, professional, and communal lives, we must recognize that to engage empathy in its positive dimensions requires the honesty, genuineness, and authenticity which Rogers prized in his principle of congruence. This explains why, to Rogers, congruence is "the most important element" in his three interrelated attitudes (1980, pp. 160–161; this volume, Chapter 15). Congruence operates together with a strong ethical and social regard to direct empathic, rhetorical collaboration toward positive ends. Without congruence and ethical norms, empathy (as Rogers and Kohut noted) and rhetoric (I would add) can be used for inimical ends. Teachers of communication, rhetoric, and writing, especially, have an opportunity to offer responsible alternative principles, like the Rogerian, to teach new means for personally and socially beneficial collaboration through language.

The figurations of empathy connoting resonance and going out of one's self to understand and collaborate with others are evident in many commentaries on social conditions today. They emphasize the need for less destructive competition, less self-centeredness, less egotism, and more cooperation, more understanding, more reconciliation in personal relations and social actions. Psychoanalyst Arno Gruen (1988) wrote that the ideology of domination, power, and control in contemporary society has led to conditions of dehumanization, inner emptiness, and betrayal of the fundamental human expressions like love and empathy. This "betrayal of the self" can originate in flawed nurturing experiences and become reinforced by undesirable social and educational conditions. In a specific plea for less competitiveness in school and sports for young children, Dr. Benjamin Spock decried the emphasis on winning in our "excessively competitive society." Margaret Chesney, one of the pioneers in the study of "type A" behavior, concluded:

> I don't think the really worthwhile contributions are being made by aggressive, angry, overly competitive people. What we probably need in our child rearing and schooling is less emphasis on aggression and individual challenge and more on communication, cooperation, understanding, and patience. . . . While health professionals can contribute to individual health by counseling their patients on changing their lifestyles, others can contribute to social as well as individual health by promoting change in some of our outmoded cultural values. (1984, p. 82)

Empathy, as the heart of collaborative communication, provides positive opportunities for us in our personal and professional lives to contribute to more cooperative, equitable, and productive developments in society.

NOTES

1. For examples of applications in composition classroom situations, see Hairston (1982), Thomas & Thomas (1989). I distinguish here between *context* and *situation* by restricting context to describe the broad fields and extrinsic categories of organizing inquiry (e.g., therapeutic context, legal context); situation refers to local, intrinsic, specific content of particular rhetorical situations (the conditions and substance of the issue at hand).

2. Most judicial experts agree that the courtroom is the least desirable place to resolve family and personnel disputes. Agreements arrived at through mediation tend to be more acceptable to the parties and longer lasting. There are many scholarly and popular studies of nonadversarial strategies; e.g., Fisher & Ury (1981) and Fisher & Brown (1988) using Rogerian approaches.
3. Literary examples of this kind, which we as teachers probably must contribute (e.g., Schuster, 1985), are not tangential to empathic understanding. Andrew Marvell's "vegetable love" growing in his poem "To His Coy Mistress" would be an empathic challenge. In addition, examples of the rhetorical figure of oxymoron illustrate opposites harnessed and controlled by language into the structure of a new, dynamically contradictory thought with which an audience can resonate. Oxymoron is a carefully crafted contradiction: for example, *thunderous silence, open secret, genuine phony;* and such titles as "Alone Together" and "Intimate Strangers."
4. Thus, in the debates about empathy, analysts may have revealed more about themselves than they have acknowledged. Those who stress one pole of empathy at the expense of the other may indicate a defensive reaction to resist being connected with the opposite, rejected pole (Schafer, 1984, pp. 31–34; Poland, 1984, p. 335). For example, Kohut, as we saw in the previous chapter, eventually published his social and humanistic views on empathy, although he continuously asserted scientific justifications for empathy, as if to make it more palatable to his conventional psychoanalytic colleagues. Rogers, however, was free of this dichtomous perspective by his congruence with his principles of humanistic psychology and the individualistic, rebellious aspects of the human potential movement.

REFERENCES

Agosta, L. (1984). Empathy and intersubjectivity. In J. Lichtenberg, M. Bornstein, & D. Silver (Eds.), *Empathy I* (pp. 43–61). Hillsdale, NJ: Erlbaum.

Basch, M. F. (1983). Empathic understanding: A review of the concept and some theoretical considerations. *Journal of the American Psychoanalytic Association, 31,* 101–126.

Booth, W. C. (1979). *Critical understanding: The powers and the limits of pluralism.* Chicago, IL: University of Chicago Press.

Brecht, B. (1964). *Brecht on theatre* (J. Willett, Trans. & Ed.). New York: Hill & Wang.

Burke, K. (1969). *A rhetoric of motives.* Berkeley, CA: University of California Press.

Chesney, M. (1984). Interview. *Esquire, 102,* 82.

Cirlot, J. E. (1962). *A dictionary of symbols.* New York: Philosophical Library.

Elbow, P. (1986). *Embracing contraries: Explorations in learning and teaching.* New York: Oxford University Press.

Fisher, R., & Brown, S. (1988). *Getting together.* Boston, MA: Houghton Mifflin.

Fisher, R., & Ury, W. (1981). *Getting to yes.* Boston, MA: Houghton Mifflin.

Fliess, R. (1942). The metapsychology of the analyst. *Psychoanalytic Quarterly, 11,* 211–227.
Gruen, A. (1988). *The betrayal of the self.* New York: Grove.
Hairston, M. (1982). Using Carl Rogers' communication theories in the composition classroom. *Rhetoric Review, 1,* 50–55.
Hoffman, M. L. (1977). Sex differences in empathy and related behaviors. *Psychological Bulletin, 84,* 712–722.
Kames, Lord. (1836). *Elements of criticism.* New York: Conner & Cooke. (Original work published in 1762)
Kohut, H. (1977). *The restoration of the self.* New York: International Universities Press.
Kohut, H. (1978). *The search for the self: Selected writings of Heinz Kohut, 1950–1978* (2 vols.). New York: International Universities Press.
Kohut, H. (1984). *How does analysis cure?* Chicago, IL: University of Chicago Press.
Kohut, H. (1985). *Self psychology and the humanities: Reflections on a new psychoanalytic approach* (C. P. Strozier, Ed.). New York: Norton.
Marshall, D. (1988). *The surprising effects of sympathy.* Chicago, IL: University of Chicago Press.
Olinick, S. L. (1984). A critique of empathy and sympathy. In J. Lichtenberg, M. Bornstein, & D. Silver (Eds.), *Empathy I* (pp. 137–166). Hillsdale, NJ: Erlbaum.
Perkins, D. (1967). *English romantic writers.* New York: Harcourt, Brace & World.
Poland, W. S. (1984). On empathy in and beyond analysis. In J. Lichtenberg, M. Bornstein, & D. Silver (Eds.), *Empathy I* (pp. 331–349). Hillsdale, NJ: Erlbaum.
Reed, G. S. (1984). The antithetical meanings of the term 'empathy' in psychoanalytic discourse. In J. Lichtenberg, M. Bornstein, & D. Silver (Eds.), *Empathy I* (pp. 7–24). Hillsdale, NJ: Erlbaum.
Reik, T. (1948). *Listening with the third ear: The inner experience of a psychoanalyst.* New York: Farrar, Straus.
Rogers, C. A. (1980). *A way of being.* Boston, MA: Houghton Mifflin.
Schafer, R. (1984). Discussion. In J. Lichtenberg, M. Bornstein, & D. Silver (Eds.), *Empathy I* (pp. 31–36). Hillsdale, NJ: Erlbaum.
Schuster, C. I. (1985). Mikhail Bakhtin as rhetorical theorist. *College English, 47,* 594–607.
Spencer, J. H. (1984). Discussion. In J. Lichtenberg, M. Bornstein, & D. Silver (Eds.), *Empathy I* (pp. 27–42). Hillsdale, NJ: Erlbaum.
Teich, N. (1987). Rogerian problem-solving and the rhetoric of argumentation. *Journal of Advanced Composition, 7,* 52–61.
Thomas, D., & Thomas, G. (1989). The use of Rogerian reflection in small-group writing conferences. In C. M. Anson (Ed.), *Writing and response: Theory, practice, and research* (pp. 114–126). Urbana, IL: National Council of Teachers of English.
Wellek, R. (1955). *A history of modern criticism: 1750–1950. Vol. 1. The late eighteenth century.* New Haven, CT: Yale University Press.

Contributors

Paul Bator has taught at universities in Michigan and California; he is an assistant professor of English at Santa Clara University, Santa Clara, CA. He has published on contemporary and historical rhetoric in *College Composition and Communication, Philosophy and Rhetoric,* and *The Quarterly Journal of Speech.*

James S. Baumlin is an associate professor of English at Southwest Missouri State University, Springfield, MO, where he teaches rhetoric and renaissance literature. His recent publications have appeared in *College English, Pre/Text,* and *Texas Studies in Literature and Language.*

Tita French Baumlin is an assistant professor of English at Southwest Missouri State University, Springfield, MO. Shakespeare and composition theory are her specialities. Her recent publications have appeared in *College English, Rhetoric Review,* and *Studies in English Literature.*

Richard M. Coe teaches at Simon Fraser University, Burnaby, British Columbia, Canada. In *Toward a Grammar of Passages,* he explored contrastive rhetoric and the rhetoric of form. The new edition of his textbook, *Process, Form, and Substance,* treats Rogerian rhetoric at length. He is now writing *How to Read Kenneth Burke.*

Kay Halasek is an assistant professor of English at Ohio State University. Her dissertation, at the University of Texas, Austin, focused on Mikhail Bakhtin and composition theory. Her article on deconstruction and writing pedagogy won the 1989 Conference on College Teachers of English Award.

Chris Madigan has taught in public schools and universities in New Mexico, Missouri, Colorado, Virginia, Maryland, and Washington, DC. In 1988, he and other University of New Mexico Writing Institute staff received the New Mexico Council of Teachers of English award for Excellence in English Education. Currently, Dr. Madigan is a communications consultant for Sandia National Laboratories in Albuquerque, NM.

Wayne Pounds has taught language and literature in Algeria, Spain, Japan, and the U.S., most recently at California Polytechnic State University, San Luis Obispo. He is the author of a book on Paul Bowles, as well articles on rhetoric and pedagogy. Currently, he teaches English at the university level in Tokyo.

Rebecca Stephens teaches at Florida State University in Tallahassee. In her specialized study of the novel, she focuses on narrative and narrative theory. She is also an experienced technical writer with interests in software engineering as reflected in a recent paper on the cognitive dimensions of writing software documentation.

Nathaniel Teich, professor of English at the University of Oregon, teaches writing and literature, directs the Oregon Writing Project, and formerly served as director of composition. He has published in the areas of literary criticism, rhetoric and composition, and writing program administration. His current research focuses on issues of gender in writing assessment and in British romantic literature.

Richard E. Young is professor of English literature and rhetoric at Carnegie Mellon University and director of the Language across the Curriculum Program. He has published widely since the 1960s when he began working on tagmemic rhetoric at the University of Michigan Center for Research on Language and Language Behavior. His collaboration with A. L. Becker and K. L. Pike produced *Rhetoric: Discovery and Change* (1970).

James P. Zappen, professor in the Department of Language, Literature, and Communication, Rensselaer Polytechnic Institute, has published in *The Journal of Technical Writing and Communication, Rhetoric Review,* and *Rhetorica.* He is the series editor for Studies in Scientific and Technical Communication, published by the State University of New York Press.

Author Index

W

Y

Z

Subject Index